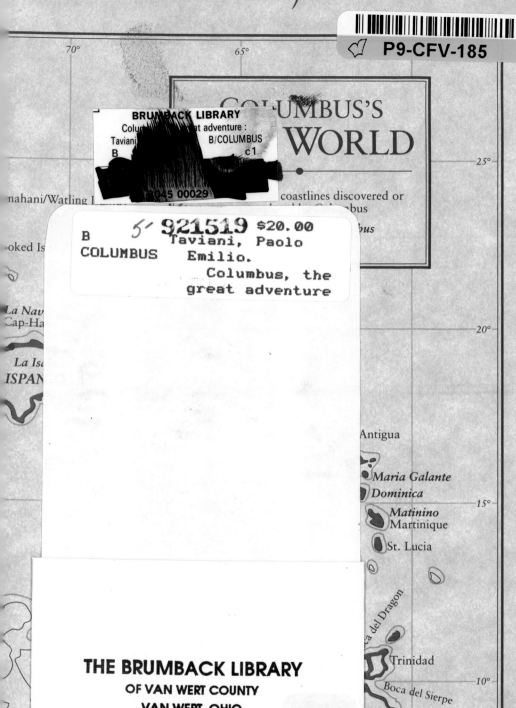

COLUMBUS'S WORLD

70°   65°   25°

...coastlines discovered or

...by Columbus

nahani/Watling I.

...oked Is

La Nav...
Cap-Ha...

La Isa...
ISPAN...

20°

Antigua

Maria Galante
Dominica
15°
Matinino
Martinique

St. Lucia

...a del Dragon

Trinidad
10°
Boca del Sierpe

P9-CFV-185

Columbus
THE GREAT ADVENTURE

PAOLO EMILIO TAVIANI

Columbus

THE GREAT ADVENTURE

His Life,
His Times,
and His Voyages

Translated from the Italian by
Luciano F. Farina
and
Marc A. Beckwith

Orion Books
New York

Published by Orion Books, a division of Crown Publishers, Inc., 201 East 50th Street, New York, New York 10022. Member of the Crown Publishing Group. Originally published in Italy in 1989 by Istituto Geographico De Agostini. © 1989 Istituto Geographico De Agostini.

ORION and colophon are trademarks of Crown Publishers, Inc.

Translated by Luciano F. Farina and Marc A. Beckwith

Manufactured in the United States of America

Library of Congress Cataloging-in-Publication Data

Taviani, Paolo Emilio.
    Columbus : the great adventure : his life, his times, and his
voyages / Paolo Emilio Taviani.
        p. cm.
    Includes bibliographical references.
    1. Columbus, Christopher. 2. Explorers—America—Biography.
3. Explorers—Spain—Biography. 4. America—Discovery and
exploration—Spanish. I. Title.
E111.T23 1991
970.01'5—dc20   91-11358
                                                 CIP

ISBN 0-517-58474-3

10 9 8 7 6 5 4 3 2

Design by Leonard Henderson

First American Edition

Contents

1 Genoa: The Spell of the Sea   1

2 Columbus's Cultural Roots   7

3 Chios: The Spell of the Orient   11

4 Portugal   14

5 Iceland and the Lost Discovery of the Norsemen   20

6 Lisbon, Marriage, and Porto Santo   30

7 Master of the Atlantic   36

8 Reaching the East by Sailing West: A New Way
   of Thinking   42

9 Scientific Support: Toscanelli   51

10 The Proposed Plan Refused by the King
   of Portugal   57

11 Spain: Father Marchena   61

12 The Consolation of Beatriz de Arana   68

13 Desperation   72

v

Contents

14 All Wishes Granted   78

15 Gomera, Womb of America   86

16 The First Ocean Crossing   90

17 San Salvador: The First Encounter   97

18 "Asia"   104

19 Discoveries in the New Lands   113

20 The Peoples of the New Lands   121

21 The Myth of Gold   126

22 Shipwreck   130

23 Discovery of the Route Home   134

24 Mockery and Triumph   139

25 The Second Voyage   143

26 Tragedy   150

27 The Gold Mine   158

28 Exploration of Cuba and Jamaica and

    Misfortunes at La Isabela   164

29 War and Slavery   173

30 Humiliating Return to Spain   185

31 The Treaty of Tordesillas, Ferrer, Vespucci, and

    Preparation for the Third Voyage   188

32 "Another World"   195

33 A Mysterious Intuition   201

Contents

34   Coup d'État at Santo Domingo   204

35   To Complete the Uncompleted: The Fourth

     Voyage   213

36   Chiriquí: The Shattered Dream   222

37   Veragua: Gold and Coca   226

38   Santa Gloria   235

39   The Last Crossing and Death   242

40   Columbus the Man, Protagonist in the Great

     Undertaking   251

   For Further Reading   265

   Index   267

Columbus
THE GREAT ADVENTURE

1 | *Genoa: The Spell of the Sea*

Antonio and Giovanni Colombo, Christopher Columbus's great-grandfather and grandfather, were peasants of Mocónesi, Italy, a village above Chiavari where grain was brought by mule from Piacenza, in the Po Valley. At Mocónesi and the nearby villages, the mills that ground the grain were powered by water from a sizable river. The flour was then taken by mule to Quinto, today a district of the city of Genoa but then a coastal village five miles east of the city ("Quinto" is short for *quinto miglio,* "fifth mile").

Columbus's ancestors had probably come to Mocónesi from Piacenza along the mule track, called Via del Pane ("Bread Route") because it was used to transport grain. By it Giovanni moved to Quinto, where he continued to farm. There was born his son Domenico, who learned the craft of weaving wool and later moved to Genoa.

From 1439 to 1447 Domenico practiced his trade in Genoa, where there was a sharp struggle between the partisans of the Adorno and those of the Fregoso. Here is an account by a nearly contemporary historian, the celebrated Giustiniani:

> On 4 January 1447 Barnaba Adorno was elected doge, and everything went according to the wishes of the Adorno fac-

tion. But Barnaba's rule was most brief, for on 30 January Giano da Campo Fregoso, who for four years had steadily harassed the Adorno faction, staged a coup. Doge Barnaba Adorno had a large number of soldiers, including six hundred handpicked fighters sent to him by King Alfonso of Aragon. Giano came by night in a single galley, entered the city, and stormed the ducal palace with eighty-five men. He met stout resistance, and a bloody battle ensued in which all of his men were wounded. Nevertheless, his prowess and strength were so great that he was victorious and became doge.

Domenico Columbus was among the many within the city who sided with the Fregoso. As we would say today, he was an activist, tried and true, so much so that on 4 February, just five days later, the new Doge Giano named "to the guardianship of the Olivella tower and city gate his beloved Domenico Colombo."

The sensitive and lucrative position of guardian of the gate was normally renewed every thirteen months. On 5 November 1448 the Olivella tower was no longer entrusted to Domenico Colombo. But in the summer of 1450 Pietro Fregoso became doge, and on 1 October 1450 he bestowed on his faithful supporter Domenico Colombo the guardianship of the gate.

In the meantime, Domenico had married Susanna Fontanarossa, whose dowry included a house and land in Quezzi. In 1451 Christopher Columbus was born, either in the house on Olivella Alley next to the gate or in Quinto if his mother went there to give birth, as was the custom, at her in-laws' house. In 1455 Domenico moved to a house on Diritto Alley, in St. Stephen's parish, in the district of St. Andrew at Ponticello.

In the five centuries since then the house has been repaired and rebuilt, but it is still located in the exact spot where it was—fifty yards from St. Andrew's city gate, which appears as it did then. On the ground floor was Domenico's wool shop, and on the upper levels the living quarters. The house was dark, hemmed in by the tall buildings flanking the narrow street. Behind it, between the uninterrupted line of buildings and the city walls, was a tiny space for growing vegetables, called the "gardens," though scarcely large enough to warrant the name. The land that belonged to the Columbuses later became part of the old cloister of St. Andrew, which has since been reconstructed.

The imagination of an intelligent child must have suffered in the restricted space of the shop and living area, where his mother was raising the younger children, Bartholomew and Diego. This experience constitutes the first image we have of Christopher, one in which he learned to daydream. In his youth he dreamed of endless, wide-open spaces from the corner of a dark room, just as another great Italian, the poet Leopardi, would imagine vast, distant horizons from a corner of his hedged-in garden.

Beyond the walls of the house, beyond the garden, lay the city of Genoa, called *Zena* by its residents and thus also by Christopher Columbus. Beautiful Genoa, majestically staged, a source of striking wonder for those who see it for the first time from the sea. Superb and awe-inspiring Genoa, with its churches, houses, and palaces forming a gigantic staircase topped by the fortress of Castelletto, a rich site then as it is now. Witchlike Genoa, enchanting and captivating without offering much, not because it is stingy but because it is hemmed in by the mountains and without land, blessed only with scraggly, low-yielding plants and bushes blasted by the sea winds. Genoa cannot give its children anything, but throws them back onto the sea, which is everything to the city and from which it receives everything and gives back only the service, tenacity, commitment, and genius of Genoese sons. Fairylike Genoa, with its women reserved but discerning and love-giving; with its nearly beachless sea drawing forcefully into its mysterious depths, its joyful skies clear and bright when the north winds blow; with its little churches and sanctuaries atop the mountains. Genoa is still all this today, though defiled by factories and by some architectural monstrosities. The city has remained much as it was, for the mountains have protected it from major changes, and the sea has not changed.

Genoa looks superb from the sea, with imposing palaces, churches, roadways, and spacious plazas—but what a labyrinth, with narrow alleys and passageways ill kept and neglected, obstructed by arches, bridges, trestles, stairs, banks, and even wooden buttresses reaching to the second floor on the outside of buildings, like the taverns of pre-Augustan Rome. Just as contradictory has been the character of the Genoese people for centuries: haughty and proud of their treasures—their walls, towers, gates, palaces, churches, and harbor; petty and mean-spirited—like their dark, steep, tortuous alleys—regarding everyday matters.

This is the Genoa in which Columbus was born and raised. In its narrow little streets he took his first steps with his mother and father; in these streets he had his first childhood experiences. From Diritto Alley—right between St. Andrew's gate and the hill of Molcento—the young Christopher often walked to St. Stephen's parish church; to the Ducal Palace, where the leaders of the Fregoso, Adorno, Spinola, and Fieschi families came and went on horseback; and to the Via Regia, to see the litters with their fine ladies.

Apparently he was not satisfied with these experiences or particularly interested in them. He studied in the primary school of the Wool Merchants Guild, receiving instruction—in the Genoese dialect—in religion, arithmetic, geography, and the rudiments of navigation. The Latin he wrote was very different from that of Caesar and Cicero; it was typically medieval, the official language of the Church and the legal documents of the Republic of Genoa.

At a tender age, as he would often write later, Christopher began to sail, but it is probable, indeed certain, that he had encountered the sea earlier. Where? At the harbor and on the beach. At the harbor it was not difficult for a boy to slip unnoticed and ignored into the multicolored crowd. There were ships, and sailors speaking a profusion of tongues, from every country. They came from all parts of the Mediterranean, east and west, as well as from Portugal, Flanders, and England. What an abundance of sails! How many hulls rolling and pitching, coming and going! And everywhere the overpowering smell of the sea, an exciting, exalting, fascinating scent.

This gives us a second image of Christopher, the boy of seven or eight wandering about the docks; stopping for hours to watch the movements of the ships, the handling of the sails, the rudder, and the anchor—to mention but a few elements connected with leaving port or docking alongside the wharf. He certainly dreamed of one day being on those decks and setting out to sea, the high sea, where the salt smell is undiluted, headed for other ports, other cities, the hundreds of cities where so many various and strange peoples came from.

Christopher probably did not go down to the sea at Albaro or even the mouth of the Bisagno, which is closer. It is improbable because to do so in Columbus's time would have required leaving the city and crossing several miles of open country. Leaving the city in those times was a problem for an adult, so one can imagine how much harder it would have been for a boy. Most women and not a few of the men of Genoa were born, lived, and died within the city walls. It was so in Genoa and in many other cities in Italy, Provence, France, and Flanders. That was certainly not the case with Domenico Columbus, craftsman and merchant as well as political activist, nor with Susanna Fontanarossa Columbus, born at Quezzi. If Christopher went outside the city walls, however, he must have done so with one or both of his parents. Where would they have gone? To Quinto.

At Quinto was his grandfather's house, a typical home of Ligurian peasants: four bare walls with a loft built of small boards and a narrow wooden stair leading to it. On the first floor were the doorway, fireplace, sometimes a cow, calf, and donkey, a few tools, and supplies for a spartan diet. Here the mother raised her children while spinning or weaving when she was not helping her husband farm. The older children surrounded her, working with her or watching the pot on the fire filled with homegrown vegetables seasoned with oil and salt, the *prebugioun*. In the room upstairs the parents and children of both sexes slept, separated by reed partitions.

Christopher certainly stayed in the house in Quinto when he was very young and, when he was older, during the summers or the family grape harvests in the fall. From this house it was not hard to go down to the sea, either through the meadows or over the few rocky areas. Today the whole area is covered with houses, buildings, asphalt, and raised highways, but the sea laps the gray, dark rocks as it always has.

One can sit on these rocks and reflect, ignoring the architectural chaos and the din of the city over one's shoulder, reliving the sensations Columbus must have had as a boy, sensing the limitless horizon of a sea rarely calm, its changing colors now azure streaks of light blue, now navy blue, sometimes violet or almost black. The sensations are not always pleasant, not even when the sky is serene and the water exceptionally calm. The surroundings provoke strong and violent feelings, good for tempering character, forcing one to meditate deeply and go beyond superficiality and lightheartedness. It was on these rocks, outside the port of Genoa, that Christopher first experienced the sea.

Here is a third image of Christopher: he has learned to swim in the sea, a sea dangerous for the nonswimmer because so few beaches are safe. He already possesses the sea and loves it, staring at it longingly from a rock. He is no longer simply dreaming of the horizon; it is right in front of him; he is looking at it, dreaming now of the day when he will finally reach it.

2 | *Columbus's Cultural Roots*

That Columbus was born in Genoa is not, as some have suggested, a fact unrelated to his achievement. There is no doubt, as we shall see, that the grand design of reaching the Orient by sailing west was born on the Atlantic, not in Genoa or Liguria. But where was the genius born that conceived and realized it? Where was formed that nearly superhuman character with its obsessive tenacity, its stubborn persistence, its unshakable certainty? Where were its roots? Columbus's faith—not the superstitious elements but its essence, always concerned with the mystery of the Transcendent, of the Word made flesh, a faith dedicated to the noblest cults, the two most relevant to the needs of the human spirit, those of the Madonna and St. Francis—how did it germinate? Where did Christopher imbibe it as a young child? It is in these areas that Genoa and Liguria were important.

Samuel Eliot Morison, an admiral in the United States Navy and one of the greatest Columbus scholars, writes, "Genoa was certainly a place to give any active lad a hankering for sea adventure." The Englishman Ernle Bradford, an expert sailor, adds, "It was in fact more than natural that one of the world's greatest sailors should come from Genoa."

What kind of place is Genoa and Liguria? It is a narrow strip of land between the mountains and the sea, a coast with a continuous succession of rocks, gulfs, inlets, coves, tiny bays, landings, ports, small harbors, and short beaches covered with rocks or golden sand interrupted by promontories, some rocky, others covered with splendid pines. Liguria's uniqueness springs from the Ligurian Sea. Over millennia its commerce has been only by sea: from Lerici in the east to Nice in the west there is a continual flow of people and goods by sea. By sea comes all, or nearly all, Liguria's commerce. By sea are knit the economic, cultural, and emotional ties among families of diverse nations; by sea were made marriages which over the centuries bound together the Ligurian people, preventing close intermarriage that unavoidably took place in remote villages of the interior. By sea were developed powerful ties, both economic and political, among the weak links of the loosely structured Republic of Genoa. By sea were formed religious ties along the Ligurian crescent with Genoa as the seat of the archdiocese.

Indeed, the impact of the sea on the Ligurian people is retold in the history of every century and the chronicles of every year and season. Commonly, the Ligurian personality is said to be conditioned by the scarcity of land and the forced reliance on the open sea. Ligurians link this scarcity of land to their introverted temperament and proverbial parsimony—really just honest frugality. The influence of a sea without beaches and shallows yet always open to a wide horizon helped mold analytic intelligence, a serious character, and moral commitment.

Such a historically and socially pervasive influence is wonderfully apparent in economics, finance, and trade, where two Genoese characteristics are evident: loyalty, which implies trust, and suspicion, which prevents deception. There is also tenacity, the daughter of sobriety, as indispensable as intelligence; and the Ligurians' profound sense of religion links life to God, while their sense of moral commitment guarantees righteousness undefiled by hypocrisy or compromise.

The outcome in social and political relations is different. The Genoese lack of confidence in and reluctance, even aversion, toward politics stems from their great maritime capacity and their inability to pursue agriculture. At sea—from the days of sail to steamers, until the beginning of this century—a commander won his men's esteem, respect, and devotion through his bravery. He chose the course, avoiding the thousand treacheries of the weather, mists, currents, and shallows; weathered storms; entered unscathed the mouths of rivers and channels; and drew alongside docks. All these things are difficult, as anyone who has navigated with sail knows, for shipwreck is always lying in wait, every day and every night, practically every hour. What does it matter if the captain is stern, rigid, and aloof, if he complains and is never satisfied, never gives you a word of praise? By bringing the ship to port safely he guarantees your life. A sea captain did not need the skills of a politician.

This summary of the character, attitudes, flaws, and brilliance of the Ligurians applies to their greatest son, Christopher Columbus. He was born and spent his adolescence and youth in the second half of the fifteenth century, when Genoa was becoming, as Fernand Braudel put it, "the metropolis of European capitalism." For centuries Genoa had been one of the naval capitals of the Mediterranean. From Genoa, armies and fleets had departed for the first Crusades. Blessed with a perfect natural harbor and located at the head of a deep gulf nearly in the center of the Mediterranean, Genoa had successfully wrested control of the Tyrrhenian Sea from the Saracens, Pisans, Provençals, and Catalonians. Freedom of movement and control of the maritime routes to the Ligurian Sea were vital for men and ships to explore the Mediterranean for landing places and the most developed ports, which the Genoese used in their penetration inland searching for goods and markets. A historian especially good at synthesis, Giovanna Petti Balbi, tells us that from the beginning of the second millennium the Genoese were in Sardinia and Corsica, then on the coasts of Tunisia and Spain, then in the western Mediterranean, before controlling the Levant, where they arrived with the First Crusade. They created a true colonial empire, economic rather than political, because individuals—Zaccaria, Vignoso, Ghisolfi, Adorno, Lomellini, and Centurione—controlled the deployment of capital, ships, men, and commercial undertakings in this or that part of the Mediterranean, often acting contrary to the policies and political alliances of their homeland. Genoese communities were established in Spain, on the islands, in North Africa, in Egypt, and even around the Black Sea, creating a massive network encompassing both the Atlantic (Portugal, England, and Flanders) and the Orient (Persia, India, and China).

In the fifteenth century Genoa already enjoyed an economic system that can be called capitalistic, or perhaps better, mercantilistic. It was already beyond the feudal Middle Ages, which had not been a time of free trade except sporadically and clandestinely. It was in this mercantilistic world that the young Christopher grew up: the seventy-seven notarized documents in which his father is a central figure or is simply referred to are unequivocal proof of that. *Buying* and *selling, interest* and *percentages, shares* and *profits*—these were terms unknown in the Middle Ages. With this heritage of economic culture, Columbus left Genoa, crossed British waters several times, traded in the Portuguese and Spanish islands of the Atlantic and Africa, and lived in Portugal, where he negotiated with the king before arriving in Seville and Córdoba. In Spain he would find the most conspicuous Genoese settlement, with the Adorno, Doria, Centurione, Grimaldi, Pinelli, Spinola, De Mari, and Di Negro families, the best names of the wealthy mercantile class of prosperous Genoa. And there in Andalusia, in a world of Genoese bankers, merchants, and ship chandlers, he would develop his great undertaking.

Columbus's Genoese cultural roots, clearly and unequivocally evident in trade and economics, are also evident in another, related field: geography. Genoa in the fifteenth century was already one of the capitals of nautical cartography, perhaps the most important, vying with Venice, Majorca, and the Arabian schools. As a boy at the school of the Wool Merchants Guild, Christopher learned the first elements of geography and of navigation in the center of Christendom with the deepest knowledge of those subjects.

In conclusion, Genoa was not only the birthplace of the Discoverer of the Americas, but it owns numerous archival documents concerning him, and it was his cultural homeland: From Genoa Columbus inherited his basic character and faith, his knowledge of the sea, as well as his scientific curiosity and economic initiative.

3 | Chios: The Spell of the Orient

*I*n 1459, when Christopher was eight or nine, the fortunes of the Fregoso party began to decline. Pietro Fregoso died tragically after a dramatic skirmish near the city gate of St. Andrew. Another Fregoso, Archbishop Paolo, led his party in the civil war that ensued and managed to win the dogeship, but in 1464 he was overthrown and fled to Corsica. Genoa passed into the control of the Sforza, dukes of Milan.

Between 1466 and 1470, as the larger fortunes of the Fregoso set so too did the small fortunes of Domenico Columbus, leading to his decision to move to Savona. With his party in disgrace, gone were his hopes of receiving patronage, and he decided a change of scene would help. Savona was a satellite of Genoa, with greater opportunities for commercial activity than historians generally recognize. It was, however, exploited, unjustly scorned by Genoa, and used by leaders and partisans of different factions and by troops of several sovereigns—Anjou, France, Milan, and Aragon—as a forward base for attacking Genoa or as a refuge after a failed assault or after being driven out of the city. In Columbus's time the fate of Savona was still closely tied to that of Genoa, as it had been for centuries.

In Savona Domenico pursued his craft as a wool merchant, but he also operated a tavern. What about Christopher? By now fifteen years old, he had already begun to sail in the waters of Liguria, Provence, and Corsica. Between voyages he stayed ashore, working in his father's shop in Savona on Via San Giuliano, today Via dei Cassari. Had he sailed continuously, the activity required in a sailor's life might have left him no time to dream of new and wider horizons. Instead, during the months ashore, the immense joy he had experienced on the open sea permeated his ambition, leading him into further contemplation of the future, and left him longing for the day when he could again stare at the infinite.

The maritime destiny of the man who would become the most famous discoverer of all time was thus first shaped in Savona. We do not know whether it was chance or Columbus's desire to honor Savona that led him to make it the only Ligurian name in the Caribbean: he would name a beautiful little island southwest of Hispaniola Saona, the name it retains today.

Columbus's first long voyage—a decisive one for his future—was to the island of Chios, in the Aegean Sea, for which he left from Savona on 25 May 1474. From the Middle Ages until the nineteenth century, the island was known as *Scio,* but it has since reverted to the name given to it by the ancient Ionian colonists. It covers 355 square miles, or four times the size of Elba, one-fourth that of Majorca, and a little less than twice that of the Isle of Man. Today it has fifty thousand inhabitants but was once more populous.

Chios is part of the Sporades archipelago, a chain of islands along the western edge of Asia Minor. A narrow strait separates Chios from the peninsula that forms the Gulf of Smyrna. Proud of a glorious past—Chios claims to be Homer's birthplace—it was in Columbus's time one of the pillars of the resistance by the remnants of the Roman-Byzantine world against the inexorable advance of the Turks. Genoa and Venice vied for this island in the Middle Ages until, at the beginning of the fourteenth century, it was occupied almost without interruption by the Genoese, first by the Zaccaria family (1304–1329) and then by the Maona (1346–1566), a society of ship chandlers whose members later assumed the name of Giustiniani.

On Chios Columbus fell in love with the Orient, to which the island was a gateway, a rich market bustling with trade. Merchants from the East, with their exotic and varicolored costumes, filled the port, bazaar, and shops, mingling with those from the West preparing to depart for the mysterious regions of silk, pearls, and precious stones.

Chios was and is most beautiful. The mountains are bare but majestic and superb because they are tall and close to the sea, like the Alps of the Ligurian Riviera. Their lower slopes, hills, and meadows are covered with luxuriant vegetation, providing vistas completely unlike those of Liguria. Sage, thyme, and oregano fill the air with strong, pungent aromas, and dominating them all is the perfume of mastic. Chios is called *Mirovolos* ("A Thousand Aromas"). The scent of mastic, obtained from the mastic tree, is all-pervasive and unmistakable. The mastic tree, of which Columbus would speak many times when he thought he had found it in Cuba, grows nearly everywhere in the Mediterranean, but only in the southern part of Chios does it yield the precious, aromatic mastic when its bark is cut. A kind of resin, mastic was and remains the mainstay of the island's economy.

In the Middle Ages, first the Venetians and then the Genoese jealously guarded the production of mastic, and the Turkish sultan made great use of it to satisfy the vanity of his favorite women. It is still used in the Middle East for making perfume, drinks, and sweets, as a dental adhesive, and as a digestive aid. The production of mastic and the wealth it generated—fifty thousand ducats per year—gave Columbus stimulating ideas. Considering the great change in the velocity of money since then, that figure is roughly equivalent to $7 million today.

But it was primarily the scents of Chios that excited Columbus. His exceptional sense of smell is worth noting. Everyone recognizes his sense of the sea, almost a sixth sense. There is general agreement that a requirement, not sufficient in itself but necessary, for understanding the sea is a well-developed sense of smell, allowing one to sense the play of the winds and currents. The perfume of the mastic exalts the instincts, spurs the fantasy, and provokes dreams. It is the preferred perfume of harems, and its scent is quite close to that of incense, which inspires mystical feelings and disposes the spirit for religious contemplation. The scents of Chios cast a magical spell over the young Christopher. He was enchanted by this sensation, part of the magic of the Orient, and would remain so for the rest of his life.

4 | Portugal

Columbus made other voyages in the Mediterranean besides that to the island of Chios. We know from his writings that he knew all the coasts west of Genoa as far as Catalonia. He also knew Corsica, Sardinia, Naples and Sicily, and the Barbary Coast. He never speaks of Rome, and therefore we believe that he never had occasion to go ashore at Civitavecchia or on the banks of the Tiber.

The *Historie*, attributed to his son Don Ferdinand, speaks of a pirate raid ordered by René d'Anjou against an Aragonese galley in the Gulf of Tunisia, but some have expressed reservations about the episode. Although exaggeration or bragging may have distorted that incident, there is no reason why it could not have occurred. Between 1470 and 1480 Genoa was often at war with Aragon and allied with the Angevins. By serving René d'Anjou, Columbus was following the policies of his city and his father's party.

In the summer of 1476 Columbus left the Mediterranean for the first time, sailing into the Atlantic. A commercial expedition bound for England had been organized in the spring at Genoa; the small fleet was made up of a galley belonging to Gioffredo Spinola, a whaling ship belonging to Nicolò Spinola, a galley belonging to Teramo Squarciafico, and the galley *Bettinella,* commanded by Gian Antonio Di Negro. There was also a ship of Flemish origin, called the *Bechalla,* outfitted in the bay of Noli and staffed by a primarily Savonese crew, commanded by Cristoforo Salvago.

One can imagine Columbus's emotion when the ship passed through the Strait of Gibraltar on his first voyage into the Atlantic. Beyond lay the open sea, not one of the oceans but the Ocean—the other three, the Pacific, the Indian, and the Arctic, were not yet known—the Ocean Sea, of which he, Christopher, would one day become Admiral. The ships headed northwest for Cape St. Vincent, the southernmost tip of Portugal. It was 13 August 1476. Between Cape Santa Maria and Cape St. Vincent the fleet was suddenly attacked by a squadron of French corsairs. Genoa was at peace with Portugal and France, but either because they misunderstood the intentions of the Genoese fleet or simply succumbed to the temptation of a rich prize, the French started a battle. The Genoese resisted stoutly. By nightfall the battle had ended tragically for both sides. Of the five Genoese ships, only two managed to escape to Cádiz, in Castile; the other three were burned and sunk, and many of their crew drowned. Of the corsair squadron, four large ships (according to one account, five according to another document) were sunk and hundreds of men died.

Some of the shipwrecked men, Columbus among them, were saved by fishermen from the Portuguese village of Lagos. He later wrote about his fortunate arrival on the Portuguese coast in a letter of May 1505 to King Ferdinand of Spain: "The Lord our God miraculously sent me here so I could serve Your Highness; I say miraculously because I landed in Portugal." *Miraculously* and *landed*—the first used twice—clearly and unequivocally indicate how the future admiral arrived unexpectedly on the Portuguese coast under lucky circumstances. Thus, 13 August 1476 was a memorable day in Columbus's life.

The believer sees in the shipwreck of the Genoese sailor on the coast of Lagos the hand of Divine Providence. The skeptic sees in it the astonishing and matchless role played by chance in history. Lagos is a fishing village at the mouth of a small river. The fishermen moor their boats in the river, whose waters flow softly into a bay. The houses are poor, like those of other fishing villages on the Mediterranean. The bay is large and tranquil. It appears not to open onto the ocean, but it was already tied to the history of the Atlantic Ocean: from here left many of the expeditions organized by Henry the Navigator.

Henry the Navigator, Prince Henry of Portugal—had Columbus heard of him? He could have, for the sailors of the Atlantic talked about him. Henry was part of history and more, he was myth, legend. But if Columbus had not heard of him before he certainly did hear his name and tales of his ventures from the fishermen of Lagos. Not fifteen miles from the village lie Sagres and Cape St. Vincent, where Henry had lived much of his life and established the headquarters for conducting his studies and organizing his discoveries.

The life and works of Henry the Navigator mirror the calling and history of Portugal. He gathered pilots, sea captains, cartographers, astronomers, and sailors of all origins: Portuguese, Catalans, Genoese, Venetians, Jews, and Moors. He had informers from as far away as Ethiopia and the Persian Gulf. His court became a center of nautical culture and colonial experience.

Though not a navigator or explorer himself, Henry holds the distinction of having introduced a new type of ship, the caravel; agile and swift, it was suited to navigation on the open sea. He also was the first to institute and codify the new mercantilistic methods of colonization in place of feudal ones: the station, transfer, company, and monopoly. Henry gave the cartographers a new direction, a renewed interest in the unexplored Atlantic coasts of Africa.

In the High Middle Ages the Amalfians, Pisans, Venetians, Genoese, and, later, Florentines dedicated themselves to cartography. From the thirteenth to the fifteenth century, the Genoese were the leaders in cartography, to their lasting glory. From Genoa the Jewish cartographers of Majorca learned and spread their art. The Genoese school also gave rise to the Catalan school of Barcelona, the Portuguese school of Lisbon, the Arab school, and, later, the Flemish.

I have said that it was not by chance that the greatest discoverer in history was born and grew up in Genoa, for Genoa had been the capital of cartography and cosmography since the early Middle Ages. And it is not mere coincidence that we find Christopher's brother Bartholomew with him in Lisbon. The art of cosmography and that of nautical mapmaking formed a close bond between Genoa and Portugal, more important than those created by trade, commerce, or finance. Henry made this bond even tighter; it would culminate in the conception of Columbus's great enterprise. But the maritime work of Prince Henry went beyond cartography. He and the undertakings he organized were responsible for the discovery that constituted the premise of the great Columbian discovery: the certainty that beyond the desert, beyond the torrid zone, lay a fertile, habitable land and a navigable sea.

Unfortunately, for centuries people outside scholarly circles have thought that Columbus was the first, or among the first, to sense that the earth is round. That belief is incorrect. Classical geographers knew perfectly well that the earth was round. During the Middle Ages the notion was forgotten, but by the middle of the fifteenth century it was an established principle among geographers and scholars in general. By supposing that the earth is round, then, Columbus was doing no more than aligning himself with prevailing thought.

Later, we will see that Columbus courageously set himself against the Ptolemaic and medieval geographic conceptions in his belief that the antipodes were habitable and reachable. Here I will simply emphasize the three main principles of classical geography: the earth is a sphere, the southern hemisphere is uninhabitable, and so are the antipodes.

The Phoenician, Greek, Roman, and Christian worlds knew only that an immense sea of sand lay to the south. Its coasts on the Ocean were sand—when they were not rock—devoid of the least bit of vegetation. South of Mauritania: sand. South of Numidia: sand. South of Libya: sand. South of Egypt: Nubia, all sand on both sides of the narrow strip along the Nile. From antiquity until 1400 A.D. the only land south of the Nubian Desert known to have vegetation and life was Ethiopia, a land considered nearly mythical. In the first decades of the fifteenth century no one knew about Guinea yet. The immense desert had kept the worlds of Greco-Roman-Christian civilization and black Africa ignorant of each other.

By land Marco Polo had managed to reach Cathay (China) and Cipango (Japan). By land and sea the Greeks had reached India.

By land Christian missionaries had reached the Arctic Circle and the more distant steppes of Russia. By sea the Vikings had reached Greenland and the frozen shores of North America. By going up the Nile and crossing the Red Sea Christian missionaries had converted Ethiopia. But no one had reached the fertile lands in central and western Africa and the large rivers south of the Sahara.

Many are the great rivers of Asia and Europe, but only one, the Nile, was known in Africa. Because it seemed strange that a continent should have but one river and more logical that it should have none, the conviction arose that Egypt was part of Asia. Africa was considered to start west of the fertile Nile delta, with the Libyan Desert, the beginning of the immeasurable Sahara.

The Mediterranean, the Red Sea, the Persian Gulf, the English Channel, the North Sea, the Baltic Sea, the North Atlantic itself—these bodies of water were open channels of communication for races and civilizations. While the sea was navigable, the sea of sand, the desert, was not. All would have been different had the Carthaginian merchants of the fifth century before Christ, the Christian missionaries contemporary with St. Augustine, the Arabian knights of the caliphs, or the heirs to the Prophet found the sea south of Mauritania, Numidia, or Libya. The sea would not have stopped them as the desert did.

And so the knowledge of the Christian and Arab worlds did not go beyond the northern oases. The desert wastes, ever more desolate to the south, and the lack of vegetation had persuaded the Greek philosophers that the whole torrid zone was uninhabitable. So said Aristotle and the great geographer Ptolemy. Their convictions were accepted by the Arabs, who were faithful Aristotelians, and even by Albertus Magnus, who, in the thirteenth century, still doubted that life could survive on the coasts and islands of the torrid zone.

Consequently, it was a great revelation for the Portuguese navigators when they reached the mouth of the Senegal River. It still provides a stark contrast, one of the sharpest in nature. Imagine what it must have been for the first discoverers to see the luxuriant vegetation at the mouths of the Senegal and Gambia rivers after the rocks of Morocco and the sands of the Sahara, which they had considered endless. Did they feel like the barbarians descending from the Alps? No, because the latter had known that in Italy they would find a land of sun and blue skies. Did they feel like the first men on the moon? No, because the astronauts had a good idea of what they would find there.

By contrast, the people of antiquity and the Middle Ages believed that to the south the earth ended with the torrid zone. That belief persisted among the sailors of Christendom until that grand moment in 1444 when Dinís Dias, an ancestor of the better-known Bartolomeu, reached the mouth of the Senegal River at Cape Verde. His caravel was a marvel to the Africans. Four of the bravest approached the monster that went on the water; they did not know whether it was a fish, a bird, or an apparition, and when they saw the men aboard they turned around and fled so precipitously that the Portuguese could not catch them.

The Europeans were in the land of the blacks, but the importance of the discovery lay more in the lush and unexpected tropical vegetation, which until then no one had imagined existed in Africa. Only fifteen degrees from the equator, in the torrid zone, abundant vegetation offered sustenance to numerous large animals and to strong, handsome people. Confronted with the reality of Cape Verde (today Dakar), what value could the doctrines of Aristotle and Ptolemy have? As Ruge, the great German geographer of the nineteenth century, commented so pithily, those doctrines foundered on the rock of Cape Verde. In the shade of those palms lie buried not only medieval geography but the classical Greco-Roman dogma that the southern hemisphere is uninhabitable.

Here converge the discoveries of Henry the Navigator and Columbus's intuition: with the baggage of antiquity buried, a new horizon opened for the development of scientific geography. Men began to trust their own eyes more than the theories of the ancients.

5 | *Iceland and the Lost Discovery of the Norsemen*

*F*rom Lagos Columbus went briefly to Lisbon, where he would return later. Now he had to continue his travels. A second expedition was prepared at Genoa for England. On this trip, or perhaps on an earlier one made up of some of the surviving ships that had reached Cádiz and Lisbon, the young sailor arrived in London and from there went to Bristol.

The old city of Bristol lay at the foot of a hill. Its port was no more than a channel formed by the River Avon, a medium-sized river that falls into a mountain cleft below the city and empties into the great estuary of the Severn, a true bay, more salt than fresh. Something similar, though on a very different scale, Columbus had seen at Lisbon. What he had not seen at Lisbon and was now experiencing for the first time was the incredible range of the tides. At the January full moon—presumably the month when he was in England—high tide at the Bristol docks is thirty-six feet, while at Avonmouth, where the Avon empties into the Severn, it reaches forty-seven feet. It is one of the highest tides in the world and the highest known in Columbus's time, when the sixty-two-foot tides of Nova Scotia were unknown.

The phenomenon had exceptional consequences for the security of the port of Bristol, for it rendered it inaccessible to ships during low tide, when the Avon did not have enough water for ships to navigate. These tides, a novelty for a Mediterranean sailor, would have struck Columbus, sensitive as he always was to natural phenomena.

He was also struck by the bustling docks along the waterway. They were crowded with goods: salt, grain, wine, and velvet coming in; wool and barrels of dried fish going out. Columbus was already familiar with English wool. He had seen it arriving in the port of Genoa, and he had gone to London specifically to pick up a large cargo of it. The exportation of fish, on the other hand, was new to him. Columbus had heard of herring; now he saw them in huge quantities, by the ton. The herring had been unknown, indeed impossible to find, in the Mediterranean. Columbus, familiar only with docks of sardines and anchovies, was speechless when he first saw the size and quantity of herring and other fish. Now he realized the smallness of the Genoese fish market compared with these huge mounds of fish and wondered from whence they came.

Similarly, he had seen dried salt cod imported in Genoa and Lisbon, but here were tremendous quantities of it. There was also salmon, which he had not seen in Liguria or Corsica. Where did the salmon come from? The rivers of Scotland, that is, from the north. And the cod? They came from the Dark Sea in the far north. And the anchovies? From both places, the waters off Ireland and Scotland as well as the sea of Ultima Thule (the northern limit of the world).

Acutely sensitive to nature, Columbus was interested in many aspects of such remote regions: the land, verdant yet yielding few crops because of the lack of sun; the damp and overcast climate; the river estuaries opening onto excellent ports; and the fish, abundant and unlike those of the Mediterranean. He observed everything, investigating all aspects of nature with his innate geographical sense. Although without formal training, Columbus was a geographer. Geography attracted him; its mysteries drew him on. Here at Bristol he was presented with the mystery of Ultima Thule, mysterious simply because there was nothing beyond it. And because it was mysterious he wanted to go there.

He embarked for Galway, on the west coast of Ireland, and from there sailed in a fleet bound for Iceland. In Columbus's time Iceland legally belonged to the king of Denmark, but the English had a de facto monopoly on trade with the island. Columbus may have been unaware that Iceland belonged to Denmark and probably thought that it was an English island, just as Madeira was Portuguese, the Canaries Spanish, and Chios Genoese, because islands usually belonged to those who held a monopoly on their commerce.

In any case, the Icelanders were not English but Norse. The Irish monks, in search of more pagans to convert, may have reached Iceland before the Norsemen, but it was the latter who discovered, or rediscovered, it in 874 and brought news of it to Christendom. The Norse settled Iceland, intermarrying with the Celts who later arrived in successive waves from Ireland. The island appears inhospitable to a man from the south, but not to one coming from the frozen, foggy, rocky lands of Norway. There were no forests except for a few dwarf birches, and those were all quickly cut down, but there was an abundance of pure water throughout the island, as well as geysers, which furnish natural boiling water. An enormous region—as big as England, Columbus would write later—where, despite rocks, glaciers, lava, cinders, and bogs, there were plains covered with grass in summer, perfect for raising sheep. And off the coasts was a staggering abundance of fish.

How the Norsemen reached Iceland is one of the glorious pages of a fascinating, nearly incredible history, reaching as it does the limits of human endurance. If the Phoenicians were the greatest mariners of the ancient world, the Norse were unequaled, unique in the Middle Ages. They were crude and bloody. Wherever they went they murdered, plundered, and pillaged. Terror smiled on their undertakings on land, but the sea was not dominated by their cruelty. Yet these Norsemen stoutly resisted the general fear aroused in the Middle Ages by the Dark, or Poisonous, Sea, as they called it in their harsh language.

Their undertakings at sea have something of the miraculous about them. Their ships, light and swift, still inspire awe that they were able to face the furious storms of the North Atlantic, the unknown Ocean, until then unexplored. And they did so without nautical instruments.

Floki, one of the discoverers of Iceland, left Norway with three crows. The first one he let loose promptly flew back to Norway. The second took a few turns in the sky and landed back on deck. A few days later the third was released and flew straight ahead, toward the large island. Thus Floki reached Iceland and was nicknamed Crow.

The Norsemen were the first—before Columbus—to sail the open sea. Some maintain that the Irish had done so before them. Certainly the Irish sailors were better than the English in the first centuries after Christ, but their valor and courage remain only a memory. Their deeds, in the service of the monks wishing to spread the Word among the peoples of the Atlantic islands, remain the stuff of legends, for proof and historical references are lacking.

The explorations of the Norsemen were not single, isolated undertakings by a handful of courageous sailors; instead they consisted of many ships and men; entire fleets set out on courses without knowing their ultimate goal. Not one or two Ulysses but a whole population of them! The Norse were one of the greatest and most remarkable peoples in human history. They converted to Christianity, but some magical and pagan rites survived for centuries, as did their ruthless cruelty; nor did they change their strict customs. Neither did their epic valor at sea diminish.

The conversion of the Norse brought them into Christendom, and so they became the standard bearers for Christianity in the Arctic. About 1000 A.D. the Icelandic Althing—the first parliament of Europe, which met in the open, among the rocks of the canyon of Thingvellir—adopted Christianity as the state religion. Within a century there were two dioceses on the island. Meanwhile, the Norse continued their sea voyages. In the spring of 982 Eric the Red, banished from Iceland for killing a servant, crossed from Iceland to America. This stretch of sea was called the Danish Channel, but it is a true ocean, quite treacherous because of fog, storms, and icebergs.

Bjarni and other Norsemen followed Eric the Red. They were so used to rocks, ice, and wastes of lava that they called the new land Greenland because they found the hillsides covered with lichen. They established their settlement on the southwest coast, where the climate is moderated by the Gulf Stream, and facing America. The Norse brought news of the new land back to Christendom. Traces of it are found in Genoese, Venetian, German, Arab, and Catalan maps of the early Middle Ages. About 1120 a diocese was established in Greenland.

The Norsemen did not stop there. About 1000 A.D. they reached a land devoid of vegetation, rocky and frozen, "overlooked by every blessing and good thing," and named it Helluland. It was either the Island of Newfoundland or Labrador. Pushing farther south, they came to a flat land covered with woods; its coast was without rocks or cliffs, broken up by white sand dunes. They named it Markland ("Land of Woods"). It was almost certainly Nova Scotia, in southeastern Canada. Beyond Markland the Icelandic sagas speak of Vinland ("Land of Vines").

Scientific research, from that begun a century and a half ago by Carl Rafn to the most recent—supported by chemical analysis of historic evidence—indicates an impressive agreement between the geographical data of the sagas and the results of archaeological excavations. And so it seems that Vinland must be considered not an imaginary land but some part of the North American coast.

Undeniably the Norse came to know of other lands beyond Greenland. The papal bull naming Eric Gnupson as the first bishop of Greenland calls him bishop *Groenlandiae, regionumque finitimarum* ("of Greenland and neighboring regions"). This is proof that such lands on the American continent were known to the Norse, but it is also an indication that Vinland—only a century after Leif Ericsson landed there—had become no more than a memory, that no definite knowledge of it or of fertile, hospitable lands remained. No knowledge of it reached the peoples of the Old World.

The Norse knew America but did not discover it. In geography the term *discovery* does not signify simply being the first to reach a place; rather it means going there, returning, and reporting the experience so anyone who wants to can duplicate the discoverer's experience. The Norsemen's remarkable experiences in America bore no fruit. Vinland, Markland, and Helluland, that is, the American mainland, were, unlike Greenland, visited only occasionally and never colonized.

Unlike the evidence of the Norse in Greenland, their alleged traces in North America are all unsubstantiated. The most controversial archaeological find, clearly a hoax, is the Kensington Stone, a rock with an inscription in runes discovered on the property of a Swedish farmer at Kensington, Minnesota, in 1898. It bears the following inscription: "8 Gotlanders and 22 Norwegians set out to explore from / Vinland to the west. We camped near two islets / a day's march from this stone, toward the north. / We rested and fished for a day. After / returning we found ten men red / with blood and dead. Hail Mary! / Deliver us from evil!" On the side is this note: "We have ten men by the sea to / watch our ships, a fortnight's / journey from this island, year 1362."

The most renowned modern critic considers the Kensington Stone spurious. The great German runologist W. Krauss considers it a modern fabrication. Another well-known runologist, the Dane Erich Moltke, declared the inscription apocryphal. Moltke, followed by other prominent Scandinavian runologists, maintains that the runes of the Kensington inscription cannot be from the second half of the fourteenth century because runes had fallen out of use in Scandinavia before 1300. He says the inscription was probably imitated from some old Swedish almanac written in runes and still available in the eighteenth century. The archives of the Minnesota Historical Society contain what appears to be a rough draft of the inscription that was later carved in the stone. "Common sense should have dismissed this as a hoax," says Samuel Eliot Morison. "Norsemen were sea discoverers, not land explorers. . . . Every leading runologist of Scandinavia and Germany who has deigned to examine the inscription has called it a clumsy forgery."

Another monument that has stirred controversy is the tower at Newport, Rhode Island, a massive, cylindrical stone structure. In some ways its shape and architectonic details resemble typical medieval Norse structures. Dr. W. S. Godfrey made excavations at the base of the tower in 1948–49 and was able to prove that it was built by Benedict Arnold, governor of Rhode Island, about 1675, probably as a fortification against Indian attack. The excavations turned up, among other things, coins, building stones, and fragments of tobacco containers, all of which can without doubt be traced to the Colonial period. The tower at Newport was definitely built much after the time of the discoveries of Columbus and Cabot.

The Vinland Map, also called the Yale Map, deserves separate discussion, both because of the polemics aroused by its discovery and the recent determination that it is not genuine. Published in 1965 by Yale University, the western section of this world map—

that is, the North Atlantic—has geographical details not found on maps until the mid-sixteenth century, while its eastern portion is quite confused and arbitrary. In particular, Greenland appears with its complete coastal outline.

The book published by Yale, *The Vinland Map and the Tartar Relation,* claims that the map is authentic, dating to 1440, or half a century before the Columbian discovery, and that it was probably based on a map from the twelfth century. Some historians vouched for the authenticity of this document and held that the date attributed to it was credible. Many others immediately denied its authenticity. Among the latter was Giuseppe C. Caraci, who had the great merit of immediately pronouncing it "the fraud of the century."

In January 1974, after two years of careful, meticulous laboratory analysis commissioned by Yale University, Walter MacCrone Associates of Chicago determined that the map is not genuine and was probably made in this century. The publication detailing their work shows, among other things, that the crystalline structure of the ink used on the parchment map contains a pigment made of titanium peroxide that did not come into use until after 1920.

In 1903 J. Fischer summarized the experiences of the Norse in North America during the eleventh century. As he said, the Norsemen held flourishing colonies on Greenland for centuries. For evidence of that we have historical, geographical, and cartographic proof based on pontifical briefs and accounts by the papal legates. There are also numerous ruins of churches, houses, and other buildings as well as a certain number of Nordic relics.

On the other hand, Vinland, Markland, and Helluland—the North American mainland—were visited, but not colonized, as some suppose. All the theories positing the colonization of Vinland have proved baseless; more important, research has revealed not a single shred of indisputable evidence of permanent Norse settlements. Subsequent research, including the most recent by Frederick J. Pohl and especially Helge Ingstad, has not contradicted Fischer's assessment.

It is undoubtedly strange that this people, whose contribution was essential for the foundation of three of the greatest civilizations of the modern world—English, Russian, and Italian— and who founded the four countries that are in the vanguard of the modern world for their social, political, and economic organization—Norway, Denmark, Sweden, and Iceland—should have come in contact with that Eldorado that is North America without even attempting to colonize it. But so it is.

The first reason the Norse did not colonize America is that on their visits in the eleventh century, of which the sagas speak, the lands they saw were anything but Eldorado. They saw Labrador and Newfoundland (Helluland), coasts and lands that Iceland and even Greenland far surpass. They also visited Nova Scotia (Markland), superior to Iceland in its forests and therefore as a source of lumber but in nothing else. A few of them had seen or visited Vinland, for it is recorded in the sagas, but it is not even mentioned in the chronicles; it remained more dream than reality.

The second reason is that the Norse of Iceland were an unlearned people. Even their leaders were illiterate. They had no real geographical knowledge, nor did they concern themselves with the problem of the size and shape of the earth. When they did they assumed it was flat.

The third reason is that the Norse did not find in North America a civilization more advanced than theirs; they did not find well-to-do potentates or lords whom they could massacre and whose goods they could seize; they did not find capital stored or in use which they could take by force.

In North America they found thick forests, but it was easier and more convenient to bring lumber to Iceland from Norway, their original homeland, where they gladly returned to see grandparents, uncles, and cousins. They also found vast pasturage, but they faced a people more bloodthirsty and less civilized than they, a people who were not intimidated by their aggression as Europeans were and who had nothing to lose but rather something to gain by harassing and attacking them.

The Norse struck fear into the Franks and Saxons, the Byzantines and Arabs, the Slavs and Latins, but not into the natives of North America. Here, instead, it was the other way around: it was not worth the effort to conquer such poor natives who lived so simply; it was not worth the effort to stay in lands infested with such opponents. For all these reasons the Norsemen did not colonize North America, and so the discovery was lost.

By 1477 ships no longer left from the fjords of Iceland for the colonies in Greenland. The last ship to go to Greenland from Iceland did so in 1408. Nevertheless, Columbus certainly heard the Icelandic and English sailors speak of Greenland, that vast, frozen island west of Iceland. We also cannot rule out that someone told Columbus of Vinland, the land southwest of Ultima Thule bathed by the Dark Sea across from Ireland. Columbus had heard of it, probably in Galway, from those who, like him, believed that the earth was not flat but round. And so the first inkling that Asia lay beyond the Ocean began to germinate and take on consistency in his mind. Thus, something of the tremendous Norse experience was not lost; part of it did affect the Genoese sailor who had reached the coasts of Iceland aboard a British ship.

On these same coasts the Norse had landed six centuries earlier, discovering the Ultima Thule of Christendom. From these coasts the Norse had departed five centuries earlier to find Greenland and visit other lands farther west. This is the link that binds the Norsemen's concrete discoveries (Iceland and Greenland) and their lost one (the North American continent) with Columbus's glorious discovery.

The voyage to Iceland put in his mind the first piece of the mosaic that would become Columbus's grand design. But it did more. Between England and Iceland lie hundreds and hundreds of miles of open sea; navigating it in a sailing ship is difficult and dangerous. The voyage to the north tempered Columbus's character, and in this way, too, it was fundamental to the conception of the undertaking that would make him famous.

After seeing Chios and after the fortunate landing at Lagos, Columbus's voyage to Iceland was but one more stop along the long road in the development of his grand discovery. It was a stop teeming with conjecture, theories, imaginings, and fantasies. If other lands lay to the west of Iceland, why couldn't other islands be found to the south as well? The ship on which Columbus had embarked went to Iceland regularly, so far west and north of the European mainland, and thence one could sail even farther west. To the north the land did not disappear in fog and air, as the ancients believed and as many in the Mediterranean still believed. To the west there was no abyss but still more lands. Why couldn't similar voyages be carried out farther south, in a sea less stormy, less wrapped in mists? Such questions Columbus surely had on his trip to Iceland.

Quite commonly, men who feel themselves destined for great

things are preoccupied with a single idea for long periods of their lives. Every action, every thought becomes a means to that end. So Columbus, tempered by the seas of the north, did not remain ashore there long. Soon he was at sea again in Icelandic waters—as a fisherman?—but already acting like an explorer. By the time he returned to Portugal and settled there, he had taken another giant step down the road to his grand design: he had gained confidence on the Atlantic.

6 | Lisbon, Marriage, and Porto Santo

On his return from Iceland and England, Columbus settled in Lisbon. Many Genoese lived there, including the agents of his shipowners, the Spinolas and Di Negros. In the State Archives of Genoa is a deposition made 25 August 1479 before the court of Genoa by Christopher Columbus as an agent employed by Paolo Di Negro. It concerns a civil suit over an agreement made in July of the preceding year regarding a shipment of sugar from Madeira. The deal went badly, for Di Negro did not send Columbus the money to pay for hiring the ship and for the merchandise.

The details of this legal proceeding do not interest us. We are, however, interested in the statements that the witness "Columbus Cristophorus" was about twenty-seven years old and a citizen of Genoa residing in Lisbon. Also of interest is his statement that he had to return to Lisbon early "the following morning."

Columbus could have given his deposition in Lisbon. Instead he came to Genoa; no doubt he visited his parents and brothers in Genoa itself or Savona. Some have suggested that Columbus had already conceived of some Atlantic venture and took advantage of this trip to speak about such ideas with his shipowners or even with officials of the republic. That hypothesis cannot be ruled out even if there is no documentation to support it.

The development of the grand design could not have been complete in 1479. It is, however, possible that Columbus spoke with his shipowners and with Genoese officials in general terms about possible new Atlantic discoveries and of the importance of the islands already known (such as Madeira).

In any case, he did not find an attentive audience. The exploit of the Vivaldis had been disastrous; that of Lanzarotto Marocello benefited only Spain. There were still some bold Genoese, and Columbus was one of them. But the republic, the Banco San Giorgio, the shipowners, and the merchants felt that although Genoa was quite wealthy, it was too small a state to expand permanently into the Atlantic.

If Columbus had discovered America under the Genoese flag it would not have flown long over the new lands. It would soon have been supplanted by that of Spain, France, Portugal, or England. That was precisely what had happened with the island of Lanzarote and other islands in the Atlantic. Thus, no matter how bold the sailors born and bred in Genoa, in one way or another their efforts ended up profiting others, and so it was only logical to let them conduct their enterprises in the service of other nations. If Columbus spoke with anyone about the Atlantic, about his as yet undefined Atlantic plans, the response he received was no doubt along these lines.

On 26 August 1479 Columbus left Genoa never to return. He left with a conviction bitter yet realistic, for the Genoese are bitter realists. He was convinced that if he was to undertake voyages on the Atlantic, if he was to search for new lands there, he would have to seek support and organization for his undertaking from the Atlantic nations, from the states that already had power and established interests in the Atlantic and were most likely to feel the need to expand there.

In late spring or early autumn of 1479, Columbus married Felipa Moniz Perestrello. According to Don Ferdinand and Las Casas, he fell in love in church, as did so many Italians, Spaniards, and Portuguese of the time. Only in the half light of a church could one stare at a nice girl without causing a scandal. He married for love, but while Columbus truly loved Felipa we cannot rule out that he had other reasons for marrying her, of which there were two principal ones. First, Felipa Moniz Perestrello was a noble, impoverished perhaps but a full-blooded noble, both on her fa-

31

ther's side, that of the Perestrellos, and on her mother's, for the Monizes were one of the oldest noble families in Portugal. All his life Columbus sought either to acquire nobility or to have the titles he had been granted recognized. Nobility was the first demand—even ahead of monetary reward—he made for a successful voyage. Felipa's family was decayed nobility, just as Columbus wanted to believe and perhaps persuaded himself was the case with his father's family.

The second reason for the marriage is more understandable today. Bartolomeo Perestrello, Felipa's father, had been, according to Don Ferdinand and Las Casas, "a great seafaring man." Historians consider this an exaggeration; it certainly is that, but not as great as they imagine. Bartolomeo Perestrello, the son of Filippo Pallastrelli from Piacenza and Caterina Sforza, was born in Portugal at the beginning of the fifteenth century. The surname was modified into the Portuguese form of Perestrello, and the king confirmed their patent of nobility. Bartolomeo's second or third wife was Isabella Moniz, daughter of one of the most illustrious families of the Portuguese nobility. From that union was born Felipa. When she married Columbus, her father had been dead some twenty years.

Bartolomeo Perestrello was not a great navigator, much less a discoverer. He was, however, governor of the island of Porto Santo. If that great organizer and judge of men, Prince Henry, had awarded Bartolomeo an island so important for the exploration of the Atlantic, it means he was a man of some stature, not only because he was descended from high Italian nobility but because of his knowledge of the sea. After his death, the husband of one of his other daughters, Columbus's future in-law Pedro Correa de Cunha, was named governor of Porto Santo. There can be no doubt that Columbus was interested in maintaining a relationship with him.

Two things, then, combined with romance—nobility and the traditions and knowledge of the Atlantic possessed by Felipa's family. Columbus's meeting with Felipa Moniz Perestrello and their consequent marriage had a great effect on the genesis of the great discovery.

The route from Lisbon to Funchal or Machico—Madeira's ports in the fifteenth century—doubled the island of Porto Santo on its last leg. Columbus, then, was not only well informed about the existence of the island but had already visited it before marrying Felipa. He became familiar with Porto Santo after his marriage. Lying 27 miles northeast of Madeira and covering only 16.4 square miles, Porto Santo is a satellite of Madeira. From any point on the island one can smell the Atlantic, see its immensity, and, during storms, hear its waves crash on the shore.

There is no doubt that Columbus went to Porto Santo after his marriage, probably with Felipa. His son Diego may have been born there. In any case, Columbus lived there and was able to consult his father-in-law's maps, of which Don Ferdinand speaks: "His mother-in-law gave him the writings and maps which her husband had left her. They excited the Admiral all the more, informing him of other voyages that the Portuguese were making to Elmina and along the coast of Guinea."

Although Bartolomeo had been dead for many years, his maps spoke a living language. What they were no historian says, but clearly they were maps, *portolanos* (navigation manuals), commentaries, and manuscripts transmitted to sailors by the cosmographers and geographers of Sagres in the time of Henry the Navigator. Columbus rummaged among these papers and learned about the area of the Atlantic bounded by the Iberian Peninsula, the Azores, and Cape Verde. He understood theoretically what he had begun to understand under the stress of prolonged, hard sailing in this portion of the Ocean Sea, just as he had done in the Mediterranean, from east to west.

He rummaged—and the word is appropriate—not only among his father-in-law's papers but among the rocks and sands, probing the most hidden secrets of the beaches and heart of Porto Santo. Was it here that Columbus first thought of his grand design? Was it here that he refined his idea of "reaching the Orient by sailing west"? There are no documents to prove it, but the island of Porto Santo was probably the birthplace of this thinking.

Porto Santo is like a boat in the middle of the ocean, a kind of skiff compared to larger ships, a kind of outpost, simple and bare, of that part of the earthly paradise that is Madeira, with her sandy southern shores, pleasant and wide, and her rocky northern ones, dark and continually battered by agitated, often stormy waves. It is an island of black volcanic rock projecting to the southwest into the so-called unknown, a nesting ground for gulls, a sentinel encircled by turbulent waters. Here Columbus lived, with the vision of Madeira always in his mind. A magical island, Madeira was for him both the end of the known world and a clue to the existence of other lands farther west. His thoughts turned that way when he learned that a piece of well-carved wood and some reeds larger than those native to the island had washed up on its western shore.

Here he wandered about from one cove to another, staring at the horizon and trying to decipher the unknown, for now he was sure that there, beyond the meridian of nearby Madeira, must lie land, not the abyss. He expected some evidence of that land from the waves that broke against the rocks of Porto Santo. The idea that possessed Columbus had already taken its first concrete form: the West. And so he was obsessed not by sunrise but by sunset. At sundown he was either at Ponta da Calheta, Ponta da Canaveira, Ponta do Umal, or on the slopes of Pico Ana Ferreira watching the sun go down and thinking that at Portofino and Quinto the sun had been down for two hours and it was already night. Could there be, then, someone out there beyond Madeira, someone beyond the sea, watching this same sun—for him already half set—for whom it was still high above the horizon?

On the same parallel as Lisbon and the Algarve lie the Azores. Were there other islands to the west on the same parallel as Porto Santo and Morocco? Was there another Morocco, another Africa? Could there be another land with the same strange trees like those found only here on Porto Santo, like the *dragoeiro* ("dragon tree"), for example, found only in the Madeira archipelago and in the Canaries, which are also exposed to the west? And could the *marmulano* be there, found only on Madeira, Porto Santo, and Cape Verde, also exposed to the west? Neither tree is found in Africa—so he had been told, and he would confirm it for himself on his voyages to Guinea.

It has since been confirmed that the winds and currents enriched the insular flora with American plants. Indeed, on the beaches of Porto Santo and Madeira one can collect seeds from the West Indies, Mexico, and Florida. In the museum of the Seminary of Funchal are several specimens of such seeds, among them a broad legume the size of a fava bean, the *Macuna entata,* which on Porto

Santo was then called *fava do mar* ("sea bean") and today is known as *fava de Colon* ("Columbus's bean").

Was Columbus aware of this, keen and sensitive as he was to every aspect of nature and every detail of the sea currents? This question is hard to answer, but it is easy to suppose that he sensed something of what is now scientifically well established. This was another piece in the mosaic of his grand design.

There was another land to the west, whence the birds brought the seeds of exotic vegetation, a land perhaps as lovely and enchanting as Madeira. Was it an island? Why not a continent? Why not Asia? The sailors at Lisbon were certain the earth was round. And if it was round, why couldn't three or four hours of sunlight separate Porto Santo from the eastern edge of Asia since two hours separated Genoa from Porto Santo?

7 | *Master of the Atlantic*

olumbus's direct knowledge of Guinea was as important in the development of the grand design for the great discovery as his voyages to Chios, Britain, Iceland, and Madeira and his stay on Porto Santo.

We are certain he completed at least one trip to Guinea some time between 1482 and 1484. He speaks often in the *Journal* of the fort at Elmina and of the coast of Melegueta. The latter extends from Cape Mesurado to Cape Palmas. Near Cape Mesurado, Monrovia rises today, capital of Liberia. Cape Palmas is also in Liberia, near the border with the Ivory Coast. The fort is still at Elmina; actually, two forts now dominate the city of Elmina, in modern-day Ghana.

What was Columbus seeking at Elmina? Not agricultural products nor sea routes for his incipient design, for they lie in a quadrilateral of the Atlantic that, as we shall see, is north of the parallel of Guinea. It is often said that he sought gold there. The myth of gold constantly occupied his thoughts. He was only marginally interested in spices and dyes, although they were the basis of Portugal's economic interests. He would speak in the *Journal* of mastic and of the dyes that can be extracted from plants, but his *idée fixe* remained gold. He found gold at Elmina, or rather a flourishing gold trade.

It was not necessary to go to Guinea to learn the importance of the precious metal for Europeans, whose continent had almost none of it. True, the amount of gold discovered in 1471 at Elmina by the first explorers gave the Portuguese an illusory impression, for it had been accumulated over many generations. Africans had apparently sought gold for over two thousand years. For example, we know that even before the Christian era, necklaces of gold nuggets were made in Nigeria, which does not produce gold.

Making a monopoly of the trade, the Portuguese were able to import about 25,000 troy ounces of gold per year for a number of years. In 1502 a single ship carried 125 pounds of gold. Those are not large figures today considering the discovery and exploitation of the great deposits of South Africa and Siberia, as well as those scattered throughout the Americas. But in the fifteenth century such numbers were significant, enough to excite anyone thirsting after wealth, or even those with a moderate desire for riches.

From Portuguese documents it appears that the greater part of the gold in Elmina was in the form of ornaments, but there was new gold as well. Columbus was certainly preoccupied with determining its quality. The importance of the disproportion between worked gold and new gold was clear to him during his first journey to Elmina. There he learned to distinguish the two sources of gold. The people of the coast sifted river sand, gathering gold dust and occasional nuggets, while inland miners followed veins in the rocks, digging long galleries, sometimes one above the other connected by vertical shafts.

Later, when he was going from one island to another in the Caribbean Sea and finding bejewelled natives everywhere, his first concern was always the same: Where did the gold come from? Where was it found? In which rivers? On which mountains? The quest for mythical gold had sent Columbus to Elmina, whence he returned believing more firmly than before in the truth of accounts of the existence of gold.

In addition to gold, Columbus's trip to Guinea gave him experience essential for his grand design, which he was still formulating. In order to reach Guinea he had to pass Cape Verde—not the islands but the mainland, present-day Dakar—and its luxuriant vegetation. He saw the Grain Coast (present-day Liberia) and the Ivory Coast, learning that those areas not only had vegetation but were lush. He also saw people, multitudes of them.

He had wanted to verify with his own eyes the collapse of the belief held by the wise men of antiquity—from Aristotle to Ptolemy—and continuing through the Middle Ages that the equatorial zone and the southern hemisphere were uninhabitable. The belief was false, the doctrine was false. People tolerated the climate of the torrid zone very well. "Below the equator, where day always lasts twelve hours, is a castle of His Highness the King of Portugal, which I visited. I found its climate mild." Thus Columbus would write about Elmina in Latin crammed with errors typical of the late Middle Ages. Not only Elmina but the whole torrid zone "is not uninhabitable, for the Portuguese navigate it nowadays, and it is quite populated."

In addition, there were always new lands, new rivers, new forests, new fields cultivated by peoples of the same race. Beyond the equator, then, was land and, what is more, land of the same continent, Africa, whose northern coasts are bathed by the Mediterranean. New horizons were opening. One could reach the southern temperate region, which clearly had inhabited lands, or at least habitable lands. This was the great news Columbus had learned in the first years he lived in Lisbon and wanted to experience for himself at Elmina. Today it would be called history-making news. It was a fundamental piece—the most important and decisive one—in the mosaic from which was emerging, clear at last, his grand design.

Even before he crossed from east to west in the greatest discovery in history, Columbus can well be said to have mastered the Atlantic. He had gone to the north, to England and Ireland and beyond, almost to the Arctic circle, to Iceland. From those voyages he had learned about tides—the full magnitude, range, and strange mechanism tied to the phases of the moon few Mediterranean sailors understood. He had experienced fogs and storms unequaled in the warm seas of the south. And he had noticed the first unmistakable signs of the marine current that gives life to so much of Europe: the warm Gulf Stream.

On his return to Lisbon, Columbus was already a seasoned sailor. Before his marriage he had made a trip to Madeira in July 1478. It may have been his first there; it certainly was not his last. To Madeira and Porto Santo he returned many times both on business and for family reasons after his marriage. One could say without exaggeration that Columbus became so accustomed to the stretch of ocean between Lisbon and Madeira that it was his home. The play of the winds and currents, the likelihood of finding this or that type of fish—he knew everything about the Lisbon-Madeira route.

He knew all the stars along his routes; before studying them in astronomy books he had seen them every sunset, every night, every sunrise. And from the stars and winds and currents Columbus learned the secrets of the art in which he has no equal: the art of sailing the ocean by dead reckoning. He mastered it by going beyond the Canaries, to the Cape Verde Islands, the Azores, and Guinea. He certainly lived for some time on Grand Canary and knew Lanzarote and Gomera. He knew the Cape Verde Islands from his return from Guinea; the Portuguese ships preferred the island route to the coastal, where they would have been forced to tack. The knowledge he demonstrated in the waters of the Azores during the voyages of the grand discovery gives us assurance that he had also navigated among these islands during his Portuguese period. Moreover, some of the most important clues—of which I will speak below—were given to Columbus by the inhabitants of the Azores.

In the waters of the Azores, Columbus gained another conviction that was fundamental for the conception of his grand design: in that latitude of the Atlantic storms were more violent, frequent, and of longer duration than those farther south. Consequently, in periods of calm weather it was easy to sail back from west to east beyond Faial, but sailing from east to west was difficult and, for long periods of time, impossible. This conviction, as important as the knowledge of the trade winds, Columbus could not have acquired except in the waters of the Azores or, more precisely, by sailing from Faial to Flores and probably to some point beyond Flores.

In the second half of the fifteenth century, traffic between the Azores and other points did not come only from Lisbon. The routes between the Azores and Galway and between the Azores and Bristol or London were also commonly traveled. There was even some traffic between Madeira and the Azores. Frequently, ships took a cargo from Lisbon to the Azores, unloaded it there and took on another cargo, which they unloaded at Galway. There they took on another and took it back to Lisbon. Some fleets even went from the Azores to Iceland and back.

We are considering, then, a large area of the Atlantic, bounded by Portugal, Ireland, Iceland, the Azores, Madeira, Cape Verde, Elmina, and Guinea, or between 64° and 5° N and 8° and 30° W. Within this wide area was a smaller one—between 40° and 28° N—that Columbus traveled from east to west, northeast to southwest, southwest to northeast, south to north, practically in every direction. At the center of both areas lies the island of Porto Santo, at 34° N and 16° W. This was the womb of the grand design; the mother of the plan was the Ocean itself, the Atlantic, the Dark Sea. Porto Santo, the Canaries, and the Azores were three points in a geographic and maritime equation whose solution granted mastery of the Atlantic. With the marine sense that distinguished him, Columbus found that solution between 1476 and 1484.

At that time only variable winds were known, for in the Mediterranean, the European Atlantic, and the North Sea between England and the Low Countries all winds are variable, shifting frequently but for different reasons. Sailors did not have precise knowledge of winds that blow in the same direction throughout the year, as do the trades. The Portuguese navigators of the fifteenth century who preceded Columbus knew only the marginal effects of the Atlantic winds in the waters of Madeira, the Canaries, and the African coast. They were familiar with the constant northeast winds, or trades, only along the coasts of Africa; they did not know what the winds would be like out on the open sea—how strong they would be and how far they would extend to the west.

The constancy of the trades derives from the continual heating of the atmosphere in the tropics, which makes the air less dense and leads to lower atmospheric pressure. Masses of nearby air are drawn in to reestablish equilibrium, much like breathing. The resultant winds would blow toward the equator, but because of the rotation of the earth, all bodies in motion in the northern hemisphere turn to the right, while those in the southern turn to the left. Consequently, the air masses in the lower part of the atmosphere in the northern hemisphere blow from northeast to southwest, and in the southern hemisphere blow from southeast to northwest. These are the trade winds, which blow all year long with the greatest regularity. The trades from the northeast and those from the southeast are separated by the zone of equatorial calms, the doldrums, caused by the ascending movement of the mass of warm air. The doldrums are near the equator but more in the northern hemisphere because the northern hemisphere has more land—which is warmer than the sea—than the southern hemisphere has.

It would be an exaggeration to maintain that Columbus knew all these scientific facts, yet he understood their practical effects empirically from his many early voyages. He discovered the potential significance of the constant winds from the northeast for sailing west; it was the most critical discovery for his mastery of the Atlantic. That it was not pure speculation but something that he had verified in his own experience can be deduced from his behavior on the first voyage. Otherwise it would be hard to explain why Columbus left Palos, headed straight for the Canaries, and from there confidently sailed west. Likewise, it would be hard to explain why, on his return, he displayed not the least hesitation in sailing north to the latitude of the Azores, where he knew the winds are variable but frequently blow from the west. Columbus not only discovered America, he discovered the two great maritime routes of the North Atlantic, which the next four centuries of navigation by sail would verify are the fastest and best.

Many other things Columbus studied and understood by sailing back and forth in the rectangle of the Atlantic between 40° and 30° N and 30° and 10° W. In those waters, and in the islands where he went ashore and lived, he developed a symbiotic relationship with the Ocean and with the constellations. He scrutinized and studied the sea and the heavens, discovering many of their secrets. He burned with love for that sea and that sky, his fancy excited by unbounded horizons. Yet only one horizon was truly unbounded for Columbus: not that to the north, where he had already sailed through many degrees of latitude and reached the Ultima Thule; not that to the south, where lay Guinea, which he already knew; not that to the east, where he had full knowledge of Portugal, Spain, the Mediterranean, Italy, Greece, and Egypt. His interest now focused exclusively on the west. There lay the unknown, there he was driven by the burning dream of his fantasy, an unquenchable passion.

8 | Reaching the East by Sailing West: A New Way of Thinking

Asserting that Columbus was master of the Atlantic is not sufficient to explain how he developed his original and brilliant plan of reaching the east by sailing west. In chapter 9 of the *Historie,* Don Ferdinand speaks of the clues that inspired the Admiral to seek the Indies. He sees them as the third cause of the discovery. The first cause related to ideas about the roundness of the earth and its measurements, going back to Ptolemy and Marinus and confirmed by the concepts of Strabo, Ctesias, Onesicritus, Nearchus, Pliny, and Alfragano. The second cause was the "many learned authorities who had stated that from the western edge of Africa and of Spain one could sail west and reach the eastern edge of India": Aristotle, Averroës, Seneca, Solinus, Marco Polo, Sir John Mandeville, Pierre d'Ailly, and Julius Capitolinus. To these were added the opinion and encouragement of the letters from the Florentine scholar Paolo Toscanelli.

In reality things came about somewhat differently. When Columbus saw Toscanelli's letter to Canon Martins of Lisbon Cathedral, he already had a clear conception of his grand design. In conceiving it he had no knowledge of Strabo, Seneca, Nearchus, Pliny, Averroës, or Solinus. Perhaps he had heard of the accounts of Marco Polo, but he scarcely knew the names of Aristotle,

Ptolemy, or Marinus. Columbus read their books in Spain after his grand design was already conceived.

The clues of which Don Ferdinand speaks, then, were not the "third cause" of inspiration, but rather the primary cause. Here are the clues in the order in which Don Ferdinand presents them in the *Historie*.

1. Martín Vicente, a pilot for the king of Portugal, told Columbus that one time when he was 450 leagues west of Cape St. Vincent he found a piece of wood finely worked but not carved with iron. Because of that and because the wind had been blowing from the west for many days, he knew that the wood had come from some islands to the west.

2. Pedro Correa, husband of one of Felipa Moniz Perestrello's sisters and so Columbus's brother-in-law, told him that on the island of Porto Santo he had seen another piece of finely carved wood blown in by westerly winds, which had also brought reeds so large that a single joint could hold nine carafes of wine.

3. The king of Portugal himself told Columbus about these large reeds and showed some to him. Because nowhere in our part of the world do such reeds grow, the winds had certainly brought them from some nearby islands or from India, for in book 1, chapter 17 of the *Cosmography* Ptolemy says that these reeds are found in the eastern parts of the Indies.

4. Some residents of the Azores told Columbus that once, when the wind had been blowing from the west for a long time, the sea threw some pines on those islands, especially Graciosa and Faial, while it is well known that no such trees grow anywhere in those parts.

5. Residents of the Azores told how on the island of Flores, one of the westernmost, the bodies of two men washed ashore; their faces were broad and different from those of Christians.

6. At Cape Verga, on the west coast of Guinea at 10° N, some dugouts with cabins were once seen. They were not from that country, and it was assumed that in going from island to island in the Atlantic the winds and currents had forced them off course.

7. Antonio Leme of Madeira told Columbus that when he once went far west in his caravel he had seen three islands.

8. Many people from the islands of Hierro and Gomera in the Canaries and from the Azores declared that every year they saw some islands to the west. They were certain of it, and many trustworthy people swore it was true.

9. In 1484 a man from Madeira came to Portugal to ask the king for a caravel to go and discover a certain land that he swore he saw every year in the same way, agreeing with the others who said they had seen it from the Azores.

These nine clues Columbus gathered before he left Portugal. Many stories and rumors, some true, some fantastic, circulated among the sailors of Lisbon and among the first colonists of Porto Santo, Madeira, the Azores, and the Cape Verde Islands. Don Ferdinand cites a few of them in the *Historie,* but there is no doubt that Columbus heard many others. For example, Columbus wrote in a postil that he had seen two corpses in the sea off Galway, brought in by currents from the west. While Don Ferdinand cites the case of the two non-European corpses washed up on the beach of Flores, which his father learned from the Azoreans, he does not mention the other case at Galway. This is proof that the *Historie* does not record all the clues Columbus assembled.

More important than these clues—all of which depend on the testimony of others—are those directly recalled by the future Discoverer: observations made in the first person, experiences, conjectures, considerations, and comparisons. These contributed decisively to planning for the grand discovery.

We have already seen what Columbus learned from his voyage to Iceland and from the experiences of the Norsemen. Most important, he acquired the first essential piece of the mosaic from which would emerge the grand design: the conviction that to the west lay no abyss but Iceland—which was not the Ultima Thule—Greenland, as well as other lands, although the last were wrapped in legend. And if land was in the northern latitudes, why couldn't there be some in the center of the Atlantic, on the latitudes of Lisbon or Ireland?

Ireland cannot be neglected among Columbus's first experiences. Although Galway lies at 53° N, Columbus had seen delicious patches of sun on the expanses of green grass around that varicolored city. He surely was told that this green is the green of all of Ireland, a tender green that knows no seasons, only the heaviness of the rains and the fleeting, almost frivolous joy of the moments of sunlight. This green, already a symbol of Ireland for centuries, would be so for centuries to come; it must have struck Columbus's fancy, sensitive as he was to all the phenomena of nature.

Columbus knew that Ireland was far north of Milan and Pavia, the cities of the duke who was already the master, at times directly and at times indirectly, of the Republic of Genoa. Whether or not his family came from Piacenza, Columbus could not have helped knowing that it snows frequently in winter at Milan, Pavia, and Piacenza. In Ireland it does not. Galway is about eight degrees north of Milan; nevertheless, its winters are less severe, and the land is green everywhere even if it is not particularly fertile in the growing season. It does not snow, but it rains continuously, and the clouds come from the west, carrying water and warmth just as the sea currents that come from the west bathe the shores of Ireland and bring warmth. All these things the Irish sailors knew; none knew better than they that to the west lies land, just as Italy lies west of Greece and Spain west of Italy.

The belief that land lay to the west was so widespread among the Irish that legendary voyages by Christian missionaries multiplied over the centuries. Some of them really took place, as did those to Iceland, which lead in turn to its discovery by the Norse. Most others were fruit of the imagination, though to what extent is difficult to say. I have already told how at Bristol Columbus learned the magnitude of the tides; he would experience it again at Galway and in the fjords of Iceland. Confronted with that experience, any intelligent schoolboy would ask an adult standing by him, "But where does all this water go when it falls?" And when the tide rises, he would ask, "Where does all this water come from?"

Columbus, being a studious observer of natural phenomena, could not have helped formulating the question himself. His reply could not have been, "The abyss! The water comes from the abyss and there it returns." The tides of Bristol, Galway, and Hvalfjördur rose from the west and receded to the west, so the tides supported the continuity of the sea from land to land, a continuity that, from east to west, was known in the Mediterranean. And the phenomenon of the tides is greater because the Ocean is larger than the Mediterranean. The confines of the Ocean, though greater, had to have limits; that is, there had to be beaches on the other side, not an abyss or darkness.

The significance of Madeira and Porto Santo for Columbus I have already suggested. He found there—by himself, without the need of help from anyone else—signs of the existence of lands to the west: the sea bean and exotic woods on the beaches; plants that are not found in European or African meadows, mountains, or marine basins; and the play of the currents—now warm, now cold—along the beaches, depending on which way they faced.

In the Canaries Columbus confirmed his impressions formed earlier on Madeira and Porto Santo. He found plants that do not grow in Europe or Africa, especially the *dragoeiro* of Madeira and Porto Santo. He also found in these islands extraordinarily fertile soil and a delightful climate, both in sharp contrast to the nearby coast of Africa, which is dry and sandy. On the Canaries, in particular, the winds and currents from the west bring fertility and abundance while those from the east bring drought and clouds of sand.

On the Canaries Columbus found a phenomenon he had not encountered on Madeira, Porto Santo, or the Azores. In none of these other islands did the first Europeans find any inhabitants. In the Cape Verde Islands they had found some blacks, the same race as those of Africa. In the Canaries, however, they found aborigines unlike any other African or Mediterranean race: they were white skinned, blue eyed, and very tall. They had no knowledge whatsoever of navigation or of shipbuilding; they painted their bodies and mummified their dead. They remained in the Stone Age. They worshipped a unique god, the terrible Great One, the Omnipotent. When Columbus arrived in the Canaries for the first time— between 1478 and 1484—this strange and bizarre people still ruled the islands of Tenerife and La Palma and were barely conquered on the Grand Canary. Columbus was certainly struck by the existence of a people unknown even to scholars, unlike any other people in the known world. At that time Temisoro, the generous king of the Grand Canary, was converting to Christianity. How many other people ripe for conversion could be found beyond the Ocean, in lands as yet unknown and in those known in the far reaches of Asia!

In the Cape Verde Islands Columbus increased his knowledge of the trade winds, of their role in the routes taken by the Portuguese and therefore their possible role for going farther west in those latitudes. Portuguese ships visited the Cape Verde Islands more often on their return than on their way out, not so much because of any whim or logistical needs but to make better use of the winds. On the way out the trades, blowing from northeast to southwest, favored the rather difficult navigation along the coast until, after doubling Cape Palmas, the ships entered the doldrums. On their return, however, the ships had to beat back to windward against the trades after leaving the doldrums. It was a course continually tormented by tacking. For the return, then, it was less perilous to sail directly toward the Cape Verde Islands and from there to the Canaries, staying well off from the dangers of the coast. From these different routes Columbus learned much about the significance and importance of the trades.

The Azores, as I have mentioned, were one of the keys in the conception of the grand design. The archipelago is considered "Europe" for modern-day tourists. It is European in the customs of the people—primarily Portuguese and, to a small extent, Flemish—who inhabit the various islands. It is European in its climate, not substantially different from that of Portugal, though more humid. It is European because Europeans introduced the fauna and a great part of the flora.

In Columbus's time the effects of Portuguese—and Flemish—colonization were just beginning to be felt. The flora were still indigenous, characterized by typically Atlantic plants. And the presence of man was not yet evident except in a few inlets or bays where the first settlements were established. The archipelago appeared to be the natural result of the play of volcanoes that had erupted in that part of the Atlantic and created a number of islands and surrounding islets: São Miguel and Santa Maria in the east; Terceira, Graciosa, São Jorge, Pico, and Faial in the middle; and Flores and Corvo in the west.

The archipelago is a unit. All the islands were and are Portuguese, and even from a geophysical point of view their unity is evident at a glance. Their volcanic origin is apparent on all the islands: all have *caldeiras,* craters that often have lakes at the bottom, and everywhere are flows of basaltic lava, hot springs, and steam vents. But because of this unity—in fact, because of the striking contrast with this uniformity—people with a sense of the sea like Columbus had cannot help noticing the profound difference in the play of the winds and currents on the eastern islands and on the western. Only during winter is the entire archipelago under the regime of winds out of the west and southwest. During the other seasons the two eastern islands, São Miguel and Santa Maria, are under the beneficent influence of the northeast trades, while the central and western islands remain under the influence of the western and southwestern winds.

It would seem that in brazenly thrusting up this confusion of craters the Ocean wished to establish the encounter of two superhuman forces, almost a divider of the marine and air currents coming from the shores of Europe and Africa and those coming from western shores. Today anyone looking to the east from the extreme edge of São Miguel or Santa Maria knows he is facing Europe, as did Columbus. If someone looks west from the edge of Faial or Flores, he knows he is facing America, whereas of course Columbus did not. But he sensed that he was not facing an abyss: from São Miguel he saw the sun rise from the Atlantic; from Flores or Faial he saw it sink into the Atlantic; just as it did not rise from an abyss in the east, the sun could not sink into an abyss in the west.

Land—the mainland, the point of reference—seems distant on both sides: it is 875 miles to Portugal, 1,054 miles to Newfoundland, really not insurmountable distances. The Azores, that crucible in the center of the Atlantic, were an important field of observation for Columbus in his endeavor to master the Atlantic. There he found the best clues among those cited by Don Ferdinand, and he must have found many others, clues that he kept secret like locked doors, opening them only when he realized his great plan. Above all he learned on the Azores not to sail from that parallel for the unknown, for he would have been thrown back by the winds that always blow in the opposite direction on the western islands. He also learned that that parallel would be appropriate for the return route.

Of his voyage or voyages to Guinea I have already spoken. There is, however, one more clue that needs to be emphasized. Columbus describes Elmina as "the place where daylight always lasts twelve hours." In Iceland he had observed that day lasts four and one-quarter hours in winter, seventeen hours in spring, and twenty-one hours at the summer solstice. These contrasting climates both supported life: plant and animal life and, most important, human life. So, superstitions crumbled in Columbus's mind; beyond the world known to the ancients lay unknown yet inhabitable lands and navigable seas.

I have listed the clues cited by Don Ferdinand and the impressions, conclusions, and considerations suggested to Columbus by his personal experiences, those same experiences that had given him mastery of the Atlantic. From these clues and experiences, Columbus instinctively drew the inspiration for his grand design. With his intuition, that sixth sense of the sea that distinguished him from others, he drew on his direct knowledge of the Ocean; on his detailed and meticulous study of the currents, winds, heavens, and stars; and on the clues he gathered along the beaches of Iceland, Madeira, Porto Santo, and the Azores.

With his intellect he gathered, analyzed, and discussed rumors and impressions of the Atlantic with Genoese, Portuguese, Spanish, and English sailors, especially the news of the marvelous, age-old experience of the Norse adventurers, gathered from the most direct sources, the sailors of Bristol, Galway, and in the ports of Iceland. With his imagination he shaped his dream in order to make it reality. Columbus's imagination was awakened by the enchanting sights of the Mediterranean coasts, those of Liguria, Corsica, Sardinia, Naples, Sicily, Chios, and Tunisia. It was set free by the solitude of the vast Ocean and buttressed by the wonders of Ultima Thule, magnificent Madeira, the blessed Canaries, the scattered Azores, and lush Guinea.

Thus was the grand design born from an inspiration, or rather from the fortunate coalescence of a series of inspirations. The letter from Toscanelli and the study of the ancient and contemporary writers came afterward, when the design was very clear, precise, and worked out. The plan germinated, then, in the Atlantic Ocean, and so Columbus would justifiably want to become Admiral of the Ocean Sea. It was born at the very moment when the myth of the uninhabitability of the torrid zones of the equator was being shattered and when the conviction was growing, not only among scholars but also among sailors, that the earth was round.

The reality of the antipodes was still wrapped up in the unknown, distorted by superstition. Common people conjured up strange pictures of a frightful abyss where men and ships would be swallowed. Scholars and more serious sailors spoke of interminable wastes of water unnavigable by ships. In short, both groups held the antipodes inaccessible by humans. A typically medieval concept is Dante's: he locates Mount Purgatory in the antipodes, rising from a sea inaccessible to the living.

Here the extraordinary innovation of Columbus's plan becomes apparent. It was born when he overcame, in the twinkling of an eye, two great fears, one a relic of the Middle Ages, the other born of following the African coast and shunning the open sea, which the Portuguese continued to do despite their productive and grand discoveries.

9 | Scientific Support: Toscanelli

The scholar Paolo dal Pozzo Toscanelli helped solidify Columbus's conviction that the land he sensed lay beyond the Atlantic was the continent of Asia. Toscanelli was born at Florence in 1397. He studied first at the University of Florence and then at the University of Padua, where the philosopher Nicolaus Cusanus, a few years his junior, became a lifelong friend. He returned to Florence at the age of twenty-seven.

Both Paolo and his brother Piero were practicing doctors, but scientific curiosity led Paolo into mathematics, physics, astronomy, and geography as well. Toscanelli's geographical knowledge was based on books on cosmography and astronomy; on maps that were multiplying not only in Genoa and Venice but in Flanders, Germany, and Vienna; on written accounts by explorers, missionaries, and business agents, especially Marco Polo's *Milione;* and on information gathered directly from contemporary travelers.

Toscanelli closely questioned travelers who came through Florence. He spoke with the Tartars from the Don basin and with Ethiopian emissaries who reached Italy in 1441 with Alberto da Sarteano. One German traveler to Italy was Johann Müller, known as Regiomontanus, who was the teacher of Martin de

Behaim, the traveler and author of the famous world map of 1492 preserved in Vienna. Regiomontanus had frequent discussions in Rome with Toscanelli in 1461 and 1463.

Toscanelli was considered the most outstanding mathematician of his time. Politian and Vespasiano da Bisticci composed tributes in his honor, Leon Battista Alberti dedicated a book to him, and Cardinal Cusanus, his close friend, dedicated his mathematical works to him and was inspired by Toscanelli's teachings when he himself designed a map of central Europe. We cannot rule out— indeed it is likely—that external events caused Toscanelli to abandon the contemplation of the stars and mathematics and to intensify his geographic studies, which before had been but a pastime or scientific curiosity for him. In the second half of the fifteenth century, the economy and learning of Europe, and especially Italy, were growing explosively. At the same time, the Turk was taking from Italy and other parts of Europe lands and peoples that had been integral to if not the progenitors of the common Greco-Roman-Christian culture: Greece, Constantinople, the Aegean islands, the coast of Asia Minor, the Black Sea ports, and Albania.

The fall of Constantinople to the Turk ruined many Venetian, Genoese, and Florentine families, particularly those involved in the spice trade. The Toscanelli family must have been preoccupied by these events and turned their gaze to the west to supplement the declining income from their commercial trade. There the land with the greatest promise was Portugal, not only because of its recent discoveries but also because it had before it an unknown and mysterious Ocean. If that mystery could be cleared up, science would be enriched. The world was growing smaller just when the need was being felt for wider spaces, new horizons.

Learning was no longer the preserve of a few monks, unmarried laymen, and ecclesiastics urged by an exceptional vocation. Sons of the nobility and the middle class were flocking to learning, to the arts and sciences; in Florence, Genoa, and Venice the sons of simple artisans and even peasants were pursuing knowledge.

The horizons of learning—of science, philosophy, and the arts— were also growing wider. Meanwhile, in the economic realm, the Europe of the fifteenth century had seen an extraordinary increase in consumer goods, indicated by the awakening of the middle classes, who were now accustomed to using manufactured goods and products that for centuries had been the monopoly of the nobility and feudal lords. Italy, particularly Florence, Venice, and Genoa, were seeing this great phenomenon translated into profits on their merchants' ledger books and in the traffic enjoyed by their ports and vessels.

For these reasons no one was in a better position than the Florentines, Venetians, and Genoese for understanding the importance of shipping avenues and trading posts and the impact on the burgeoning economic and cultural development created by the tremendous consumption of Europe and the production of Asia, which came through the Levant, the very lands the Turk had conquered or was in the process of conquering. No one was in a better position than the Florentines, Venetians, and Genoese for estimating the magnitude of the interests that the Asian trade represented and the gravity of the obstacles that would derive from the loss of the Levant.

Toscanelli was a scholar, but he participated in his family's business interests, and those interests were primarily concerned with the spice trade. A double interest, then—scientific and cultural as well as economic and familial—prompted him to look to the west. In the west learning would find new horizons; the commerce and fortunes of the Italian states would find new stability and opportunities.

Columbus encountered, then, the man who had sensed the new needs and feelings that were projected onto horizons as vast and infinite as they were yet undefined. Columbian historiography is not agreed as to how Toscanelli's ideas reached the Genoese. Don Ferdinand in the *Historie* and Las Casas speak of a direct exchange of letters, but many historians have serious doubts about such a correspondence. One thing is certain: Columbus was familiar with a letter Toscanelli wrote to Canon Fernando Martins of Lisbon. The letter is dated 25 June 1474 and came into Columbus's hands about 1480. Columbus made a copy himself, now in the Columbus Library, Seville. In it Toscanelli proposes going to the Indies by crossing the Atlantic Ocean:

> Although many other times I have argued for the shortest sea route from here to the Indies, where spices originate, which I

hold to be shorter than the one you take via Guinea, you tell me that Your Highness would now like me to give some statement or proof to make it understandable and possible to take that route.

Toscanelli proposes his prodigious idea as if it were a theorem. He foresees as the fruit of progress in geographical science an undertaking that would free Christendom from commercial servitude to the Turk. The Italian republics would be replenished with riches and the firm of Toscanelli would receive new life. He proves his theorem as follows:

> Therefore, though I know I could demonstrate with a globe in my hand and show you how the world is laid out, nevertheless I have decided it would be easier and make more sense to show that route in a map like those that are used in navigation, and so I am sending Your Majesty one I designed and made myself. It shows the whole of the west, from Ireland as far south as Guinea with all the islands that lie in between. Directly opposite them to the west is shown the beginning of the Indies with the islands and places you may reach, and it shows how far from the Arctic pole you may sail to the equator and how much space, i.e., how many leagues, you must traverse to reach those most fecund places bearing every kind of spice and gem and precious stone.

This is the famous map to which Las Casas would refer many times, saying he had seen it and held it in his hands.

A later paragraph of the letter clearly indicates how Toscanelli made the map, but more important than the technical details is the descriptive part of the letter, the passages that arouse the desire to make discoveries, and the passage on the mercantile and economic advantages to be gained:

> I have also painted on the map many places in India where one could go should a mishap due to contrary winds or some other unexpected catastrophe befall. And besides, to give you full information of those places, which you desire to know all about, you should know that in all those islands live none but merchants, and there is as great a quantity of ships and sailors with merchandise as in any other place in the world, especially

in a fine port called Zaiton, where every year a hundred large ships load and unload their cargo of pepper, and there are many more ships carrying other spices.

In the preceding passage, Toscanelli borrowed from Marco Polo's *Milione*. Toscanelli continues his wonderful description:

This country is heavily populated, and there are many provinces and kingdoms and cities without number under the dominion of a prince called the Great Khan, which means King of Kings. He lives most of the time in the province of Cathay. His predecessors wanted very much to have relations and friendship with Christians, and two hundred years ago they sent ambassadors to the pope asking that he send many wise men and scholars to teach them our faith, but the ambassadors encountered various obstacles and had to turn back without reaching Rome.

Columbus would become obsessed with finding the Great Khan and his empire. While the above passage was also inspired by Marco Polo, in the following, Toscanelli relies on another source.

And yet another ambassador came to Pope Eugene IV, who told of the great friendship which those princes and their people have toward Christians, and I spoke at length with him about many things and about the size of the royal courts and the great length and breadth of their rivers. And he told me many marvelous things about the multitude of their cities and places on their banks, and that on a single river are found two hundred cities with marble bridges, very big and long and ornamented with many columns. This country is as worthy as any other that has been discovered, and you can earn there not only the greatest profits but gold and silver and precious stones as well and every kind of spice in tremendous quantities, which kinds have never been brought into our part of the world.

Eugene IV, pope from 1431 to 1447, resided for some time in Florence (where Toscanelli lived), for the Council of Basel-Ferrara-Florence was held in Florence between 1438 and 1443. A postscript reads as follows:

Due west of the city of Lisbon the map shows twenty-six spaces, each of which represents 250 miles, to the noble city of Quinsay, which encompasses 100 miles or thirty-five leagues and has ten marble bridges. The name of this city means Heavenly City, and wonderful things are told about the greatness of her talented people, factories, and income. This area is nearly a third part of the globe, and this city lies in the province of Mangi, near the province of Cathay, in which the king spends most of his time.

Toscanelli's letter, then, solidified Columbus's notion that Asia lay beyond the Atlantic, and Columbus was comforted by the authority and optimism that the way there would not be long or dangerous. Before he read Toscanelli's letter, Columbus did not think that Asia was so close to Europe. He thought that the closest lands would be islands and archipelagoes, outposts of the mainland. Later he would find the means—by bending the facts of his own experience or simply from the need of convincing the skeptics and doubters—of placing Cipango twenty-four hundred miles from the island of Hierro (in the Canaries) instead of three thousand miles off, as Toscanelli did. But for the moment it was Toscanelli's letter that induced Columbus to consider the edge of Asia closer to the coast of Portugal than had previously been thought, and that was most reassuring for him and lent support to his plan.

Toscanelli gave Columbus both scientific and moral support. Whether they were addressed to him directly or not, the letter and map from the Florentine scholar exercised a profound influence on Columbus. Toscanelli was a prophet of the revolution in geography, as his friend Nicolaus Cusanus was a prophet of the revolution in philosophy. Toscanelli and Cusanus were two geniuses, among the most brilliant in fifteenth-century Europe. Both were forerunners of the new age, of which Christopher Columbus—the "enlarger of the world" as Paul Claudel would call him—would be the pioneer, the first protagonist.

10 | *The Proposed Plan Refused by the King of Portugal*

The idea of reaching Asia by crossing the Atlantic was no longer a dream but a plan, the project of "reaching the Orient by sailing west." In late 1483 or early 1484 Columbus presented his plan to King John II of Portugal. John refused, and so Portugal lost its chance to discover the New World. Yet Portugal more than any other nation seems to have deserved the privilege of extending its culture and trade across the Atlantic to Central and South America.

Both geography and history were in Portugal's favor. Geography had filled the Portuguese soul with love of the Ocean, and that love had been a spur to action. The history of Portugal in the fifteenth century is the history of maritime discoveries. Projecting into the Ocean, the central figure in most of the discoveries of the fifteenth century, culturally in the avant-garde, not only in arts and letters but in the sciences of navigation, geography, and astronomy, Portugal seemed predestined to discover America. Yet frequently history recants and abandons its own logic.

Was it chance that robbed Portugal of this greatly deserved conquest? It was not that alone, though chance did play a part. There is a logical reason for the lost opportunity, and that is that the Portuguese ruling class—the sovereign, the court, the scholars, and the most influential mariners—were stubbornly bent on finding the route to the Indies by circumnavigating Africa. They were not wrong, for in 1487 Bartolomeu Dias doubled the southern tip of Africa, and in 1498, six years after Columbus's discovery of America, Vasco da Gama arrived in Calicut, India.

Many Portuguese, Spanish, Genoese, French, and Irish sailors as well as numerous residents of the Azores, Madeira, Porto Santo, and the Canaries had repeatedly said, sworn, and sworn again that they had seen lands to the west, west of Madeira, or Hierro, or Flores, or Corvo. King John himself showed the large reeds to Columbus, insisting that there were many clues of land beyond the Dark Sea. Those reeds were unknown in Europe and could not have come from Africa because they were found on the beaches of the Atlantic islands when the waves, wind, and storms were blowing in from the west. The Portuguese sovereign, court, scholars, and captains, however, interpreted these clues as signs simply that other islands were to be discovered in the Atlantic. They were searching for Asia; they intended to be the first there and to establish their own trade. What could interest them in other Azores or Madeiras? No one among them, not Columbus nor anyone else—scholar, artist or philosopher, sailor or merchant, holy man or magician—no one in Europe imagined there could be a fourth continent.

Here lies the point that explains John's refusal and the opportunity lost to the Portuguese. But it is only a partial explanation. Had he still been alive, Henry the Navigator would have recognized the validity of Columbus's plan to reach new lands beyond the Azores and Madeira. It would have made all the difference had a talented astronomer and learned Franciscan priest, such as Father Marchena, been at the Portuguese court instead of the Spanish to make them all listen to Columbus's plan and accept it. John himself would change his mind when he wrote a letter to Columbus in 1488, but it was too late: history was already favoring Spain.

What would have happened if, with or without Columbus, Portuguese ships had anticipated Cabral's expedition and discovered America? For one, all of South America would speak Portuguese; for another, Spain would have followed what at the beginning of 1492 appeared its historic destiny: the reconquest of Moorish Africa from Morocco to Tunisia and the transformation of the western Mediterranean into a Spanish lake. But it is vain to get lost in *ifs*.

King John's momentous refusal was also influenced by the magnitude of Columbus's demands in case he succeeded. The conditions he requested in Spain, according to Las Casas, were that the king make him a caballero so he and his descendants could style themselves *don;* that he be named Grand Admiral of the Ocean, with all the rights and privileges that belonged to the admirals of Castile; that he be named perpetual viceroy and governor of all the islands and mainlands that he should discover; and that he should retain one tenth of all the king's revenues (gold, silver, pearls, precious stones, metals, spices, and other things that should bring a profit; all kinds of merchandise bought, traded, found, or won within the confines of his admiralty).

It seems likely that these exorbitant demands tipped the scales in the decision when one considers that John reached an agreement with two of his subjects to attempt at least part of Columbus's plan: they proposed to discover Antilia, which the Portuguese called the Island of the Seven Cities. Fernão Dulmo of Terceira requested permission to sail with two caravels "to search for the large island—or islands or mainland near its coasts—which is thought to be the Island of the Seven Cities, and to do all this at his own expense." The king granted him anything he should discover and promised to confer on him appropriate "titles of honor" should he succeed. Not possessing the means to carry out the expedition by himself, Dulmo joined a certain João Estreito of Funchal. The king confirmed his agreement with both men: Dulmo was to command the fleet for the first forty days after leaving Terceira and receive all the lands discovered during that time. Command was then to pass to Estreito, to whom would belong everything that should be discovered from then until they returned. Contrary to the traditional policies of the Portuguese kings toward explorers, John promised he would support Dulmo and Estreito with his own naval forces should the inhabitants of Antilia resist.

The date fixed for the departure of this important expedition was 1 March 1487. From an indirect reference by Don Ferdinand to the land that Fernão Dulmo "tried to discover" and from the account the latter proposed to write one may conclude that Dulmo and Estreito did in fact sail, but he never did. But complete silence on the subject in the Portuguese chronicles shows that the voyage was a total failure. As Morison correctly observes, the cause of its failure was the starting point, the Azores. Like their compatriots who had preceded them in exploring the Atlantic, Dulmo and Estreito found themselves on the latitude of the Azores, facing winds and currents that made it impossible to reach the western shore of the Ocean. Columbus had sensed that would happen, having mastered the large portion of the Atlantic surrounding the Azores, and that was one of the most important elements of his secret.

Was this the clandestine expedition, organized by King John to steal Columbus's plan from him, that Don Ferdinand and Las Casas speak of? Both historians report that the leaders of that expedition returned, having found nothing, before Columbus left Portugal; that is, before 1485, making it two years before the expedition by Dulmo and Estreito. But was there ever really a clandestine expedition? It is not certain whether John sent caravels to realize Columbus's plan. Whether this expedition was real or imaginary, Columbus believed in it and held that he had been deceived.

For diplomatic reasons or out of loyalty to John, Columbus managed to maintain good relations with him, blaming others for the refusal or the deception. However, he could no longer remain in Lisbon. What should he do? The grand design now possessed him. Felipa, his wife, was dead, buried in the Carmelite church. His son, Diego, was still a child; at four or five years old he was old enough to stand on the deck of a ship with him. And so Columbus found a ship and secretly sailed for Palos, Spain.

11 | *Spain: Father Marchena*

When Columbus and Diego landed at Palos, they went to La Rábida, a church annexed to a Franciscan friary three and a half miles from the port. Columbus, a devotee of St. Francis, was in the habit of attending mass at the end of a voyage or during stops along the way. He also needed a place to stay on his first night ashore, as well as specific directions to his in-laws. Violante Moniz Perestrello, sister of his late wife, lived with her husband, Miguel Muliart, in Huelva, a city near Palos.

Visiting La Rábida was the first thing Columbus did in Spain. The visit was as essential to the greatest discovery in history as his being washed ashore at Lagos, for at La Rábida Columbus met Father Marchena. Many historians have been unclear about the figure of Father Marchena. In the sixteenth century some confused him with Father Pérez, creating a figure who never existed: Father Juan Pérez de Marchena. Even today some popular books on Columbus and La Rábida speak of Father Juan Pérez de Marchena. They were two separate people, both Franciscan monks. Father Pérez was the monk who later introduced Columbus to the court of Queen Isabella. At La Rábida in 1485 Columbus found Father Antonio de Marchena, who would become the spiritual father, the guardian angel, to the future Discoverer during the seven difficult years Columbus spent in Spain.

Father Marchena was not only a cleric of great piety and reputation but also a cosmographer and astronomer. Columbus had needed scientific support and found it in Toscanelli. He did not think he needed religious support, given his extraordinary faith, which bordered on fanaticism. But he did need it, for nothing radically new could be done at that time outside of the Church or without its support. Through Father Marchena Columbus gained—rather than simply adversaries, skeptics, the indifferent, and doubters—some powerful friends in financial and political circles.

The encounter between Columbus and Father Marchena probably occurred the evening of the day he landed at Palos. Friaries gave free lodging to pilgrims, and Columbus slept in one of the cells at La Rábida with his small son. One can imagine the enthusiasm with which he related his ideas and plans to the head of the friary as soon as he learned the monk was interested in cosmography and astronomy. Columbus spoke at length and grew excited, baring his soul. One source says he spoke *en poridad*—he "told everything." Everything? According to some, Columbus confided in the monk during confession so the priest could tell no one. (We will return to this suggestion later and show that there is no support for it.)

Things were actually simpler than that. Columbus revealed all his thoughts. He told of the clues of the Atlantic islands and of Galway. He spoke of his voyage to Iceland and of the information he had gathered there. He described his voyages to Madeira, the Canaries, the Azores, the Cape Verde Islands, and Guinea. He told of living for a long time on Porto Santo, sifting his impressions, clues, and experiences. He did not hide what he had learned in the Perestrello house. He described his ups and downs at the Portuguese court. He showed Father Marchena Toscanelli's letter to Canon Martins. He recounted at length his convictions about the play of the sea currents and the winds in the Atlantic, in particular the constant ones on the parallel of the Canaries. He expressed certainty that beyond the Dark Sea lay Asia, Cipango, and Cathay (Japan and China), vast, rich, densely populated lands, their peoples waiting centuries for salvation, people who did not reject the

Gospel of Christ as did the Muslims but were simply ignorant of it. Are we to believe he recounted all this in confession? With or without the bond of the sacrament, Columbus certainly confided in Father Marchena under a pledge of secrecy.

Many of the things said to Father Marchena in that decisive meeting, which surely extended over more than one evening, Columbus would tell no one else, because he feared—not without cause—that they would steal his idea. For example, he would not speak of his experience in Iceland, of Toscanelli's map, nor of the route—or rather the two routes, for going and coming—that he already had clearly in mind. We will see the arguments Columbus would find, with Father Marchena's aid, for scholars, arguments based on classical and religious texts. They were not the arguments that had originally convinced him and Father Marchena.

It is not necessary to look for a secret explanation for the bond that so quickly knit Father Marchena to Columbus. The key is found in a psychological phenomenon as simple as it is common. A man of thought is often attracted to a man of action and devotes himself to him, living vicariously through the actions of the other. This phenomenon can be observed today in the fields of social relations, politics, science, and religion. It occurs today just as it always has, for human nature has not changed, or at least not since the fifteenth century. This is what happened between Father Marchena and Columbus. The Spanish Franciscan was fired with the enthusiasm of the Genoese sailor, reliving in his experiences his own dreams as a cosmographer and astronomer.

Meanwhile, Columbus's son, Diego, stayed at La Rábida until Columbus could meet his in-laws, Violante and Miguel Muliart. Columbus stayed with them for a few days because, once that contact was made, Diego would go to live with his aunt and uncle in Huelva, and Columbus would be free to move about.

Father Marchena would introduce Columbus at court and would support him during the most difficult and trying moments of the seven years from his arrival in Palos until his first voyage. He would be by Columbus's side frequently, even after he left La Rábida to head the Observants in Seville. And he would introduce Columbus to Father Juan Pérez, who was responsible for making the last, decisive contact with the Spanish monarchs.

Columbus would write of Father Marchena, "I never received aid from anyone, other than Father Antonio de Marchena, besides the help of the everlasting God." Thus, Father Marchena was his guardian angel: only he and God aided Columbus. Father Marchena used the vast network of the powerful Franciscan order to open the many heavy doors of the royal court to the Genoese sailor. On 20 January 1486 Isabella and Ferdinand received Columbus in the city of Alcalá de Henares, not far from Madrid.

Columbus presented his plan with the fervor and faith of a convert, in the tones of a man possessed of the truth. To inspire more faith in his arguments, he displayed the world map he had made with his brother Bartholomew depicting the lands and seas to be discovered. Two years later Bartholomew would present a copy of this map to the king of England when he offered the project that had not yet been accepted in Spain. Columbus would take this same map with him on the first voyage of discovery.

On 24 February Father Marchena presented himself at the court of the monarchs in Madrid to tell them that what the foreign sailor had told them "was the truth." But Isabella and Ferdinand did not believe Columbus. Of greater weight for them was the contrary opinion held by the learned men of their council. They did, however, show a certain curiosity for the strange project. That same year, 1486, the Catholic king acquired a Ptolemy; Honorato Mercader bought it from the bookseller Jaime Serra for 160 sueldos and sent it to the king from Valencia. Columbus undoubtedly cited Ptolemy in expounding his singular cosmographic theories on that historic 20 January 1486, and the name must have made an impression on the monarchs.

I must stress that from the time he arrived in Spain, Columbus went over his books with a fine-toothed comb, scrutinizing every sentence, every hint, that could support his project and making heavy use of these citations in his conversations and perorations. As already mentioned, however, he did not speak of his experiences in Iceland, Galway, Porto Santo, and elsewhere in the Atlantic, nor of Toscanelli's letter. Both his experiences and the letter were his secret; as to the first, scholars would scarcely have believed him, while from the second they could have learned too much, stealing his idea.

Columbus used arguments based on classical and religious texts before the council of scholars called as a result of his direct appeal to the monarchs in January. However, progress was slow. The council heard him and examined his plan from November 1486 to

April 1487. Throughout 1486 Columbus followed the court as it moved from Madrid to Avila to Guadalupe and finally to Córdoba. At Guadalupe Columbus worshipped at the most famous sanctuary in Spain, Our Lady of Guadalupe. At Córdoba he fell in love with Beatriz de Arana. The two loves—divine and human—would leave deep and lasting marks on his life and undertaking. *Guadalupe* would be one of the first names used in the new lands. Columbus would make a vow to Our Lady of Guadalupe when he found himself in extreme danger on the return trip of the first voyage during the worst of many storms he experienced. Beatriz de Arana would give him peace of mind as well as physical pleasure during the anxious and difficult years of his long wait in Castile.

Columbus did not limit himself to praying to the Madonna and making love to Beatriz. He continued to work his way into the inner circles of the court. Many people made fun of him, others listened to and appreciated him, some were fascinated. There is no doubt that despite his suspicious, reserved, and proud nature, he had charisma when he bared his soul to his listener. Once he began to speak, he did not stop, becoming excited and persuasive. Had he not convinced King Ferdinand to read Ptolemy? Had he not impressed the serious and modest Queen Isabella with his proud boldness?

But these things did not help him with the council of scholars; in fact, they hurt him. Intellectuals who want to retain power cannot do so unless they stifle all innovations. That has been so throughout history. Every revolution in knowledge—because it affects behavior—threatens the very basis of their power. They are obsessed with following a strictly formal line of thought, ignoring and despising feelings. They do not perceive the reality of life, which seems so irrational and ruled by chance, which can be mastered only by a free spirit, by imagination, by openness to different points of view. They would not have understood Columbus if he had spoken as he did to Father Marchena. But he did not want to disclose to them his most important, secret maps. So, instead Columbus used his world map and cited classical geographers and the Old Testament.

In Castile Columbus began to read and reread the first printed books on cosmography and geography. They are preserved with his numerous annotations in the Columbus Library in Seville.

They include the *Tractatus de imagine mundi* by Cardinal d'Ailly, printed at Louvain between 1480 and 1483; the *Historia rerum ubique gestarum* by Enea Silvio Piccolomini (subsequently Pope Pius II), printed at Venice in 1477; the Latin summary of Marco Polo's *Milione* by Francesco Pipino of Bologna, published at Anversa in 1485; Pliny's *Historia naturalis,* translated into Italian by Cristoforo Landino and published at Venice in 1489; Plutarch's *Lives,* translated into Castilian as *Vidas de los ilustres Varones* by Alfonso di Palencia, published at Seville in 1491; the *Sumula confessionis* of St. Antonino of Florence, 1476; and a folio palimpsest containing Seneca's *Tragedies.* Columbus knew and read other works that have not found their way into the Columbus Library. For example, he certainly owned and read Sir John Mandeville's fantastical *Travels* and Julius Capitolinus's *De locis habitabilibus;* so said Andrés Bernáldez, in whose house Columbus was a guest. It also appears from a postil that he knew the Alfonsine Tables, a monumental compilation of astronomical lore made at Toledo in the thirteenth century by a commission of astronomers under the patronage of Alfonso the Wise of Castile.

Columbus read these books not before he conceived the grand design but after the plan had been translated into a concrete project. Most historians confuse two distinct processes: the genesis of the plan for the discovery and Columbus's scientific learning. The two were perfected at different times. The genesis of the plan occurred without any scientific learning or support whatsoever except for Toscanelli's letter. It was made on the decks of the ships on which the future Admiral traveled from east to west, south to north, and north to south over great tracts of the Atlantic, from Iceland to the equator, from Sagres to the farthest Azores.

Columbus gained his scientific knowledge from reading the books cited and from the information and suggestions provided by Father Marchena, a competent astronomer. Columbus resorted to obtaining this knowledge in order to persuade the scholars of the council. There is a common thread running through all the postils Columbus made in the books he read at various times, though without doubt he read them all after he reached Spain. That thread, evident at first glance, is the humility of the student in the face of what he is reading, the elementary simplicity, often outright banality, of some of the concepts that he selected in the texts and marked in the margins of the books.

In fact Columbus was not learned, as Gómara assures us. According to Bernáldez, "He was a man of the greatest genius, though not the most learned." But it is not necessary to invoke the testimonies of others; Columbus's judgment on himself is sufficient. A letter of 1501 to the monarchs contains a revealing confession: "Perchance Your Highnesses and all the others who know me and to whom this may be shown, privately or publicly, will reprove me in various ways as a man of little culture, an ignorant sailor, a frivolous man." The last adjective Columbus used was *mundanal,* which today means "worldly" but then indicated "frivolous."

He was at least partially correct. Certainly he was not frivolous, but he had little scientific training. His stock of theoretical knowledge was definitely inadequate for successfully confronting the scholars of Castile charged with examining his grand project. Nevertheless, his project remained grand, and the discovery that would stem from it would be the greatest in history, for everything is not reducible to scientific knowledge, nor can science do everything.

Columbus's intuition, brilliant even in its errors, did not stem from scientific deduction. It was the intuition of a sailor, a self-taught man who merely sought to buttress it scientifically. He did what he could and arrived at the conclusions he was capable of. But the limits of the geographic conception with which he sought to cloak his intuition and the grand design do not diminish the value and significance both would have in human history; they do not diminish his extraordinary genius.

12 | The Consolation of Beatriz de Arana

T he tiring study, the exhausting work, of perfecting the presentation of his project accomplished nothing. It may have served to prolong the discussion, but it did not cause the council to change its recommendation, a recommendation absolutely opposed to the project. The Catholic monarchs gave Columbus a negative reply in August 1487.

That might have been a moment for despair, but Columbus did not despair. His brother Bartholomew did not abandon him. Beatriz de Arana still loved him. The relationship between Columbus, a widower for several years, and this Spanish Beatriz is one of the romantic episodes of a fascinating life.

Beatriz Enríquez de Arana was the daughter of Pedro de Torquemada and Ana Nuñez de Arana, modest working people in Santa María de Trassiera, a mountain village about ten miles from Córdoba. Her father died when she was a child; her mother died on 2 June 1471. Beatriz and her brother Pedro went to live with their grandmother and aunt. These pious women were determined that Beatriz learn to read and write, uncommon skills at that time. But her grandmother died soon thereafter, as did her aunt in 1478, and Beatriz went to live with her mother's cousin, Rodrigo de Arana.

Rodrigo had some culture and was intelligent and rich. Extant documents reveal his business and personal ties and even indirect relationship to Luciano and Leonardo Esbarroya, Genoese pharmacists in Córdoba. It was probably through them that Columbus, who resided in Córdoba for many months in 1486 and 1487, got to know Beatriz. He was thirty-seven years old, she twenty. In August 1488 the young woman gave birth to Ferdinand, Columbus's son. There can be no doubt that he was born out of wedlock.

At the end of the nineteenth century, those in Italy, France, and Spain who tried to prove that Columbus had legalized his romantic relationship, at least in the eyes of the Church, produced no convincing proof. They were obsessed with a single idea: to make the great Discoverer into a saint. Columbus is worthy of myth, for his maritime genius, his fanatic stubbornness, his faith, his charm, and for the colossal undertaking that he brought to a successful conclusion. But it is the myth of a genius, of a great man of history, not that of a saint. The desire to make him a saint at any cost was the compulsion of clerics during the fourth centenary of the discovery, when blatant and violent anticlericalism spawned an equally crude clericalism.

Columbus conscientiously discharged his duties as a father. He legitimized Ferdinand, who acquired the title of *don,* became very learned, and merited greater fame than his brother, Diego, legitimate by birth. Columbus did not, however, feel that he had discharged his duties to Beatriz de Arana, as is evident in this request made in his will to his son and heir Diego:

> May he take care of Beatriz Enríquez, mother of my son Don Ferdinand, so that she may have the means to live honestly, as a person to whom I owe so much. May that be done to lessen the burden on my conscience, for it is something that weighs much on my soul. The reason is better not discussed here.

In fact, Columbus was not very generous to the woman to whom he owed so much. A small pension of ten thousand maravedis per year, invested in the slaughterhouses of Córdoba, given to her in 1493 after his return from the first voyage, and another, of the same amount, authorized in the will of 1502—these were the sole proofs of his generosity, indeed quite modest. Beatriz's unhappy existence came to an end about 1521, the date of the last public writing we have of hers. Don Diego's testament, written at Santo Domingo on 8 September 1523, gives instructions for paying her heirs the pension, which had not been paid for the previous three or four years.

That is all we know about Beatriz Enríquez. Is it much? It seems like a lot, but there is little substance. We cannot determine, as some claim, whether the young Beatriz was a temptress who seduced Columbus or, as others maintain, she succumbed to the spell of his personality. Nor do we know how she behaved after Columbus left for the first voyage or on his return, when it was clear that he would abandon her. Some say she was untrue to her first love, others claim the opposite. It is unnecessary to assume the worst about her to explain why Columbus never normalized their relationship. As admiral and viceroy of the Indies, elevated by royal decree to the highest honors in the Kingdom of Castile, he was explicitly forbidden by royal laws from mingling his blood with the likes of Beatriz Enríquez, the humble woman from Córdoba, daughter of modest winepressers and utterly without blue blood.

Canon law did not bar marriage between persons of different social ranks, but civil law did. Obsessed by the desire for nobility, Columbus would not or could not pay the debt he owed the young woman of Córdoba, so for the rest of his life he was often tortured by remorse, evident when he believed his time had come to render his final account to God. Hence the provision in his will.

We find no exaltation of sex nor interest in romantic love in any of Columbus's numerous, if fragmentary, writings that have survived. History cannot tell us his personal feelings on this subject. His dalliances with the young widow on Gomera are cloaked in legend. The suggestion that Queen Isabella fell in love with him is sheer fable, rejected by all serious historians. She may have felt his charisma, but nothing more. She was virtuous and above all deeply and passionately in love with her husband. It is not difficult, however, to suppose that the love of Beatriz Enríquez sustained Columbus in one of the darkest moments of his life. This woman who silently, almost furtively, appears at his side at the moment of his greatest discomfiture, when everything and everyone seemed to urge him to give up and abandon Spain, the country destined to manage his grand undertaking, this woman takes on pathetic qualities.

Having examined earlier the essential stages that led the Discoverer to conceive of his grand design, we have now reviewed the specific stages by which he finalized it. There were two, both fundamental: the encounter at La Rábida with the astronomer monk, Father Marchena, and the love of Beatriz Enríquez. Without the latter Columbus probably would have despaired and followed his brother Bartholomew to Portugal and England. Instead, when Beatriz gave him a son he baptized him Ferdinand, after the king of Spain. Columbus still hoped; he still believed in Spain. And in Spain fortune would smile on that stubborn hope, that obstinate faith.

13 | Desperation

*I*n the spring of 1489 Columbus was
again in Castile. Discouraged, he was
beginning to think of going to France. Once more he bared his soul
to Father Marchena, who advised him not to leave and told him to
seek an audience with the powerful duke of Medina Sidonia, Don
Enrique de Guzmán. The duke was one of the rich and powerful
grandees of Spain. Las Casas says there was no one richer in all of
Spain. But Columbus obtained nothing from him.

Columbus then turned to Duke Don Luis de la Cerda Medinaceli, who lived at Puerto Santa María. Medinaceli made minute
inquiries about Columbus's plan and became intrigued with it, as
Las Casas tells us:

> He sympathized with Columbus's prudence and good sense,
> forming a positive judgment of the voyage which he wanted to
> undertake and considering irrelevant any expenses deemed
> necessary, the more so as Columbus asked very little for
> himself. In those days, knowing that Christopher Columbus
> had little means for ordinary expenses, he ordered that he be
> provided with everything he should need. . . .
> Being convinced by the arguments presented by Columbus
> and having understood the importance and economic value—

if not the glory—of the proposed undertaking, the duke decided to discuss no more whether it would be successful and, with magnanimity and liberality, as if he were dealing with a sure thing, ordered that Christopher Columbus be given everything he needed up to three or four thousand ducats to obtain three ships or caravels, provisions for more than a year, sailors, and all that was necessary, making very sure that the ships be built in the shipyard of the port at Santa María and that construction not be interrupted until it was complete.

However, to get official authorization, he petitioned the king and queen to approve the favors and assistance that he, with his own money and his family's, was giving to a man who gave every indication he could discover such fantastic things and such great wealth.

Isabella thought otherwise. Such an enterprise, if it was to be undertaken at all, was the concern of the Crown and the Crown alone. The queen herself, continues Las Casas, would assume responsibility, and the royal council would arrange for necessary expenses; such a project could only be the exclusive province of the monarchs.

Thus, even the good intentions of the duke of Medinaceli could not effect the plan, but they did have an important result: Queen Isabella reestablished contact with Columbus. She sent a courteous letter inviting him to come to court immediately. Isabella received Columbus in Jaén in the summer of 1489. She was alone, for King Ferdinand was taking part in the siege of Baza. During their conversation she gave "positive hopes that, when the business of Granada was settled," the problem would be resolved. Columbus would have to be patient and await the successful conclusion of the campaign at Baza, with which the monarchs hoped to put an end to the centuries-old crusade against the Muslims. In the meantime he could live at court.

Columbus felt secure. He had the queen's promise. He followed her and the court to the field of Baza. Twenty-seven days after Isabella arrived, the chief Moorish fortress fell. It was 4 December, the feast of St. Barbara. Events continued at a dizzy pace. On 22 December the Catholic monarchs entered Almería, and on 30 December they entered Guadix. The war seemed over. True, Emir Boabdil was still in Granada, but he was a vassal to the Spanish monarchs and bound, by a pact signed in 1487, to surrender the capital of the Moorish kingdom as soon as circumstances allowed. The moment had arrived now that his hated rival, the king of Guadix, had disappeared from the political scene for good.

The queen had given Columbus "sure hope" that she would reconsider his plan as soon as the war was ended. Now was the decisive moment. But once more his hopes were dashed. The war was not quite over. "The Moor replied that he could not do what he had promised": so report the historians laconically. There followed an exchange of ambassadors and messages between Ferdinand and Boabdil, with the result that the war for the final conquest of Granada was resumed.

Months stretched into years, and the promise of July 1489 was not redeemed until 2 January 1492, when the surrender of Granada ended the war and removed the last remnants of Moorish power on the Iberian Peninsula. During that time Columbus, a guest now of the duke of Medinaceli, now of Quintanilla, now of the Franciscans at La Rábida, alternated between hope and despair. The duke, the chief treasurer, Father Diego Deza, and Father Marchena all counseled patience, but Columbus was fed up with being patient; desperation gripped him. The idea of abandoning Spain and trying his luck in France was growing more appealing to him all the time.

At La Rábida, where he went for the second time in autumn 1491, Columbus met, through Father Marchena, Father Juan Pérez. These two monks, Columbus would later say, were the only ones always faithful to him, never ceasing in their support. Father Juan Pérez had been the queen's confessor and still could obtain an audience. He rode from Palos to court by mule. The queen told him she had not forgotten the foreign sailor and sent Columbus twenty thousand maravedis with a summons to present himself. Thus, Columbus went to court once more, and once more he was accompanied by a Franciscan, this time Father Pérez. That was in December 1491. The court was in Santa Fe, and the war was nearly over.

On 2 January 1492 Columbus took part in the monarchs' entrance to Granada. "I saw," he would write in the preamble to his *Journal*, "the royal banners of Your Highness rise over the towers of the Alhambra, and I saw the Moorish king come out of the city gate and kiss the hands of Your Highnesses and the prince." The war was over; the last Muslim was leaving Spain, ending the Moorish kingdom on the Iberian Peninsula that had been established in 711 at Jerez de la Frontera. So concluded an epoch of nearly eight centuries.

Isabella, who had never forgotten Columbus's project, who had understood and respected him, summoned a special council for a definitive opinion. It consisted of three archbishops, fourteen bishops, two heads of orders, nine dukes, four marquesses, and ten counts, as well as philosophers, astronomers, and cosmographers. In earlier meetings in Salamanca and Córdoba, everyone had rejected the project; all had considered Columbus's proposal impossible. On this occasion, however, "opinions were divided." This important detail is given to us by Monsignor Geraldini (born in Amelia, in Umbria, Italy), a most important witness because he had been present at all the discussions and deliberations.

In Santa Fe the cause of the future Admiral was probably defended by the local cardinal, Mendoza; it was certainly defended by Geraldini, who had ties to Columbus both directly and through his late brother, a benefactor of Columbus's in Seville. Las Casas says some scholars probably supported him too. If they did so they were timid about it because the majority of the council was again opposed. Other courtiers, friends of Columbus's, backed his plan enthusiastically. The majority nevertheless was still against the project.

Under these circumstances, what could Father Fernando de Talavera, president of the special council of Santa Fe and confessor to Queen Isabella, do? He could only advise her not to sponsor an undertaking that, in the judgment of the wise men of the kingdom, appeared unattainable. Not only that, but this impudent foreigner was demanding, in addition to considerable economic rewards, the highest honors and titles: the perpetual office of admiral and viceroy governor, until then granted only to Don Alfonso Enríquez, King Ferdinand's uncle. Considering this final point, one can understand how the atmosphere in the council would not have permitted Father Talavera to intercede with the monarchs for Columbus.

After this definitive defeat Columbus bade farewell to his friends, grateful for all the attention and help they had given him during the years he had spent at court, and prepared to leave camp for Córdoba. He would go elsewhere to pursue his grand design.

But where? Not to Portugal or England. He had already charged his brother Bartholomew with making a final presentation to the king of Portugal and then going to London to propose the undertaking. Thirteen years earlier Columbus had known the courage, tenacity, and innate maritime sense of the English, and so he had hoped they would appreciate the value of his project. But things did not go well in London either. Bartholomew obtained nothing and was preparing to go to France.

Columbus was now thinking of going to France himself; he even thought of going to Genoa again. Ramusio, writing about 1535, reported that he understood from Peter Martyr of Anghiera, the court historian, that Columbus, at the age of forty (in 1491), had proposed the Atlantic enterprise to his homeland. Peter Martyr of Anghiera was a man of uncommon intelligence, sober and precise in his reports. A friend of Columbus's when Columbus became admiral, Peter Martyr is a most reliable source for this kind of information. His testimony is confirmed by the greatest Turkish geographer of the time, Piri Reis. That is an important proof, for Piri Reis learned it from a Spanish slave, who had been close to Columbus and moreover was incapable of inventing the story.

Columbus, then, thought once more of Genoa when his efforts at the Spanish court came to naught. He thought of the city even though in 1479 he had realized that there was little to hope for in that quarter. His Genoese friends at Seville and Córdoba must have asked, "Why don't you try our homeland again?" Columbus probably did, although he could not have avoided another denial from the leaders of Genoa, who had no faith in the eventual success of the Atlantic enterprises. It was not that they did not believe. In fact, the Genoese had been the first to face the problem of the Atlantic and the first to overcome the medieval superstitions regarding the southern hemisphere and the antipodes. They did not consider Columbus a dreamer any more than did the Genoese of Seville and Córdoba, who associated with him all along and supported and financed him.

As already indicated, the reason for Genoese skepticism lies elsewhere, in the temperament of the Ligurian people. Ligurians never overreach themselves, know their own limitations, are terribly realistic. The Genoese well knew that they could discover other islands and lands, as their countrymen Antonio da Noli, Lanzarotto Marocello, Usodimare, and Niccoloso da Recco had done. But if they were successful others would enjoy the fruits, just as others had with the earlier discoveries. The Genoese knew their limits in an age when national powers throughout Europe—except in Italy and Germany—were supplanting regional and municipal powers. The Genoese gradually decreased their role in ship chandlery and turned to banking. By the eighteenth century they were creditors to all of western Europe, at which time Genoa became a metropolis, a rapidly expanding center of what would become capitalism. It was useless, then, to try to deal with Genoa, either through the republic or by involving the Banco San Giorgio. There was no possibility of returning to Portugal, especially after Bartolomeu Dias's expedition had opened the eastern route to the Indies. His brother Bartholomew's mission at the English court had failed. Columbus was desperate. He had to leave. On muleback he departed from Santa Fe for Palos, intending to sail for France.

14 | *All Wishes Granted*

At court Columbus's friends did not give up. The theologian Father Deza, the prince's tutor, insisted. The treasury chief, Quintanilla, insisted. The grand chamberlain to the king, Juan Cabrero, insisted. The marquess of Moya insisted with the queen. The affectionate and aged governess, Doña Juana de Torres, insisted with the prince. The Genoese, Florentine, and converted Jewish bankers, to whom the entire court owed money, insisted. Father Marchena and Father Pérez insisted with prayers and deeds, convincing the courtiers. Even Father Fernando de Talavera, the queen's confessor, who had suggested that she heed the council's recommendation, sought a means of reversing that suggestion, which in conscience he had felt necessary at the time but which was not in the best interests of the Crown.

At this point enters the keeper of the privy purse, the Valencian Luis de Santángel, whose family had converted from Judaism. He was the son of a merchant and cousin of a bishop. His father, also named Luis, in collaboration with the Genoese, Milanese, and Aragonese merchants, developed systems for collecting customs and taxes in the ports of Catalonia. The younger Luis had close business connections with some Genoese, in particular Francesco Pinelli—Pinelo in Castilian—a friend of Columbus's. Santángel went back to the queen on the same January day when Columbus left court, and presented the arguments of those who supported the enterprise. Those arguments are easy to imagine. According to the Spanish writer Juan Manzano, they can be summarized as follows:

True, the men of science who were consulted rejected the foreigner's proposals. But one must also consider that some of these experts left many of Columbus's reasonable claims and arguments without a satisfactory response. In contrast, he always answered his adversaries' objections. Moreover, not everyone recently consulted had rejected the project. Columbus was no fool; he was balanced, prudent in speech, and knew how to present his arguments. If the undertaking were as crazy as his adversaries said, he would not even have proposed such a voyage, asking the sovereigns for only a million maravedis and pledging to supply the remainder himself.

He was not asking for rewards or compensation in advance. The royal recompense he sought was to be granted after he discovered new lands. The risk to the sovereigns was minimal, while their benefit could be greater than the human mind could imagine: reaching long-sought India, with its abundant mines of precious metals and costly spices, and acquiring for the Spanish Crown immense territories—in a single stroke transforming the Catholic monarchs into the most powerful sovereigns in Christendom, nay, the entire world.

What doubts could possibly remain to make it not worth the effort? Yes, the enterprise could fail, but didn't the example of the Portuguese say anything? They were constantly risking men and money in maritime expeditions, some of them as problematic as the one now submitted to the court. Yet no one in the world criticized the Portuguese efforts, however vain they might seem.

On the other hand, Father Fernando de Talavera must have reasoned as follows: "If I persist in rejecting the enterprise and if as a result of my intransigence Columbus is dismissed and goes to another country where he receives the support he seeks and manages to reach the Indies, what great remorse I should have for the rest of my days, having deprived my nation and sovereigns of such glory and riches! I have done my duty and my conscience is clear because I explicitly told the king the feelings of the men of science as well as my own on this question. Yet if Father Deza, Cabrero,

Santángel, and other friends of Columbus's persuade the king and queen of the likelihood of successfully concluding the plan, I should not continue to oppose it lest I become an irresponsible obstructionist. The only thing that remains for me to do is to urge the greatest prudence on the sovereigns so that the risk of the adventure is minimized."

With these or similar reflections Father Talavera reached his decision. He, Deza, and Cabrero counseled King Ferdinand to "undertake the experiment even if it cost a great deal because of the immense profit and honors that were hoped for from the Indies." It is curious to observe that the scientific and nautical arguments now counted for nothing. Admittedly, the uncertainties were being acknowledged; there was a fifty-fifty chance. If all went well it would bring prestige, power, and riches. If it went badly, what was there to lose? There was no worry about losing prestige after the splendid triumph over the Moors. As far as risking life was concerned, that would be done by Columbus and those who decided to sail with him of their own free will. The only risk to the king and queen would be the cost of outfitting three ships. And Santángel had come up with some creative financing.

He was not only keeper of the privy purse but treasurer of the Santa Hermandad ("Holy Brotherhood"), a medieval institution for the defense of Christian civilization, and treasurer—along with the Genoese Francesco Pinelli—of the Fund for the Crusades. Both organizations were deeply in the red in 1492. There were, however, in addition to Pinelli, Genoese merchants who had plenty of money to invest and nothing to invest it in. Contemporary chroniclers list the names of several. And there was Gianotto Berardi, a Florentine merchant willing to lend money for the undertaking with the risk of losing it if things did not go well but demanding that he be paid a hundred to one if things turned out as planned.

But Spanish honor had to be preserved. Letting such an enterprise be financed entirely by foreign money was unthinkable. Santángel reminded the Catholic sovereigns that, as punishment for smuggling, the city of Palos had to outfit two caravels for the monarchs. This would provide a good portion of what was needed. For the balance Santángel would provide from the funds that he administered. The problem of money, then, was solved.

Even King Ferdinand was convinced. Queen Isabella did not wait for anything else; her husband was now convinced, while she had been convinced for some time. She immediately recalled Columbus. A messenger on horseback caught up with Columbus, riding his mule, at the bridge of Pinos, four miles from Santa Fe. Columbus returned.

The sudden reversal of fortunes was so rapid and dramatic as to border on the theatrical. Did Columbus plan it as a trick to convince the sovereigns? Or did they stage it in order to overcome the stubborn resistance of scholars, courtiers, and cosmographers toward the undertaking? We do know that Columbus came back without the least sign of penitence. The vicissitudes, hardships, and pains of so many failures had not changed him; his demands were no less than before. But did that matter? If the undertaking did not succeed, all concessions in the Capitulations (the agreement between Columbus and the sovereigns) would be worthless. If it succeeded, the anticipated profit would justify the pain of signing any concession.

Genoese, Florentines, and Jews invested in the venture. Indeed, the sovereigns had a proper respect for them when it came to money. The sovereigns could not help but follow their example, so they signed the Capitulations, and the project began to take shape. The project was financed as follows: 1,140,000 maravedis was loaned by Luis de Santángel. The money was either his or Francesco Pinelli's or, more likely, both of theirs. Columbus contributed 500,000 maravedis. Who lent it to him? His only problem was choosing someone. The names of the Genoese bankers are known, and their ties with Columbus are revealed in more than one document: Francesco Rivarolo, Francesco Doria, Francesco Castagno, and Gaspare Spinola definitely contributed to the Admiral's portion of the expenses for the fourth voyage (one-eighth). Father Aspa lists the backers of the first voyage as Jacopo Di Negro, a resident of Seville; Zapatal, a resident of Jerez; and Luigi Doria, a resident of Cádiz. Finally, there was the rich Florentine merchant living in Seville, Gianotto Berardi, who was undeniably involved in Columbus's business affairs beginning with the first voyage. That left only 360,000 maravedis to make up the balance of the 2 million needed. It was supplied by the citizens of Palos to discharge the royal fine mentioned earlier, which required them to outfit two caravels. Genoese, Florentine, Jewish, or Castilian money—it was paid punctually, and once it changed hands no one cared where it came from.

The rights were agreed on and the Capitulations signed after long, drawn-out negotiations. They gave Columbus all he sought in case of success: titles, honors, and riches. But, with all due respect to economists and lawyers, money is not everything, nor are rights. Men were still needed. There was a commander, Christopher Columbus, but where were the sailors? On Wednesday, 23 May 1492, in the church of St. George in Palos the royal proclamation of 30 April addressed to the Paleñans was promulgated. Present at the solemn ceremony, besides Columbus and Father Pérez, were the two mayors, three councilors, the city notary, and many citizens. Columbus handed the authorities the sovereigns' letter, which the notary read out loud. The sovereigns named Christopher Columbus commander of a fleet of three ships which was to go, in their service, to "certain parts of the Ocean Sea." For this voyage the citizens of Palos were requested to provide him with two caravels completely fitted out with men and supplies. The Paleñans were to work for the monarchs on the caravels for two months, obeying the new captain. Thus would the city discharge its fine. Men and ships were to be at the disposal of the captain.

Columbus had obtained another royal order, which pardoned, or rather suspended, legal action and any sentence for criminals who signed for the expedition. In other words, Columbus could ship delinquents, men condemned to prison or death, and he did. But how many were there? Contrary to tradition, careful research of extant documents shows there were only four. To recruit others, Columbus had an ace up his sleeve: Juan de la Cosa, owner of the *Gallega*. Renamed *Santa María,* it would be the flagship for the fleet. Juan would ship as master. Columbus had known Juan since Columbus had been a guest of the duke of Medinaceli in 1488 and 1489. When the duke decided to finance the enterprise, Juan was probably inclined to participate in it with him. Now, with the two caravels outfitted by the Paleñans, the addition of the *Santa María* resolved Columbus's anxieties about the preparation of the fleet. Juan de la Cosa brought some sailors with him, but we do not know whether they were enough to man his ship, let alone the other two.

Columbus had three ships, then: a *nao* and two caravels. He had the master and part of the crew for the *nao:* Juan de la Cosa's men and four delinquents. He had a marshall of the fleet, the chief administrator whose main responsibility was the drinking water. In this post, one of the most delicate, Columbus put a man who had his absolute trust: Beatriz Enríquez's cousin, Diego de Arana of Córdoba. Columbus still needed sailors and captains for the two caravels. He needed at least sixty more experienced men, some of them specialists, and no one was volunteering. Columbus was a foreigner, just an ordinary fellow, a poor, deluded dreamer dedicated to achieving the impossible. The Paleñans knew nothing about his maritime skills—they had seen him only on dry land. What assurance could this poor man, protected by the patronage of the friars of La Rábida, offer expert seamen? None, and therefore everyone was refusing to ship with him.

The seamen of Palos and Moguer were not cowards by any means. On the contrary, they had given proof of a strong character and of courage in the dangerous trips to Guinea and in naval battles with the Saracen corsairs and with the neighboring Portuguese. But the enterprise being proposed to them was entirely different; it was a "new and unknown adventure," a "voyage never before attempted." And because, as Mosen Diego de Valera told the sovereigns, "sea voyages are always most uncertain," what Columbus was proposing was downright audacious.

Confronted with the stubborn and reluctant Andalusian mariners, Columbus was forced to rely on the court. Those were bitter days for him. Luckily he had at his side his great friend and long-standing protector, Father Antonio Marchena. Marchena was known, venerated, and loved in Palos. In this difficult job of recruiting sailors, the astronomer-friar was more than once the right man at the right time, for he had a strong friendship with one of the best captains of Palos, Martín Alonso Pinzón. Like Columbus, Pinzón had gone to sea in his early youth, rising to pilot and captain. He had sailed the Mediterranean as far as Italy and the Atlantic to the Canaries and Guinea. In the war with Portugal, he had acquitted himself with courage and demonstrated maritime skill. He had accumulated a good fortune, owning one ship and hiring one or two others.

Pinzón's son would later maintain that Martín Alonso Pinzón had learned in Rome—through a cosmographer friend at the Vatican—of lands that "were yet to be discovered." When Father Marchena spoke to Columbus about Pinzón, he indicated that the latter was then in Rome. He had gone there, however, not to look at documents on navigation and discovery, but to unload barrels of sardines. That is not to say that Pinzón was not a key figure in this initial phase of the preparation for the discovery. As soon as Pinzón returned to Palos from Rome, Father Marchena visited him, spoke about the undertaking, and put him in contact with Columbus.

In contrast with what he held from others, Columbus did not hide from Pinzón the objective of his oceanic voyage: India and the Great Khan. In order to win the able Paleñan to the cause, he showed him the dispatches he had brought from Santa Fe, the most important being the Capitulations and the letter addressed to Oriental sovereigns. More important to Pinzón than the royal backing, however, was Columbus's great experience, his tremendous sense of the sea. The meeting of the two men was an encounter between two outstanding seamen. The data, clues, and intuitions Columbus had gathered in Iceland, Ireland, the Atlantic archipelagoes, and Guinea may have counted for nothing with the scholars at court, but they definitely counted with Pinzón. Being a sailor and having been to the Canaries and Guinea, he was in a position to understand those things and appreciate their importance.

Martín Alonso believed the foreigner, because he listened to him and realized that he was an exceptional sailor; so he became involved. He spoke with his brother Vicente Yáñez, also a skilled seaman, and offered him, on Columbus's behalf, the command of one of the caravels. With Vicente in the enterprise, the two brothers enthusiastically began to recruit seamen. Sometimes alone, sometimes with Columbus, they went through the three cities of the region—Palos, Moguer, and Huelva—in search of pilots, seamen, and other crewmen. Columbus, Martín Alonso, and Vicente Yáñez would be the three captains of the fleet. The first would go as supreme commander on the *Santa María*, while the two brothers would command the caravels.

Historians are divided in their judgment of Martín Alonso Pinzón. Carried away by nationalism, the Spanish tend to overestimate the role of the captain from Palos, while the Italians tend to underestimate it. Some of Columbus's detractors go so far as to give Pinzón most of the credit for the enterprise, while others consider Pinzón a primarily negative force. The dispute is aggravated by the differing judgments that can be made on Pinzón's behavior during the return of the first voyage. During the preparations for the voyage, however, he was a key figure. No one can contest that. From the meeting between the two mariners sprang the solution to the final problem lying in the way of the realization of the grand design born at sea, on the Ocean. The solution to the last big obstacle to carrying it out came from the sense of the sea held by these two outstanding seamen.

15 | Gomera, Womb of America

The *Santa María* and the two caravels left Palos between five and six in the morning of Friday, 3 August 1492. There were about ninety men aboard: eighty-four Spaniards, mostly Andalusians but including Galicians, Catalans, some Basques, and a black from the Canaries; two Genoese (Columbus and Jacome el Rico); a Venetian; a Calabrese; and a Portuguese. The pilots had no doubt about the course, for Columbus's order was simple: to the Canaries.

Columbus had selected Gomera in the Canaries as the point of departure for crossing the Ocean. There were many reasons for choosing it. The first was geographic. The magnificent bay of San Sebastián—chief city of the island—was the last good port of the known world, on a latitude far enough south to take advantage of the trade winds. Farther south lay the Cape Verde Islands, owned by Portugal and so out of the question. West of Gomera lay two more islands, La Palma and Hierro. But the Spanish had not yet conquered the former, and the latter did not have a good port or offer the certainty of provisions.

The need for provisions was the second reason for his choice and can be summed up in three words: water, meat, and wood. Gomera had an abundance of water, more than it has today. The *barranco* ("ravine") that ends on the beach of San Sebastián has a river, today sometimes dry but then carrying fresh water the year round from the spring of the Citron Grove, running among the houses of that pretty little town, under the battlements of the fortress, and down to the sea. Fresh, pure water was also drawn from wells; the one from which Columbus's sailors drew water on the evening of 5 September before beginning the great crossing is shown to tourists today.

The pasturage was and is good on Gomera. Before the Spanish came, goats, pigs, and rabbits furnished excellent roasts for the original Guanche population. The natives even roasted dogs, castrated and raised for eating. It was not the dogs that interested Columbus and his Spanish crews but the goats and pigs as well as cattle, which had already been introduced in substantial numbers. Some live goats or pigs may have been taken aboard to be eaten during the voyage, but most of the provisions were butchered meat, because high-quality meat was found on Gomera, where it was salted. Ships coming from the Iberian Peninsula normally provisioned there and departed, returning eight to ten days later.

As for wood, Gomera had, and still has, many pines, not to mention some of the best beech groves of the Canaries. Beech is one of the best firewoods. Columbus knew that quite well. His grandfather, who taught him about it in their house in Quinto, was familiar with the beeches of Mount Caucaso just behind his village of Mocónesi in Liguria. Good firewood was essential for the crossing because when a ship put out to sea it always kept a fire burning in the stern to avoid having to use the tinderbox all the time, a task that is not easy when waves are sweeping the deck and spray is breaking everywhere. The fire was used for sending signals when ships were proceeding in convoy, as Columbus would do. From the stern hung a cresset, in which the sailors produced *humo* ("smoke") by day and *fuego* ("fire") by night, using wet canvas and a resinous pine torch. Different numbers of *fuegos* and *humos* indicated different commands: change course, strike or reduce sail, approach the flagship for verbal orders, and so forth. It was important, then, to get good pitch pine for the torches and beech to keep the fires in the cressets. On Gomera Columbus found both.

Gomera offered not only a fine port, water, wood, and food but also the beautiful Beatriz de Bobadilla, widow of the governor, Hernán de Peraza, killed by the Guanches in 1488. According to

Michele da Cuneo, his boyhood friend who accompanied him on the second voyage, Columbus was "touched by love" for this Beatriz. This is the only occasion, in the long and complex writings about the voyages of discovery, that reference is made to the amorous feelings of the Genoese. Cuneo, a sympathetic chronicler, does not linger on this subject. He simply reports it. What reason would he have to relate false gossip? One could perhaps consider the story exaggerated, that Cuneo interpreted a normal congeniality and exchange of courtesies as romantic dalliance. But Beatriz was not a woman to stop with congeniality or the exchange of courtesies. Her temperament and adventurous life indicate Cuneo was a faithful and credible chronicler.

The future Discoverer could not be called a lady's man. Quite the contrary. His reserve when writing to the pious Queen Isabella can be attributed to opportunism, but he used the same style elsewhere, for in his other letters and the postils Columbus's unmistakable personality shows. He was a careful observer of natural phenomena and therefore of women and sexual behavior also, but he wrote about sex with clinical detachment. Nonetheless, Columbus exuded a remarkable charm that won for him both profound esteem and love and just as profound hate and rancor. His charm had impressed the great Isabella without exciting a real feeling of love, as she loved only her husband deeply. But Beatriz de Bobadilla did not share Isabella's monogamous temperament and virtues. History cannot prove or disprove the possibility that the love between Beatriz and Columbus began much earlier, when he was trying to turn his dream of reaching the Orient by sailing west into a solid undertaking.

In any case, there is no need to compare Beatriz with Dido or the sorceress Circe. Columbus's obsession for his project was stronger than any romantic passion, for he was profoundly honest and sincerely religious, with an almost mystical devotion to the Madonna and St. Francis. He sought—even if he did not always succeed—to bend all reasoning, every plan, to the service of God, spreading the faith and the triumph of Christianity. On her side, Beatriz was not a woman to fall madly in love, like Dido; and unlike Circe, she had no intention of holding back an undertaking of exceptional interest to both her Spanish homeland and the Rivarolo, a rich Genoese family of Seville and the Canaries with which she was closely associated in business. Besides, after Columbus left there would still be "men of honor"—as he calls them in the *Journal*—with whom to console herself.

These men of honor, "who lived on the island of Hierro and whom he met on Gomera with Doña Peraza," assured Columbus "that every year they saw land to the west of the Canaries, and other inhabitants of Gomera swore it was so." Columbus had heard so many stories like this, not only in the Canaries but on Madeira and Porto Santo, in the Azores and Ireland, that he probably attached little importance to it. He records such news in the *Journal*, however, because he used it to give hope and security to the sailors. It was all the more useful since the flame bursting from the Peak of Teide had spread superstitious fear among his men.

On 4 and 5 September the *Santa María, Pinta,* and *Niña* took on a substantial supply of well-salted meat. Piles of pine and beech were stowed in every available corner. The casks were filled with water. All was ready. At dawn on Thursday, 6 September, Captain General Columbus heard mass in the Church of the Assumption, went aboard, and gave the order to set sail. Thus began the voyage of the grand discovery. Gomera, the island in the Canaries, can justly claim to be the "Womb of America."

16 | *The First Ocean Crossing*

*T*he first Atlantic crossing, begun on 9 September, when Columbus passed the last known lands, ended 12 October. There had been Norse expeditions before that, in the north, but at high latitudes the routes are much shorter. Had there been others farther south? by Christians—Irish, Genoese, Catalans, Portuguese? by Phoenicians or Egyptians? Many people speak of them, scholars and explorers and, unfortunately, especially dilettantes. Every year some new theory is advanced, some old theory revived. But what does it matter? Any discovery that is not handed down to others is lost to history, and so Columbus's crossing is the determining, the unique, event leading up to the greatest discovery in history.

It was not, however, the most arduous nor the most agonizing voyage. Indeed, other hardships awaited Columbus, from his return on the first voyage to the trials in the Caribbean on the fourth. Only in legend was there general fear of the Sargasso Sea, terror over the strange behavior of the compass in the zone of magnetic declination, and mutiny over the length of the voyage on the unknown sea. No reliable historians force the drama. Differences in their accounts are limited to a greater or lesser emphasizing of the events that actually took place and from which legend has created dramatic myths. The facts to be considered are these:

- The ships entered the Sargasso Sea on 16 September and left it on 8 October.
- The western deviation of the compass needle, noted on 17 September, was first hinted at in the *Journal* on 13 September.
- The voyage on the unknown, seemingly infinite, sea was a lengthy one.

Sargassum is seaweed with air bladders and rolled fronds like leaves. The bladders look like fruit but are filled with air and give buoyancy. This seaweed accumulates, through the action of the waves and currents, in a vast area of the Atlantic roughly between 30° and 75° W and 22° and 40° N.[1] Living in the seaweed is a fauna of exceptional richness and variety: worms, crustaceans, mollusks, fish, and innumerable species of insects. The Sargasso Sea has been known since antiquity. In the fourteenth and fifteenth centuries, sailors searching in vain for the islands of Antillia (the Seven Cities), and St. Brendan spoke of weed covering the sea to the west. This weed kept alive the hope that land was nearby, but it also caused anxiety, fear, and terror.

So it is certain that before departing for the great voyage Columbus must have had at least indirect knowledge of this extraordinary phenomenon. He probably also had direct experience with it from some of his earlier voyages; one must remember that Flores and Corvo, the extreme Azores, lie beyond 30° W. On 16 September about nine hundred miles from the Canaries, at 28° N and 35° W, the three ships sailed "into patches of the greenest seaweed." Columbus adds poetically that the air was as temperate "as April in Andalusia, and that it was a great pleasure to 'taste' the morning air, which lacked only the song of a nightingale." On 17 September the weed grew thicker, appearing like a river. A living *cangrejo* was found. In his *Historie*, Alfonso Ulloa translates *cangrejo* as "crawfish," but that is an error; it was a type of crab common in the Sargasso Sea.

---

[1] The figures are approximate, but not because of differences of opinion among geographers. The area changes as a result of currents and storms, appreciable differences occurring from year to year and even from season to season.

On 19 September the sounding lead was dropped, and with two hundred fathoms of line out it did not touch bottom. On 21 September, at 28° N and 48° W, the accumulation of sargassum became so great "that the sea seemed completely curdled with it." On 22 September they saw almost no weed, but on the next day it was again "quite thick." On 26 September "the sea was like a river and the air sweet and most mild." On 29 September Columbus repeats his earlier poetry: "The air was so sweet and delicious it lacked nothing but the sound of the nightingale's song." There was "still much weed." "Much weed" again on 30 September and 2 October, but now "it came from the east and went toward the west, contrary to the way it had gone until then." This motion results from the action of the waves, a constant flux that confines the seaweed to the large area of the ocean indicated above. On 3 October the weed, still abundant, is partly old and partly very fresh; on 5 October "no weed." But on 8 October "some of that weed appears again." That is the last time it is noted. The three ships had probably just crossed 72° W. Thus was the barrier of the Sargasso Sea conquered—without any drama. Columbus was the first to cross it.

In contrast with the phenomenon of the sargassum, that of the western magnetic declination was absolutely new and until then unknown. Magnetic declination is the angle toward the east or west that a magnetized needle forms, under the influence of terrestrial magnetism, with the ideal straight line from the center of the needle to the astronomical pole. This angle varies from place to place. The eastern declination had been known for some time, especially in the Mediterranean. No case is known, however, of anyone recording the western declination until 13 September 1492. At nightfall on that date, Columbus noticed that the needles deviated to the west from the polestar, while in the morning they deviated to the east. He writes in the *Journal:* "Today at nightfall the needles turned to the northwest, and in the morning they went the same amount to the northeast."

It must be remembered that in its apparent daily motion the polestar describes a circle around the celestial pole. The amount it seemed to shift in 1492 was about 3° 27' (today it is less). At sunset on 17 September, through the addition of this shift to the right of the pole and the western magnetic declination, the needles made a strong deviation to the left. The sailors said nothing, but they were anxious. They badly needed reassurance, and Columbus gave it to them with an ingenious explanation. He knew of the little circle around the pole described by the polestar, while most of the pilots did not. Profiting from their ignorance, he called them together and pointed out the deviation at dawn. In the meantime the polestar had moved to the left, and so the deviation of the needles was lessened, though not eliminated. The needles—said the captain general—did nothing but follow the polestar. It was moving, and the needles retained their ability to show direction.

The *Journal* reports that Columbus ordered the pilots to repeat the observation at daybreak and, heading north, they found that the needles were good. Thus, the deviation must have occurred, the sailors thought, not because the needles moved, but because the polestar was moving. Columbus did not believe such arguments; in fact, he continued diligently to note the deviations shown on the compass, modifying the course to compensate for the mysterious angle. From day to day the deviation of the needles to the left grew larger. On 30 October, the fleet having probably reached the line of seven degrees declination to the west, the needles deviated a point to the west at nightfall. This angle, added to the seven degrees of magnetic declination, gave a total of a little less than a point ($11\frac{1}{4}°$). At dawn, Columbus observes, the needles "point precisely in the direction of the polestar," which in the meantime had moved west of the celestial pole, and the initial angle of $11\frac{1}{4}°$ should have been reduced, though not eliminated. "From this it seems clear," he insists, "that the polestar moves like the other stars and the needles always tell the truth." Was it optimism that convinced him he was dealing with a natural phenomenon, or was it his unshakable faith in success that sustained him? The answer is both, evidence of two contradictory aspects of the Discoverer's personality that make him at once enigmatic and engaging.

Neither the sargassum nor the magnetic declination significantly affected the great crossing. Instead, the greatest disturbance came from the length of the voyage, aggravated by the constant push of the trades from east to west. This phenomenon, unforeseen by the men, created ever-increasing anxieties about the possibility of returning. The sailors did not know the plans of the captain general. Columbus, suspicious as always, carefully avoided revealing them. He refrained from saying that precisely on account of the constant winds from the northeast he had chosen his course, counting on taking another route, in the zone of variable winds, to return. To the men's specific fear of the constant winds, which seemed to preclude the possibility of returning, must be added their feeling of traveling toward the unknown, which always creates fear: the greater the fear, the longer it seems it will last.

Columbus had foreseen both anxieties. For the first he was aided by luck, because he managed to remain almost always within the limits of the trades, and those limits are not absolute, changing with the seasons. Nor are they the same from one season to another. Those of September–October 1492 turned out to be particularly propitious. The sudden appearance of a contrary wind (22 September) was more good luck: "This contrary wind was rather convenient for me," writes Columbus. "My people were heartened by it, for they thought that in these seas no wind would blow toward Spain." The next day something extraordinary happened: the sea grew very rough even though the wind had not risen. On the one hand it frightened the sailors, but on the other it calmed them because earlier, when the sea was always even, they had muttered that because the sea was never rough "there would not be wind to return to Europe."

Finally, Columbus was lucky when, approaching 70° W, he risked going north of the upper boundary of the trades. At that moment a providential flight of birds caused him to change course and head southwest. He had left Gomera on 28° N. He found himself, on Sunday, 7 October, at about 67° W on 26° N. He had descended two degrees to the south thanks to the northeast wind, which, though the course was to the west, pushed him strongly to the southwest. That day, at sunrise, the sailors of the *Niña* hoisted the colors, believing they had seen land. False alarm! Land did not appear that day nor that night. A multitude of birds did appear, however, flying

from north to southwest, so one could easily believe that they were going to sleep on dry land or perhaps fleeing winter, which could be descending on the lands whence they came. So the Admiral agreed to leave his western course and turn west-southwest, intending to hold to this new course for two days.

With the change of course, the fleet sailed in four days to 24° N. Thus, they stayed within the trades and entered the sea of the Bahamas before the wind.

As to the more general and serious fear regarding the long voyage into the unknown, Columbus had thought about it before departing. The day Hierro disappeared from the horizon, he writes in his diary, "We proceeded that day [9 September] 15 leagues, and I decided to count less than I was covering so that, if the voyage should be long, the crew would not grow afraid or disheartened." As the days and weeks pass, the *Journal* repeats this refrain; he writes a good twenty-five times that the leagues indicated in the pilot's log are less than those actually run.

How many miles did he believe had to be covered? He had two points of reference: Cipango (Japan), which he located 2,400 miles from the Canaries, and Quinsay (Hangchow), a city in Cathay (China), which he placed 3,550 miles away.[2] Now then, on Tuesday, 25 September, the ships had covered 2,400 miles. According to Columbus's calculations (we will see how exact—or inexact—they were), that was the expected distance between the Canaries and Cipango. That same day Martín Alonso Pinzón, from the poop of the *Pinta*, shouted to the captain general: "Land! Land, sir!" Many believed they saw land. But they were mistaken.

On 3 October Columbus says pointedly that he has seen "as many indications of land in the past week as in these days." Nevertheless, he adds that they did not have to tack, knowing very well that there were islands in the vicinity. His goal was to reach the Indies, and it would have been "foolish to linger." Here the *Journal* seems to argue with the anxieties of the crews. But between 5 and 6 October the anxiety must have affected the captain general as well. He thought that they had covered 913 leagues (3,652 miles), 100 more than the distance he had calculated from the Canaries to Cathay, that is, to the Asian mainland.

And land was not in sight. Anxious days passed, the last days of the crossing, but it was not long enough for the tension aboard the ships to become drama. I am convinced that genuine drama was never there; that is mere legend. As to the evidence from the

[2]I have so far spoken in leagues and miles, using Columbus's terms. The league was 4 miles, while the mile was the Mediterranean mile, or 1,480 meters (4,856 feet). By contrast, the modern nautical mile is 1,852 meters (6,076 feet), so Columbus's league was equal to 3.18 modern nautical miles, not 4.

original sources, the *Journal* speaks only of grumbling and pro-
tests, never of violence or actual revolts. The most important
voyage in history had the calmest seas of Columbus's eight
transatlantic crossings. Except for a few hours—on 23 September—the ocean was never rough nor terrible nor dark. The
ships glided lightly on waters always as calm "as the river at
Seville." Then, on the very last day, "there were heavy seas,
heavier than they had seen on the whole voyage." The waves
covered the sterns, strengthening the push toward the goal. History borders on fable: the ships seem guided by a fairy's hand.

17 | *San Salvador: The First Encounter*

*L*and, foreshadowed by a flight of many birds, was indicated by a feeble light in the darkness of night. On the evening of Thursday, 11 October, Columbus was standing on the sterncastle, slightly higher than the prow, and from there, at 10 P.M., an hour before moonrise, saw, or thought he saw, a light in the darkness, "like a little wax candle rising and falling," as he writes in the *Journal*. Columbus told Pedro Gutiérrez to look, and he saw it too, while Pedro Sánchez de Segovia saw nothing because of where he was standing. After this historic consultation, the light appeared once or twice and was seen no more.

On this light have been spoken, written, and printed comments, observations, explanations, and polemics. The suggestion has been made that the entire episode was invented, that it is an outright fraud. Columbus wrote about seeing the light after land was discovered. The entries for 11 and 12 October are not separated in the *Journal;* hence the suspicion that he invented the episode to gain the honor of being the first to see land as well as the annual pension of ten thousand maravedis promised to whoever should discover land.[1]

[1]A little less than $500 today if one ignores the tremendous difference in the velocity of money. When that is considered, it would be $2,000 to $2,500.

The suspicion cannot easily be refuted. Only fools or detractors try to deny the maritime genius of the great Genoese. In this area the myth corresponds with reality. But quite unreal is the myth created by those who wish to attribute to Columbus all virtues while denying him the least defect. Subsequent events confirm that Columbus was quite capable of concocting the fraud that many historians attribute to him. There is, however, one particular item that gives weight to the belief that the incident really occurred: the testimony of other seamen, one of whom is specifically named. Columbus seems to have anticipated suspicions and takes care to cite proper testimonies in the *Journal*.

If it was not fraud, could it have been illusion? That explanation was ruled out after on-site experiments were made. They conclusively eliminated the possibility that the light came from a torch, the only light that the natives had at their disposal. There remained the possibility that it was a bonfire, which looked like a torch only because of the distance. Ruth Durlacher-Wolper and I made direct experiments and can assert that the episode Columbus describes was possible. At a distance of twenty-seven nautical miles and under identical conditions of moonlight and visibility as those at ten in the evening on 11 October 1492, bonfires burning on the cliffs seen by Columbus's ships are visible.

Why would the inhabitants of San Salvador have lit bonfires? The answer is simple. In October the rainy season is ending. Lakes and ponds are full of water, and insects, especially sand flies, are positively intolerable. To keep them away the "Indians"—as Columbus called them, thinking he had reached the islands off India—burned great fires at night in front of their huts. Archaeological excavations have revealed that well-identified Indian villages lay in front of Columbus's ships, which were coming from the east. It was not a supernatural light, as someone has said. The episode does, however, have mystical and romantic overtones. First with a flight of birds, then with a tiny light, did the New World introduce itself to the men of the Old.

At 2 A.M. on 12 October the moon, in its last quarter, was in the best position to illuminate whatever lay before the ships. At that moment Juan Rodríguez Bermejo,[2] from the forecastle of the

[2]There is a question about the sailor, whom tradition calls Rodrigo de Triana but whom the most recent research—especially that conducted by Ballesteros Beretta—has identified with the name given above.

Pinta, caught sight of a whitish sand dune; another lay a little to the south, and in between was a mass of dark rocks. This time there could be no doubt. Land! It really was land, six miles ahead of the caravel, which at that moment was at 74°20' W and 23°57' N. It was the cliffs of High Cay and Hinchingbrooke Rocks, the southeastern edge of the island of Guanahaní, as the Indians called it. Columbus named it San Salvador. About thirteen miles long and six wide, it lies at 24°N and 74°30' W and has a surface area of sixty square miles. It is part of the Commonwealth of the Bahamas, an independent member of the British Commonwealth. Like all the Bahamas, San Salvador is a coral island and consequently flat.

The first novelty at the landfall of the great discovery was the coral barrier reef that entirely surrounds San Salvador. Columbus was familiar with true coral, *Corallium rubrum,* found here and there in the Mediterranean and the Canaries. The Republic of Genoa was one of the major markets for it, the center for its collection, both from nearby and distant waters, as well as its working and sale. But coral barrier reefs are so called only through an etymological fluke, since in English the word *coral* is applied to all calcareous organisms that create madreporic reefs and islands.

No sailor in Christendom before Columbus's time knew of this extraordinary phenomenon. Marco Polo did not speak of it in the *Milione.* Yet it does not appear from the *Journal* that Columbus realized the importance of the discovery; he simply notices that "a reefy shoal surrounds the island." He does not linger in describing the sea, preferring to speak of the land and its inhabitants, though the wonders of that sea undoubtedly enchanted him.

Within the coral reef the water is warm and transparent, with a range of colors running from deep blue to a changeable green like that of spring leaves. From the waterline, thick clumps of mangroves advance into the sea; their roots seek, deep below the salt and the sandy surface, the indispensable sustenance of fresh water. Where mangroves do not grow are colorful gardenlike areas, palms and trees with tall trunks growing right down to the shoreline, gently lapped by waves at high tide. This phenomenon of plants and forest in direct contact with the sea was unknown to Europeans. That contact is permitted by the stillness of the water—"as in a well," Columbus writes. The stillness is assured by the madreporic barrier reef on which the sea breaks and grows quiet in a constant play of foam that is never the same; its movements, whiteness, and noise are endlessly diverse. Columbus did not really understand the phenomenon of the barrier reef at the time, but his seafaring skill led him to act as if he did.

As soon as he was certain that there was finally land to the west, about six leagues ahead, he gave the order to reef sail and proceed with only the lower courses, lying to till daybreak. Anyone who has navigated with sail knows how difficult it is to approach before the wind because of the risk of running against a rock. But why should there have been rocks so far from land, which had scarcely been glimpsed? Nevertheless, rocks there were, though they were a kind of coral unknown until then to seamen and geographers. Columbus sensed the danger, and so he stopped.

In the light of day the splash of white foam from the waves breaking against the rocks could not be missed. Like a picture frame, the barrier reef surrounds the entire island of San Salvador. Off High Cay, Hinchingbrooke Rocks, and Low Cay—the three rocky islets that make up the southeastern point of the island—the reef, running parallel to the shore, breaks up into a fan of rocks perpendicular to the shore, forcing navigators to double the promontory well out to sea, which Columbus did. Approaching the west coast, where he could come in to leeward, he spotted a gap in the reef, and the three ships passed through it and came up to the beach.

The Admiral—at this moment Columbus acquired the title he so coveted—went ashore in an armed boat accompanied by the two Pinzóns. He stepped on the fine white sand, kissed it, raised his eyes to heaven, thanked God, and wept. That emotional and joyous crying in which the Genoese and the Spanish captains joined, before an awestruck crowd of naked men and women—that crying summed up the outstanding significance of the most important encounter in human history. *Encounter* is more accurate than *discovery* because it was not humanity discovering a new and deserted land but two portions of humanity, two worlds, coming together that morning on Guanahaní–San Salvador. The Admiral unfurled the royal standard and the Pinzón brothers the two flags with green crosses, one bearing an *F* (Ferdinando) and the other a *Y* (Ysabel). The Admiral summoned Rodrigo de Escobedo, secretary of the fleet, and Pedro Sánchez de Segovia, a seaman, and "told them to acknowledge and witness how he, before them all, was taking, as in fact he took, possession of the island for the king and the queen." The appropriate formulas were drawn up in writing.

After the ceremony the encounter proceeded. Two worlds until then unknown to each other grew acquainted. Unfortunately, they did not understand each other. Here is the first impression of the encounter: "Right away they saw naked people." In its graphic adherence to reality the expression has no sexual connotation; it is merely an expression of surprise.

They all go naked as their mothers bore them, even the women, and one of these was very young. But all those I saw were young, for I didn't see anyone who was over thirty, and they are all well formed, with handsome bodies and a graceful physical appearance. They have coarse hair, almost like a horse's tail, short and falling into their eyes except for a tuft which they throw behind and let grow long, never cutting it. Some paint themselves gray (the color of the Canary Islanders, neither black nor white), others white, red, or another color. Some paint their face, others their whole body or only the eyes or nose.

They do not carry arms nor do they know about them. I showed them swords and they took them by the blade through ignorance and cut themselves. They have no kind of iron. Their spears are sticks without iron; only some have a fish's tooth on the tip.

Some people I saw bore marks of weapons on their bodies, and I asked them with gestures what they were. They made me understand that from other, neighboring islands people used to come to capture them, and they defended themselves. I believed then and do now that people come here from the mainland to capture and enslave them. They must be good and clever servants; they repeat immediately whatever I say to them, and I believe that they could easily become Christians because it seems to me they belong to no sect. God willing, when I leave here I will take six of these people with me to bring to Your Highnesses so that they can learn to talk like us.

Such are the impressions of the first day. On the second day Columbus says that he was primarily interested in learning where to find gold. He noticed that some of the Indians wore "a little piece of gold inserted in a hole in the nose." They told him—or so he understood—that by "sailing to the south he would find a king who possessed great vessels and many pieces of gold." The Admiral would have liked one of the Indians to lead him to that blessed land, but he realized that they refused to go with him.

Thus did both sides begin to misunderstand. The European scale of values was different from that of the natives. "They give everything they have for a trifle"; obviously what was a trifle on the European scale was not so for the natives. For them "a potsherd or a broken glass cup" was worth "sixteen skeins of cotton." Columbus warned that that would never do, because from unrestricted trade between the two mentalities, the two conceptions of value, grave injustices would result, and so he immediately prohibited the cotton trade, allowing no one to take any and reserving the acquisition of it entirely for the king of Spain. A just prohibition, not easy to impose on ninety men—what strength could it have when nine hundred, nine thousand, or ninety thousand Europeans would arrive? Such were the first troubles in an encounter between two worlds that did not understand one another.

On Sunday, 14 October, the Admiral went by boat along the coast of the island and visited the villages. Some of the natives brought water, others food, and still others threw themselves into the sea and swam out to meet the boats. "As far as we can understand," writes Columbus, "they believe we came from heaven." The Spaniards were received as gods. The Admiral was so moved that while searching for a site on which to build a fortress, he notes in the *Journal,* he decided

> that it would be unnecessary to build one because these people are so simple in deeds of arms, as Your Highnesses will be able to judge from the seven that I ordered taken so they could be brought to Spain, taught our language, and then brought back to their homes.

He immediately adds,

> If Your Highnesses should order either to bring all of them to Castile or to hold them as *captivos* on their own island it

102

could easily be done, because with about fifty men you could control and subjugate them all, making them do whatever you want.

Capitivos means slaves. It is difficult to give a more generous interpretation. Columbus lived in his own time, was a man of his own time, thinking like the leaders—and others—of his time, not like the saints.

18 | *"Asia"*

The Spanish ships reached San Salvador on Friday, 12 October. The next day they visited the island. The Admiral went only a couple of miles into the dense woods of mastic and lignum vitae, to the large lagoon, Great Lake. Beyond it stands the highest point on the island, Mount Kerr, which rises 141 feet. On Sunday, 14 October, Columbus completed the exploration by boat as far as Graham's Harbor (a port protected by the barrier reef, capable of holding "all the ships of Christendom"), on the northern side of the island. He saw two or three villages. Others were found on the eastern side, the side he had seen first. One may readily suppose, on the basis of archaeological discoveries, that more people lived on San Salvador than the seven hundred of today.

On Sunday evening he departed, sailing to the southwest. Reaching Santa María de la Concepción (Rum Cay), Fernandina (Long Island), Isabela (Crooked Island), Columbus stopped at each island and always put the same question to the Indians: "Where is the gold?" The parrots he had found. The spices he expected were there. But the gold? At island after island the inhabitants pointed south. There lay a large island called Coba or Cuba—so all asserted with signs and words, although difficult to understand. A dead calm and rain impeded navigation, but finally, before night fell on Saturday, 27 October, the sailors discovered land. Land that was really extensive at last. At dawn the next day it appeared with its mountains, valleys, and plains, with its thick trees, flowers of a hundred colors, fruits of a hundred kinds, and numerous birds, big and small, sweetly singing. Columbus had never seen "a more beautiful spot." He had no doubt that Cuba was Cipango (Japan). The great design had been realized; they had reached the Orient by sailing west.

At the first landing Columbus immediately thought that San Salvador was one of the many islands that tradition and Marco Polo had located east of Cathay. That conviction was confirmed during the trip through the Bahamas. But what made San Salvador, Santa María de la Concepción, Fernandina, and Isabela appear to be Asian? For us there is very little, indeed nothing. But for Columbus? There were palms, yet he knew that palms are found in Africa as well as Asia. There were majestic trees and new species of plants. But Columbus and the Spanish sailors who had sailed in the Canaries and to Madeira—and there were many— should have known that flora so different from that of Europe is not conclusive evidence of Asia, being common to all tropical and subtropical lands. There were snakes and lizards bigger than those of Europe. But the Admiral had seen their equals in Guinea.

Columbus's conviction was based on four clues: parrots, spices, gold, and the racial characteristics of the natives. As soon as he landed on San Salvador, he experienced great joy: he almost considered it a sign from Providence that the first Indians he met offered him parrots. And he was very happy to write in the *Journal* on the day of the great discovery: "On this island I didn't see animals of any species except parrots." On Long Island, on 16 October, he repeats it: "On land I didn't see animals of any species except parrots and lizards." And on 21 October: "The flocks of parrots obscure the sun." Parrots symbolized the Indies. Marco Polo and other medieval travelers who described the wonders of far-off Asia had spoken of parrots. Columbus knew that parrots do not live in Europe or anywhere in the Mediterranean. Some species are found in parts of Guinea, a land known to the Portuguese and Columbus. No one had spoken of these African parrots, however, perhaps because they live in the forests of the interior, where neither the Portuguese nor Columbus had penetrated, or perhaps because they are usually parakeets, which do not display the variety of brilliant colors typical of their Asian, American, and Oceanic cousins. So Columbus did not know that parrots are found in all the tropical and subtropical regions of the world, from Kenya to Papua and Polynesia. He believed, as did all his contemporaries, that they were proof positive of Asia.

As for gold, the reports of the time leave doubt as to the quantity brought home on the first voyage. It is said that the Royal Chamber in Barcelona and the tabernacle of the Blessed Sacrament in Toledo Cathedral were gilded with gold from the Indies, but that has not been proven. It appears that only small amounts were brought to Europe from the first voyage. Nevertheless, the belief that the precious metal was to be found in the newly discovered lands was not an illusion, for signs of it, however modest, were to be seen right from the first. True, many years passed before the biggest gold and silver mines were discovered. And Columbus's belief was not a mere illusion but a clever enticement, opening the gates to the gold-bearing regions.

The final evidence that convinced Columbus he was in Asia was the physical characteristics of the people. They were unlike the Europeans, the Moors (Arabs), and even the Africans of Guinea. Columbus attempts to emphasize their difference the following day, 13 October: "Their hair is not kinky [evidently an allusion to blacks] but straight and coarse like horsehair. . . . They have a large head and forehead, much larger than any other race I have seen before, and their eyes are very beautiful and not small." He emphasizes that they are not blacks: "None of them is dark." On the contrary, they are the color of the Canary Islanders or of sunburnt peasants. "Their stomach is not large and is well formed," whereas many of the blacks of Guinea had swollen stomachs from protein deficiency and the resultant pathological changes.

Despite the parrots, racial characteristics, some gold, and hope of spices, there were elements that diverged sharply from Marco Polo's accounts. "Right away they saw naked people" was the immediate impression of the first encounter. All were naked on San Salvador, and all were naked on Santa María de la Concepción. Painted black, white, red, or brown, the natives had decorative rings and pieces of gold on their arms, legs, or neck, in their ears or nose—and were always naked. How could he forget that Asians were dressed, very well dressed? Furthermore, from the first day Columbus records in the *Journal* that the natives did not know "any kind of iron." Having read the *Milione,* or at least an abstract of it, he must have known that Asians were as familiar with iron as were Europeans.

Ignorance of iron, nakedness, the construction style of the houses and villages—all indicated a primordial state, inferior even to conditions in Guinea. Being better nourished, they were not as miserable looking as the people of Guinea, but their material development was, on the whole, inferior. How could they be Asians? Columbus persisted in his error because he believed that he had come to the outposts of Asia, small islands far removed from the civilization of Cathay and Cipango. Indeed, the *Milione* itself mentions the islands of Socotera (Socotra) and Zenzibar (Zanzibar), where the people go naked or wear only a loincloth. Columbus may have thought that only on the mainland and the large islands would he find the rich, splendid civilization of which Marco Polo spoke. Cipango, Cathay, and India were his objectives.

The natives told him of "a very large island." The Admiral had no doubts: "I think it must be Cipango, judging from the information which the Indians I have with me provide." So he writes on 21 October, and he repeats it on 23 October and 26 October, a disconcerting conviction. The Admiral was also fooled by his conception of geography, to which he remained stubbornly faithful. He held that the distance by land from Portugal to China was much greater than it is. Not only Toscanelli but Piccolomini's *Historia rerum* and Marco Polo had given him the idea that Cathay and the land of the Great Khan extended much farther east than they do. Hence his certainty—having accepted the principle of the roundness of the earth—that Asia was three thousand miles beyond the Atlantic Ocean from Lisbon, twenty-four hundred miles from the island of Hierro.

Had he not been so certain, Columbus would not have elaborated his project with such enthusiasm, would not have pressed it on the scholars and rulers with such passion, would not have convinced Pinzón to follow him, would not have faced the adventure of the crossing. Now that he had found land, or rather lands, right where he expected them, right where his calculations indicated, right where "his" geography said they should be, how could he abandon his goal, an obsession and a polestar for him during years of hopes, fears, confrontations, and arguments? For

107

years he had maintained that beyond the Dark Sea, beyond the Atlantic, was Asia, that he could reach the Orient by sailing west. Now he had found many islands and finally a large landmass beyond the ocean. There were parrots, gold, spices (according to him), and people unlike Europeans or Africans. How could he not have believed that he had reached Asia?

Las Casas sought to explain Columbus's error with frequent references to the map of the physician Paolo Toscanelli, saying "he held this opinion"—that is, that these were the lands of the Great Khan—because "the map of Paolo the physician and the information Paolo had sent in his letters strongly encouraged him to do so." But many other times the Genoese explorer, forced to choose between theory and experience, trusted his experience, bending theory to it by introducing necessary modifications or corrections. After arriving in the New Lands, Columbus continued to be an acute observer, a first-class mariner, and a good geographer because he trusted his own experience. But on this occasion he did not give the least consideration to the many indications that he was in lands far different from the Asia of the *Milione*.

The *Milione* describes kingdoms full of pomp, of numerous cults and major religions, of pearls, diamonds, ivory, sandalwood, and ambergris, even of goods from Russia and the Arctic, an unequaled phantasmagoria of civilized peoples and countries. In addition, a large part of the *Milione* is devoted to the diverse Asian fauna: tigers, leopards, cheetahs, lynxes, timber wolves, elephants, rhinoceroses or unicorns, baboons or mandrill apes, Tibetan dogs "as big as donkeys," deer, wild boars, monkeys, and snakes. All of this finds no echo in the experiences and descriptions of the Genoese: his conviction, his *idée fixe,* prevailed despite reality, despite the nature of the New Lands. Why? Because of other deceptive evidence and especially because the Discoverer was obstinate and ruled by ambition and pride. Through his obstinacy he found the strength to persist for seven years—the best of a man's life, from thirty-four to forty-one—while waiting for a decision from the Spanish monarchs. Having finally found land beyond the ocean, of which he was not grand admiral, his persistence grew into pig-headedness, blocking his reason.

Obstinacy is often a characteristic of great men. In Columbus it was so intense and unrelenting as to be both a virtue and a vice. Early on it was a virtue: in Lisbon, in his Mediterranean and oceanic voyages from Iceland to Porto Santo and to Guinea, later on in Spain, and finally for thirty-three days in crossing the Atlantic. Now it was a vice, when the Admiral of the Ocean Sea had discovered the most wonderful and enchanting lands without realizing that they were not Asia, that they could not be Asia.

Just as he had nourished the secret of his grand design for seven years, convinced that he was to accomplish a divine mission, so now, having reached the land beyond the Dark Sea, he was more convinced than ever of accomplishing a work willed by God, laden with undying glory for him and power and riches for his descendants. In fact, glory he had obtained, but the thought never even crossed his mind that such glory was due him for having discovered new continents, vast, rich, and nearly as important as Asia, much more so than Europe and Africa.

A new continent was beyond every scientific theory, beyond imagination. The justifications of Las Casas are very much to the point. Paolo Toscanelli and other scholars unanimously ruled out the existence of other continents besides Europe, Africa, and Asia. These lands therefore had to be islands—no matter how distant— off Cathay and India. Discovering Atlantic islands would not have been a divinely inspired mission, for which he felt himself predestined, would have had no impact on the course of history. There were already many islands, real or imagined, on every map of the Dark Sea; the discovery or rediscovery of the Canaries, Madeira, and the Azores had not changed the course of history.

To admit that the New Lands were not Cathay and Cipango would have required humility, impossible in Columbus. He was too proud to humble himself. Precisely because of his proud and stubborn character, he had succeeded in an undertaking which to many appeared impossible, even absurd. To become master of the Atlantic, to conceive his grand design, it had been easy for Columbus to bend theory to his own experience and maritime intuition, because doing so matched his desires, his thirst for glory. Now he would have had to subordinate theory to reality again, the reality of the Caribbean, an interesting and striking environment but with modest architecture, furniture, and utensils—in short, an entire social structure and level of civilization far below what he expected.

Subordinating his own theories to such evidence would have required a virtue Columbus did not possess. Had he had humility and a spirit of renunciation before 1492 Columbus would not have achieved the greatest discovery of history. Had he had them after 12 October of that momentous year he would not have committed this great error; he would have been freed from the fixation that followed him to the grave, robbing him of the honor of immortalizing his own name by giving it to two of the greatest, richest, and most important continents on earth. On the other hand, his fixation would prove exceedingly productive. Convinced that he had found Asia, Columbus would return three times, always stubbornly trying to reach the fabled cities by sailing west, always animated by the hope, indeed the faith, that he would reach India. In his frantic search for India, the great discovery was expanded well beyond Cuba and Hispaniola to other islands in the Caribbean and, above all, to the mainland, to the mouths of the Orinoco, where he discovered Venezuela in South America. He did determine it was not Asia, but he was not interested because of his obsession with reaching India.

Cuba, which now lay before him, had a fairylike fascination, emanating as it did a perfume like that of which he had had his first exciting, unforgettable whiff when a youth on the island of Chios. It was probably Cipango, or Cathay itself. It was, in any case, Asia! At dawn on Sunday, 28 October, the three ships entered the mouth of a river and dropped anchor "a lombard shot from the shore." Columbus named the river San Salvador and the new land Juana. Neither name has survived. The large island today bears the native name, Cuba. The village named San Salvador has disappeared, yet many villages in Oriente Province claim they are on the original site. There is, however, no doubt that the natural harbor, which Columbus said was "without danger of sandbanks or other impediments," is Bariay Bay. On this encounter with the first large island of America, as earlier with the little outlying island, I will let the Discoverer speak for himself: "This island is the prettiest that human eyes have ever seen. It is full of very beautiful and very high mountains, though they are not very long, and the rest of the land is high, as in Sicily." On 29 October the fleet tacked to westward. In the evening it made the mouth of "quite a large river," today Puerto Gibara, far larger and easier to use than any of the natural harbors encountered earlier.

On 30 October Columbus "found a cape covered with palms, to which he gave the name Cabo de las Palmas." Today called Punta

Uvero, it still has great numbers of palms. Then the wind shifted to the west, growing so strong that on 31 October the fleet was forced to sail close-hauled. The wind shifted again, to the north, and the temperature dropped; a storm was making up. Columbus knew that it would be impossible to tack with a north wind along a coast running to the north-northwest, so he gave the order to reverse course. He returned to Puerto Gibara at dawn, 1 November, and stayed eleven days. They left on Monday, 12 November, for an island "which many of the Indians on board call Babeque," the modern-day Great Inagua.

A new storm came from the north, so Columbus decided to seek shelter somewhere on the coast of Cuba. He spotted an inlet about two hundred yards wide. The middle of the channel was over forty fathoms, so the fleet was able to enter. At the end of a tortuous passage Tánamo Bay opened up, well protected by a high mountain and with numerous islets emerging sharp as "diamond points" or flat "as tables." At Tánamo the fleet stayed four days. On Monday, 19 November, Columbus sailed in the early hours of the morning, his course north-northeast, six points off the wind. Here occurred an incident about which Columbus scholars of all times have conjectured and debated endlessly, the so-called desertion of Martín Alonso Pinzón. The *Journal* reports as follows:

> Today Martín Alonso Pinzón in the caravel *Pinta* left the other two ships without having received an order and against the Admiral's will. Pinzón acted thus through desire for gain, thinking that he would find much gold by following the advice of one of the Indians which the Admiral had taken aboard. And so Pinzón left without waiting for the others, without any excuse of bad weather but only because he wanted to. And many other nasty things he said and did to me.

It was not desertion per se. Pinzón went to Babeque in search of gold, then landed on the northern coast of Haiti, where he knew the Admiral was headed. He did not take with him—nor did he even try to—his brother, Vicente Yañez, who stayed with the *Niña* beside the Admiral. He later sent messages to Columbus and, receiving no reply, went to rejoin him.

Let us return to the voyage of the *Santa María* and the *Niña*. For two days and nights—22 and 23 November—the current carried them west. Finally, on the morning of 24 November, they made

Cayo Moa Grande, Cuba. The place is enchanting. The abundant pines, straight as spindles, Columbus imagined as beams in the sides of caravels and masts in the largest ships in Spain. The forest was already a fleet; untouched trunks in the American woods were already raw material, goods for the metropolis, a source of incalculable riches and of naval power. Two days later the vision would become even more concrete and detailed: the king and queen could easily subjugate the new islands, convert the inhabitants, and build cities and fortresses. To ensure that their empire would be long lasting, they would do well not to allow "any foreigner to trade or set foot there except for Catholic Christians." Only six weeks earlier, comments Gerbi, Columbus the stranger had set foot in America; now he was already jealous, in the interests of Spain, of every other "immigrant." The paradise was no sooner discovered than annexed to the Crown of Castile.

On 26 November the ships left Puerto Cayo Moa and the next day reached "a very striking port," Puerto Baracoa, surrounded by fields and villages. Here Columbus stayed a week and had the opportunity to explore the surrounding area, make contact with many of the natives of Cuba, and take stock of his discoveries. He was euphoric. The small islands of the Bahamas had already made him enthusiastic, but in this great land the exuberance of nature, its novelty and beauty, far superior not only to the vistas of Europe but also those of Guinea as well, stirred and inspired him. Columbus appears to have been dominated by three sentiments: enthusiasm for the novelty of the flora of the Antilles, admiration for its exceptional beauty, and frustration at not being able, through lack of time and ignorance of botany, to evaluate fully its medicinal and nutritive values. Nature on the discovered lands was diverse and surprising, even unusual. On the aesthetic level it was beautiful and pleasant; on the practical level it had to be most usable and exploitable.

19 | Discoveries in the New Lands

*A*fter leaving Cuba the *Santa María* and the *Niña* entered, on 6 December, a natural harbor that Columbus named San Nicolás on the island of Hispaniola. The port is outstanding, but it is even more memorable because of its resemblance to Spain: "the island seems completely cultivated, or nearly so, and the fields look like wheat in May in the Córdoba countryside . . . many species of trees are the same as in Spain, for example, ilex, oak, and arbutus." The sailors "catch sole and other fish like those of Castile. They find myrtle and other plants and herbs, and the vegetation, soil, and mountains resemble those of Castile." Even the rain and cold were "like Castile in October." All these things induced the Admiral to name the island Española, which Peter Martyr would translate into Latin as Hispaniola, the name still used when one wishes to indicate the entire island consisting of the two nations of Haiti and the Dominican Republic.

Later in the *Journal* Columbus would say that what he found on Hispaniola "is a wonder." What did he find in the New Lands? His first concern was to identify the trees and plants. He thought he recognized the aloe and decided "to have about ten hundredweight of it cut and stowed aboard, because they say it is a most valuable wood," and so it is. Its leaves have been cut and its sap collected to produce a medicine since antiquity. A belief of the late Middle Ages, current down to the last century, held that an elixir for longevity could be made from aloe. So Columbus was not mistaken about the value of the aloe, but he was mistaken in identifying it: the trees he brought back were not aloe but simply a strong-smelling wood.

Another error, regarding mastic, must have occurred right afterward, though this time the Genoese was not mistaken in identifying it. Mastic is still found today in the Caribbean. It has quite large leaves and the same fragrance as Mediterranean mastic found on the Aegean islands, Sardinia, and in Liguria. When Columbus caught a whiff of mastic coming from a large fire built for caulking the ships, he remembered very well the mastic trees of Chios and their value and decided to search for the tree. After discovering it on Cuba the sailors found it again, or at least a tree similar to it, in great quantities on Hispaniola, which was "thick with mastic trees, from which they collected a great deal of resin, but it was not yet harvest time, for in this season the trickling drops from the tree do not harden." So Columbus records for 10 December. The following day, he writes, "Men were again sent ashore, and they again found a great deal of mastic resin."

Recalling his experience of Chios, Columbus notes in the *Journal* entry for 12 November that from the mastic of Chios Genoese merchants earned "a good fifty thousand ducats per year." Here, then, was a source of riches. He could not yet guarantee gold and pearls, and he could not positively identify the spices. But mastic, yes. In reality, however, the mastics are not the same. Caribbean mastic is similar to that of the Mediterranean; however, neither produces riches: common medicine, yes, but not a product of great commercial value. The mastic of Chios is an exception, almost a trick of nature, and only on the southern part of the island do the mastics produce enough resin to make it a valuable product for both small businesses and industry.

It was not mastic alone that excited Columbus. On Cuba "when he smelled a wonderful odor he was certain they had found aromatic trees and herbs" (2 November). Columbus's sense of smell did not deceive him. The Caribbean islands are lands of spices; many Asian spices were introduced later, different from the native ones but no less aromatic. Hence the seesaw of disappointment and hope continued on Haiti, where Columbus was convinced that the peppers were really a spice: "Their pepper," he writes, is "much better than ours, and no one eats without the seasoning of this spice, which is a great aid to health. One could load fifty caravels a year with this spice from this island." Peter Martyr would comment later that "they also brought from there some wrinkled grains of different colors, more piquant than Caucasian pepper, and cut dried tree branches similar to cinnamon, but as far as taste and smell go the bark and the pulp were like hot ginger." These are the fruit and stems of a plant until then unknown to the Old World, bell peppers. Today, bell peppers and cayenne are cultivated and used on all continents. They are found pickled not only in the homes of every country but also in the standard international cuisine, as flat as it is universal.

The palms of Cuba impressed Columbus because of their quantity and difference from those of Guinea and Spain. The first he saw were of medium height: "They have a large trunk without bark at the base and quite large leaves, with which the natives cover their houses." So the Admiral wrote on 28 October. As mentioned in the preceding chapter, on 30 October he named a promontory Cabo de las Palmas; the palms are still there. The *Journal* entry for 14 November speaks of "unending palm groves." And finally, on 17 November, he came across "palms quite a bit higher than those which he had seen until then." Ten days later, among various kinds of palms, he discovered the "tallest and most beautiful ones" he had ever seen. They are the royal palms, until then unknown in Europe. The other palms, which Columbus immediately discovered, were not the well-known date palms of Spain and Mediterranean Africa nor, as some believed, coconut palms. The latter, very numerous in the Caribbean today, were imported later. Nor were they oil palms, like those of Guinea, as Columbus observed. They are a different kind, still found in the Bahamas and here and there on the other islands of the Caribbean, called dwarf palms because their height, although completely normal, is far less than that of the stately royal palm.

But the most important botanical discoveries were not the majestic and impressive royal palms, nor the fantastically abundant pines, nor even the new spices, but plants whose introduction into the European and world economies would create an authentic revolution: corn, potatoes, tobacco, and new species of cotton. A few statistics are sufficient to indicate their present-day importance, which no one would deny. Every year over 330 million tons of corn are grown, nearly half in the Old World; over 330 million tons of potatoes are grown, nearly two-thirds in Europe and Asia; and over 5.5 million tons of tobacco are grown, nearly three-fourths in Europe and Asia.

When he first saw corn, Columbus mistook it for a kind of millet, and on Haiti he would confuse it with barley. Don Ferdinand is more precise, speaking of "another grain, like kneaded flour, which they call *mahiz* and which has the most wonderful flavor either cooked, roasted, or ground up in mush." Peter Martyr had never seen a field of corn and created confusion by saying that there was a great abundance of this kind of "wheat or fodder" among the Lombards and Spaniards of Granada. This assertion, made in 1493, is absolutely impossible. Columbus brought the plant back to Spain on his return from the first voyage, but years and even decades were to pass before the new crop spread throughout Europe. This plant seems marked by destiny for confusion, for even the name which it would assume in everyday speech—*granoturco* in Italy, *Turkey wheat* in England, *blé de Turquie* in France—stems from an ambiguous term: corn had nothing to do with Turkey, but in the sixteenth century *Turkish* was applied to anything foreign to Christendom.

The potato does not appear in the *Journal* for the first voyage, nor would it appear in accounts of later voyages. The true potato cannot be counted among Columbus's discoveries. It did not grow in the Caribbean, nor is it cultivated there today because it cannot adapt to the climate. It was found several decades later in the Andes of northern Chile, Peru, and Ecuador. But if the potato is not technically one of Columbus's discoveries, it may be so considered because its near relatives are—the sweet potato (called *ajes* by the Indians) and manioc (then as today called *yuca* in Central and South America). These are not relatives in a strictly scientific, botanical sense, but the potato, sweet potato, and manioc are all tubers with the same nutritional properties and may be substituted for one another or, with some deficiency, for grain, corn, or rice. And so the discovery of the sweet potato and manioc may be considered an anticipation of the discovery of the potato.

Columbus at first thought these Caribbean sweet potatoes were the same as *ajes*, the yams of Guinea. "These lands are very fertile;

they produce great quantities of *niames,* which are like carrots with the flavor of chestnuts," he writes on 4 November on Cuba, and on 6 November, "the soil is very fertile and cultivated for yams." On 15 November he mentions "roots with which the Indians make their bread." This bread, "which is quite white and good," he mentions repeatedly in the *Journal* during the exploration of Haiti.

The great news, then, of the Columbian discovery is these tubers. It was not only the people of Guinea who ate yams, which grow underground, resemble roots, and are, botanically speaking, roots or parts of roots. The peoples of the New World cultivated and ate them too. Columbus and the Spaniards ate them and discovered that cassava bread, which tastes a bit like a chestnut, is delicious, and they became accustomed to eating it. After the sweet potato they tried *yuca*—manioc that has had the poison removed—and found it nutritious and palatable. Nor did they disdain the Caribbean yams, washing and chopping or grinding them and adding them to soups or meat dishes. So began the gastronomic revolution that would explode with the potato.

The true potato appeared only in the middle of the sixteenth century. It scarcely held its own in the American colonies, and its entrance into Europe would be humble. A century later, however, its success was evident. In 1645 Germany survived a terrible famine thanks to the potato. In 1771 a prize was offered in France for a product that would substitute for cereals in the basic French diet. Parmentier, returning from prison in Germany, suggested the potato. It ultimately drew the attention of Louis XVI, who called it "the bread of the poor" and promoted its cultivation.

As "the bread of the poor," the potato replaced rye bread, for hundreds of years the staple of European peasants. When one considers that rye bread, because of ergot fungus on the grain, was the cause of one of the most frightening epidemics in medieval pathology (St. Anthony's fire or ergotism), the improvement in health brought about by the use of the potato instead of rye—at least until the modern means for disinfecting rye were discovered—becomes clear.

The potato, then, created a true revolution in the agriculture, economy, gastronomy, and, above all, health of the peoples of the Old World by its decisive contribution to the elimination of the greater part of the scourges of famine and epidemic. The revolu-

117

tion extended even to military strategy. It has been justly observed that Napoleon could not have achieved his victories without the potato. The rapidity of his movements—the keystone of the great Corsican's strategy—would not have been possible if his tens and hundreds of thousands of soldiers had not been able to transport huge quantities of potatoes instead of flour, which is much more costly, spoils more easily, and is much more difficult to handle.

Europeans took less time to learn to use tobacco than they did the potato: nearly two centuries for the potato, some seventy years for tobacco. Columbus discovered it immediately on landing at San Salvador. On Fernandina, 15 October, he speaks in the *Journal* of "some dried leaves which these people valued highly, because earlier they offered some as a gift to me on San Salvador." On 6 November two Spaniards he sent to explore the interior of Cuba refer to "having met on the way many people who were going back to their villages, men and women, with a firebrand in their hand and herbs to *tomar sus sahumerios* [drink the smoke] as is their custom." I have quoted the original Castilian because it is the first European mention of smoking. *Tomar sus sahumerios* in fact means to inhale the fumes. On San Salvador and Long Island, then, the Europeans first learned of tobacco leaves, and on Cuba two Spanish sailors saw its strange use for the first time.

Don Ferdinand reports without change the simple account of the *Journal*. From Las Casas's more precise account we learn, not without surprise, that the cigar was practically the same then as it is now. I should add that the word *tabaco* in the Arawak language meant "cigar" and not, as it does today, the plant from which the leaves are gathered. The two Spanish sailors, as Las Casas gives the details of the appearance of the cigar, noticed that the men and women held "a firebrand in the hand, . . . dry herbs" placed in a dry leaf, like the little firecrackers Castilian boys make for Pentecost. They burned one end and from the other inhaled the smoke; intoxicated with it, they did not feel tired.

Among the discoveries spoken of thus far, tobacco had a great influence in changing the habits of men and women of the Old World, greater than the potato, corn, tomato, bean, and bell pepper, all of which revolutionized the diet of Europeans and Asians. It is an influence greater than many other discoveries that are more important from a scientific point of view.

I have mentioned tomatoes and beans; one could add cocoa to

the list of products which have revolutionized the agriculture, gastronomy, and economy of the entire world. But Columbus did not know these three plants, or at least he does not indicate that he was familiar with them, except for a reference to cacao seeds used as money by Indians on a boat encountered off the coast of Honduras on the fourth voyage. Of that I will speak later.

There is, finally, cotton, not one of Columbus's discoveries, but the species and subspecies found in the New World were unknown in the Old. Along with mastic, it is one of the few things known to both sides in the encounter. If Columbus was mistaken in predicting great economic gains from mastic, he was not mistaken about cotton. He reported it after his first landing on San Salvador. "Cotton grows on this island," he notes in the *Journal* on 13 October, adding that he saw the natives trade sixteen balls of yarn weighing twenty-five to thirty pounds for a few cents. He immediately "forbade this trade and permitted no one to practice it, reserving the acquisition of it entirely for Your Highnesses should we find large quantities of it."

On 6 November on Cuba the Admiral says the Spaniards "saw a great quantity of coarse cotton, spun and woven, and they estimated that in just one house were gathered more than five hundred arrobas[1] and that every year one could gather four thousand quintals."[2] The Admiral adds that he believes they did not plant it and that it bore all year round; the cotton was quite fine and had very large bolls. A different species from that of the Old World, it is shaggier and has leaves divided usually into three lobes instead of five, and white, spotless petals. Old World cotton has yellow petals with a red spot. Columbus did not report all these differences, but he realized that the cotton of Cuba "has a very big boll" and is "quite fine," so he must have known the cotton of the Old World, probably from Andalusia, where the Moors had introduced it in the ninth century, although on a small scale. Columbus's two details show, as always, his keen observation of nature, not only at sea, where his ability was exceptional, but also in the plant kingdom. The cotton of Central America does have shaggier, bigger bolls with a more pronounced tip.

Columbus already foresaw that a great quantity of cotton could

[1]The arroba is a Spanish measure equivalent to twenty-five pounds.
[2]A quintal is a hundredweight.

be produced in Cuba, as Las Casas reports, and that much of it could be sold. The development of the cotton industry in America completely fulfilled the Discoverer's intuition. However, while corn, potatoes, tobacco, tomatoes, beans, peppers, cocoa, and other plants produced a revolution in the customs of the entire world simply by their introduction, the economic revolution touched off by cotton began only with four great mechanical inventions in the eighteenth century.

Beginning in 1738, Wyatt, Hargreaves, Arkwright, and Crompton invented and perfected various devices that finally culminated, in 1779, in the famous spinning jenny, the mechanical spindle that allowed a man and four boys to do the work of six hundred women. In 1785 James Watt invented the steam engine, freeing industry from dependence on animal or water power. In the same year Edmund Cartwright invented the mechanical loom, which wove as much in one day as eight thousand hand weavers. Finally, in 1792 Eli Whitney of Massachusetts patented the cotton gin, which simplified removing the seeds.

One can realize the significance of these events by considering two figures. In the middle of the eighteenth century, England imported a few tons of cotton from America; in the second decade of the nineteenth century it imported 385,000 tons. The cultivation of cotton, with its many varieties and adaptable species, spread to all the tropical and temperate regions of the world. The spiraling development of technology, with the creation and ever-increasing spread of synthetic fibers, has not stopped or even slowed the spread of cotton. Recently, the use of cotton as an oil-bearing plant has made it even more widespread, so that almost everywhere the plant is cultivated for two purposes, either for fiber or oil-bearing seeds.

The "threads of the devil" employ 10 million people in America, 12 million in the British Commonwealth, and perhaps 100 million worldwide. White gold takes its place with yellow gold and black gold (petroleum). Of the three, Columbus did not even imagine the existence of the black. He immediately saw the importance of the white and predicted its development in the lands of the great discovery. As for yellow gold, he continued his passionate search for it.

20 | *The Peoples of the New Lands*

A s we have seen, Columbus describes the physical characteristics of the peoples of the New Lands many times in the *Journal*, beginning with the first encounter of 12 October. They were a tall, handsome people. Their hair was not curly, but smooth and coarse like a horse's tail; their foreheads and heads were wide, wider than almost any other race; their eyes were beautiful, not small; they were not dark skinned, but colored like the Canary Islanders; their legs were unusually straight; and their bellies were not big, but well formed.

They were Tainos, the original peoples of all the Bahamas, Hispaniola, and Cuba—in short, of the Greater Antilles. Their language was Arauco, or Arawak. They are now completely extinct; only a few of their features remain among the blacks, with whom they intermarried. In the fourteenth and fifteenth centuries, the Tainos had spread from Hispaniola to the eastern parts of Cuba, to Jamaica, Puerto Rico, and the Bahamas, expelling or enslaving the earlier inhabitants.

Archaeological diggings in the areas inhabited by the Tainos reveal significant cultural development in the decorative arts, used in rituals and in sports. They had three classes: nobles, commoners, and slaves. Caciques (chiefs) had the power of life and death over their subjects. They oversaw the festivals, work in the fields, hunting, and fishing. Their position, like their goods, was passed down matrilineally.

The Tainos were of a mild and hospitable nature. As Columbus noted, the men went naked, while the women sometimes wore small aprons or cotton skirts. They used a variety of colors—red, white, black, and yellow—to paint their bodies. They practiced deformation of their skulls and perforated the nasal septum and their ears. The few ornaments they had were made of stone, bone, shell, and sometimes gold. On some islands of the Bahamas and once on Cuba the Spaniards came across Indians with pieces of gold or silver in their noses. In their dances they wore feather ornaments and masks. The wooden drum used during the dances was like the Mexican two-toned drum.

The Taino religion featured a celestial deity, the sun, and its mother, the moon, from which sprang the human race. They kept and worshipped *zemi* ("statuettes") in their dwellings. Each *zemi* had a name and an individual history and was connected with some dead cacique. Each functioned as a kind of spokesman—whose use was secret—for making oracles. The images found here and there on cliffs were probably also based on the conceptions that inspired the *zemi*. The dead were buried in the prenatal position. The cacique's main wife followed him into the tomb.

Columbus and his men did not meet any other races during the first voyage. The *Journal* speaks often of the Caribs (Cannibals) and reports the Tainos' terror of them, but they appeared only on the second voyage. For now the new peoples were only the Tainos. They spoke, as I have already said, one language. "In Guinea," Columbus observes, "things are different: they speak a thousand languages, and the inhabitants of one place cannot understand those of another." On 11 December the Admiral could report in the *Journal* that "every day we can understand these Indians better and they understand us much better, though as often as not we misunderstand them or they us." This explains why it was not difficult to obtain interpreters. One of them, brought back to Spain and baptized Diego Colón, was a translator on the second voyage also.

The Tainos were not highly civilized, but neither were they primitive. Their nakedness and disinclination to work do not indicate primitive conditions but rather the natural consequences of the environment. There is no need to dress in the wonderful climate of the Caribbean, and it is not necessary to work hard for food. Nature offers a variety of tasty, nutritious seafood, still abundant along the coasts of the Bahamas, Cuba, and Hispaniola. The fact that fish were eaten raw would scandalize Don Ferdinand, but it does not surprise present-day gourmets. As for spiders and white worms, they are not filth, as Don Ferdinand calls them, but rather foods no less delicious than escargots, so prized in French and Italian cuisine. Besides the foods offered freely by nature, one required real work to obtain: bread, made from grated sweet potatoes or from pounded and ground corn, which the Spanish called cassava or *cazzabì* bread. Obtaining *yuca* required rather heavy labor, especially removing the poison from manioc.

Taino dwellings were made of straw or palm fronds, similar to those often found today in tropical America, Africa, and Asia. Usually rectangular with a sloping roof, they were also circular with a conical roof, and sometimes were built on pilings. Taino settlements had playing fields. The game was played with rubber balls that could not be touched with the hands. This discovery was of considerable significance when one considers the importance acquired in this century by soccer, another game in which the ball cannot be touched with the hands.

Rubber, in the form of a ball, made its entrance bouncing and jumping into history on Cuba and Hispaniola before the awestruck gaze on the men from the Old World. Oviedo noted the difference between these and the balls already known in Christendom: "These balls bounce much more than others, because as soon as they are thrown to the ground they come back and make another bounce and another and another, the bounces gradually diminishing by themselves." Hard rubber from various species— the best known is the *Hevea brasiliensis*—was known to the Indians of the pre-Columbian New World. Europeans gained fuller knowledge of it through the work of La Condamine; Goodyear discovered how to vulcanize rubber in 1839.

To return to the dwellings, they were "quite large and resembled tents in a military camp, but they were not lined up and so did not form roads but just sprang up here and there." In one of these houses Columbus found, on 3 December, "palm fibers, ropes, a hook made of horn, harpoons made of bone, other items for fishing, and many fireplaces inside." The seats were made from a single piece of wood and shaped like animals with their tails raised to form a headrest.

The most unusual discovery the Europeans made in the Indians' houses was the hammock. Columbus first noted it on 18 October on the island of Fernandina: "The beds and covers on which these people sleep are a kind of cotton net." On Cuba, 27 October, he visited two houses and found "nets of palm fiber in both." On 3 November he defines them as "nets in which they sleep, which are hammocks." Las Casas is more minute and precise in his description. He perceptively associates the custom of sleeping in hammocks with the structure of the houses:

> The hammocks are shaped like a sling, their long threads not interwoven like nets but loose enough that the fingers can be inserted between them. These threads are attached to other thick threads, like the lace of Seville. They are comfortable and long, and from their ends protrude the threads of which they are made, forming many ends. Each end is tied to other fine threads of a material stronger than cotton, similar to hemp and an ell [about 45 inches] wide at both ends. These are tied into a knot resembling a fist and attached to pillars on both sides of the house so that the hammocks are suspended in the air and used in that position. They are three or four yards wide, and to use them they are opened up like a giant sling.

The Indians collected water in hollowed-out gourds. They wound spun cotton into balls. On more than one occasion the Spanish found wooden statuettes, rough figures of women, and well-made masks in the houses. But they could not determine whether the statuettes were religious or art objects. Columbus speaks of their assegais and javelins in the *Journal* right from the beginning, 12 October. He mentions them again on Hispaniola on 15 January: "These Indians' bows are as big as those used in France and England, and their arrows are just like assegais." Arrowheads, always very sharp, were of wood or a fish's tooth. Usually, however, they did not do great harm. Also on 15 January Columbus repeats that "the inhabitants of this land do not possess iron or any other known metal," which he had noted on San Salvador.

The canoe aroused particular interest. Don Ferdinand compares it with the *artesa*, a Castilian dugout. There were big ones and little ones, long and narrow, all made from a single tree trunk hollowed out with razor-sharp stones. The ends of the craft were rectangular. The oars had a handle, and the blade was considerably longer than that of oars used, then and now, by Europeans and Arabs. Columbus speaks of canoes in the *Journal*, beginning with the first encounter. On 13 October he writes as follows:

> They came to my ship in well-fashioned boats made in one piece from a single tree trunk. Some were large enough to hold forty or forty-five men, others could hold only one. Their oars were like baker's peels, and they could make the boats go so fast it was a wonder to behold. If a boat overturned everyone began swimming, turned it over, and used gourds to scoop out the water.

On 30 November he writes, "Near one of these rivers they saw an *almadía* or canoe, ninety-five palms long, made from a single trunk, very handsome, which could hold at least 150." The latter figure must be an error in transcription. Closer to the truth is the entry for 3 December: "They came across a well-made, covered boathouse, which gave protection from sun and water. Under it was another canoe, made from a single tree trunk like the others, shaped like a galley with seventeen benches for the oarsmen; its beauty and workmanship were a pleasure to behold." These, then, were the implements of the new peoples, in truth quite few, but sufficient in that climate and with nature's abundance to obtain an adequate living.

One episode will illustrate the docile and rather cowardly nature of the Tainos. On 3 December Columbus was in a boat on a river in Hispaniola. Many Indians gathered on the bank; one of them came into the river and made a menacing speech. The Indian with the Spaniards held up a loaded crossbow and told them they would all be killed because the crossbow was lethal at a great distance. Then he drew a sword from its scabbard, brandishing it and saying the same thing, whereupon all the Indians fled. Before recounting this episode Columbus had already drawn a simple, harsh conclusion: "These Indians are so cowardly and fearful ten of our men could put ten thousand of them to flight." This is just one of many misunderstandings between the world of the discoverers and that of the discovered.

21 | *The Myth of Gold*

*I*T is not true, as some have said, that Columbus was deluded, as far as gold is concerned, by the first voyage. True, he did not find the roofs and bridges of gold, the gold-inlaid porcelain described by Marco Polo, or the gold mines. But he did find gold right from the start. The inhabitants of the Bahamas and Cuba had gold, admittedly in small quantities. They were simple, almost primitive in their dress. Columbus emphasizes their nakedness for a reason. If these people, he seems to think, naked and poor, adorn themselves with little pieces of gold, who knows how much gold we will find where the civilization and dress match Marco Polo's descriptions? The facts seemed to support this belief. On Haiti, where the land was cultivated everywhere, the Indians were more handsome, better fed, and sharper traders. There, where the level of civilization proved to be higher and the countryside like Europe, the Genoese found gold at last.

On 12 December the sailors captured the prettiest woman of the voyage and then released her; she had a little piece of gold in her nose, "clear evidence that there was gold on the island." On 17 December the *Journal* mentions the episode cited earlier of the cacique who bartered a leaf of gold in little pieces. That same day the Indians said there was gold on Tortuga, the little island off the northwest coast of Haiti that would later become a famous base for pirates. On 18 December a cacique gave the Admiral "a belt with two pieces of worked gold." On 21 December an Indian chief, receiving the Admiral's ambassadors in his own village, "presented them with some pieces of gold." On 22 December the *Journal* reports that the Indians bartered a piece of gold for six glass beads, and a cacique gave the Spaniards "three very fat geese and a few pieces of gold." On 23 December two Indians the Admiral had sent to the villages near the ships returned "with the news that a great deal of gold was there."

Similar episodes occurred every day. Particularly significant is the gift Columbus received on 22 December from Cacique Guacanagarí. It had the best craftsmanship they had seen so far. A belt of cotton quilted with white and red fish bones, it was woven like a Castilian chasuble embroidered with gold thread. It was four fingers wide and so tightly woven that it could not be pierced even with a shot from a harquebus. In the middle of the belt was a mask with ears, tongue, and nose of solid gold.

Columbus became convinced that he had finally found the land where gold was mined. The coastal inhabitants no longer indicated the islands but rather the interior, which they called *Cibao*. Once again chance played a trick, but the Genoese was responsible too, eager as he always was to believe what he wished. The Indians said "Cibao" and he translated "Cipango." That was on 24 December, and then his ship wrecked (of this incident I will speak below). The cacique knew Columbus wanted lots of gold, so on 26 December, to cheer him up, he "indicated through sign language the locality, not far away, where large quantities of it were and that he [Columbus] should be content, for he would have as much as he wanted."

The *Journal* entry for 26 December says that the Admiral received "a large face mask with big pieces of gold in the ears, eyes, and other places; the cacique gave it to him along with gold jewels which he put on his head and around his neck, and he gave the other Christians jewels. Thus the Admiral was pleased and consoled." Two days later, on 28 December, he received another "large plate of gold."

On 29 December "a nephew of the cacique said that four days' journey to the east was an island called *Guarioné,* and there were others on which an infinite amount of gold was found. . . . But there is so much, and in so many places, on this island of Hispaniola," the Admiral writes, "that it is a marvel." On 30 December "two caciques came in the morning to Guacanagarí and the Admiral, and each gave the Admiral his own large gold plate." So Haiti had gold, and in dependable quantities.

The subject of gold has a singular and anomalous place in Columbus's experience, beginning with the first voyage. One could discuss at length—and never arrive at an unequivocal answer—as to what was uppermost in his mind: ambition or pride, scientific curiosity or spirit of adventure, a fascination with the unknown or the mystical feeling of being chosen for a divinely inspired mission. At different times one of these drives predominated, or perhaps they were all present simultaneously. What is certain is that the search for gold was not an end in itself. Like a good Genoese, Columbus knew how to look after his own interests; he wished to secure riches for himself and his descendants. While that is undeniable, it was not his primary consideration. It was not *the* motive but *one* of his motives, and not the most important at that. The most important motives—and I will repeat them—were ambition, pride, scientific curiosity, a spirit of adventure, a fascination with the unknown, and a mystical feeling of being chosen for a divinely inspired mission. This last driving force is part of the worldview derived from Joachim of Floris, by whom Columbus was more or less consciously influenced, as were so many Franciscans of his time.

Columbus unquestionably sought gold; a mystical obsession with it possessed him. What is significant is that gold for him was not only a source of riches, of economic progress, but above all an instrument of power for Christianity, a means for a victorious war against the Turks and for the reconquest of the Holy Sepulcher; it was even—and why not?—the necessary means for ushering in the third Joachimite age, that of general well-being and perfection. And so one could consider the search for the Indies a Renaissance reincarnation of the obsessive search for the philosopher's stone in the late Middle Ages.

Unfortunately, during his second voyage gold would become an evil obsession for the Admiral, a source of iniquity, of exploitation, slavery, destruction, and death. On the first voyage none of these things occurred, but already in the *Journal* for the first voyage Columbus mentions gold 134 times, while only 36 times does he speak, either in general or specific terms, of spices. Beginning with the first voyage, then, the primary motive for seeking a new route to the Indies changed, switching decisively from spices to gold. This pursuit would become fevered and spasmodic during the second voyage, but from the first voyage one can see that this turning from spices to gold was a fundamental and determining change. From the mastic of Chios to barrels of gold: thus can one summarize the switch from one goal to the other in Columbus's mind.

If we wish to see the other side of the coin of the grand discoveries and fix our attention on the economic consequences of this shift from spices to gold, we must note that it was not by chance that a Genoese was the protagonist in these events. Already in the fifteenth century, as in the following centuries, the Genoese, growing wealthy from their maritime trade, did not have the chance to invest in agriculture—as did the Venetians—because of the scarcity of land in Liguria, and so they invested in palaces, paintings, precious collectibles, and especially in gold. They covered their furniture and ceilings with gold leaf; they loaded their rooms with gold objects and filled their coffers with gold coins. To make their gold work for them they lent it out, becoming creditors (and so more hated than loved) of businesses, great families, sovereigns, and the powerful in almost every corner of Christendom.

22 | Shipwreck

*C*hristmas Eve. The *Santa María* was tacking along the northern coast of Haiti, going against the trades, which come from the east. The flagship advanced slowly until it was off the promontory today called Picoulet Point, northwest of Cap Haitien.

Eleven o'clock. The ship's boy turned over the hourglass. A new helmsman took over. The Admiral went to his cabin, said his prayers, and slept. "He had been two days and a night without sleep." No sooner did he disappear below than the men on deck—lookouts and boys—stretched out and went to sleep. Juan de la Cosa, officer of the watch, showed the helmsman the easy course: follow the *Niña,* its sails filled and lit by a pale moon low on the horizon. The sea was "dead calm, like water in a still bowl." Juan de la Cosa told the helmsman to call him if wind or weather should change or if anything should happen, then he went below too. The helmsman was dead tired and shook the ship's boy, whose only duty was to watch the hourglass, gave him the tiller despite Columbus's express orders to the contrary, and stretched out to sleep. Thus, the fate of the flagship rested in the hands of a ship's boy, the only one awake.

The moon was too low to reveal the white foam where the long swell broke on the coral reef. In any event, the boy, standing on the stern, had all he could do to manage the heavy tiller, and he could not have seen the reef anyway. A current was carrying the ship over one of the shoals and roaring so loudly it could be heard at a distance, but the ship went over the reef so quietly the boy felt nothing. Only when he felt the tiller ground and heard the noise did he begin to shout.

Columbus was first on the quarterdeck, where Juan de la Cosa and the others joined him. The situation was immediately clear. The *Santa María* had run its prow onto a coral reef. Since the stern drew more water than the prow, the way to set the ship afloat was to throw out an anchor beyond the reef, put the cable through the big capstan in the prow and warp it off stern first. These were Columbus's orders to Juan de la Cosa: bring the boat (which was towed behind the ship) alongside, put in the anchor and cable, and go out beyond the reef to find some depth for the anchor. Instead, Juan de la Cosa got in the boat and headed straight for the *Niña*. When one considers that the *Santa María* was his property, it seems that he lost his nerve. Vicente Yañez Pinzón on the *Niña* did the right thing, refusing to take the men aboard and sending boats with a number of sailors to help the Admiral. But it was too late. The stern had come around, and the ship lay crosswise to the sea; every wave lifted it up and let it down heavily on the coral reef. Coral, more than almost any other rock, perforates a wooden hull.

To lighten the ship, the Admiral had the mainmast cut away, but it was not enough. The tide was ebbing, and the ship "had no respite; it rolled heavily, the seams opened up, and it filled with water from below." So occurred the first known European shipwreck in America, near modern-day Cap Haitien. Christmas Day was spent salvaging the cargo of the *Santa María* and transferring the Admiral and his crew to the *Niña*. Guacanagarí's people aided the Spaniards, showing zeal and absolute honesty. At the end of the salvage operations, Columbus noted in the *Journal* that they were missing not even a lace point.

We have come to one of the most important episodes in the extraordinary story of the great discovery: the establishment of the colony of La Navidad, the first European settlement in America. The decision was swift; it cannot be explained unless Columbus had thought of it before the wreck. Two lines in the *Journal* make it clear that he had not only thought about it but had spoken about making a settlement earlier: "It is, however, quite true that many of my men had begged me and had others implore me to let them stay in this place."

Thirty-nine men stayed, including Diego de Arana, marshall of the fleet and cousin of Beatriz de Arana, Columbus's Córdoban mistress; Pedro Gutiérrez, the king's butler; and Rodrigo d'Escobedo, the secretary. To these three the Admiral gave the powers that the monarchs had conferred on him. Diego de Arana he made commander-in-chief. Among those who stayed were Luis de Torres, the converted Jew who would act as interpreter; two surgeons, Juan and Alfonso; the tailor Juan de Medina; the varnisher Diego Pérez; the caulker Lope; the carpenter of the *Niña,* Alonso Morales; the cooper Domingo Vizcaíno; the Genoese sailor Jácome el Rico, and the Calabrian Anton Calabrés. There were also a gunner—Columbus left some lombards and ordered the construction of a tower, fort, and moat—and a boatswain in charge of a boat left to explore the coast, discover the gold mine, and found a new colony at a better site; the present one was only meant to be temporary.

The exact location of La Navidad has not been identified. We know only that it was somewhere in an area extending about four miles along the beach and two inland. Within this rectangle today are a small village (Bord-de-Mer de Limonade), a church, many huts, and some small boats belonging to Haitian fishermen; it is a sandy-bottomed expanse linked to the sea by a belt of mangrove swamps.

Another reason for the difficulty in identifying the exact site of the settlement is the fact that the coastline has changed since 1492. The alluvial plain has extended out into the sea, and the course of the water coming down from the mountains has changed: the French channeled the water of the Grande Rivière into the westernmost of the forks that existed then. Today, the Grande Rivière runs in a straight line, from south to north, flanked by two lines of tall trees planted by the French to mark clearly the new course of the river. To the east two channels remain near the sea, the vestiges of two other forks of the river predating the shift made by the French. Near one of these watercourses, which in Columbus's time was presumably the main fork, rose Guacanagarí's village. Thus, La Navidad was about a half-mile east of the present-day channel of the Grande Rivière and about a mile southwest of the present-day beach of Bord-de-Mer de Limonade, near the right bank of one of the eastern channels.

Expert builders of cities as they were, the Spanish did not usually settle on alluvial plains, and it is quite logical that Columbus thought of other places for the permanent settlement. This is clear from the *Journal*. On 31 December he indicates his intention of coasting all of Haiti "to find the best place for establishing a station where one could import livestock and other items." On 2 January he hopes that on his return "they would be able to show him the best site for the foundation of a city, because this place whence he was leaving was not convenient."

Columbus left the thirty-nine settlers "a great quantity of merchandise, all that the king and queen had authorized for trading, so it could be exchanged for gold, and everything that was aboard the *Santa María:* a year's supply of hardtack,[1] wine, and quite a bit of artillery." With so much shrewdness and foresight, the Genoese felt at ease. When he went down the channel of Limonade toward the open sea on 4 January, he saw the fort of La Navidad from the quarterdeck of the *Niña* for the last time, not imagining how sad the fate of the first European colony in the discovered lands would be.

[1]The traditional food of sailors until the first decades of the twentieth century.

23 | Discovery of the Route Home

After leaving Hispaniola Columbus wanted to visit another island before facing the Atlantic, Carib, or the Isle of Women. On Wednesday, 16 January, he changed his mind and decided to begin the return crossing. "He turned the prow toward Spain, direction northeast by east." So says the *Journal*. His objective was to sail north of the area of the trades. He realized he had left the trades about 23 January, for he writes in the *Journal*, "tonight there were many shifts in the wind." From that point on the ships sailed before the wind, headed always east and north. On 25 January they were at 60° W, on 1 February at 55°, on 3 February, 50°. At this point "it seemed to the Admiral that the polestar was as high as it is at Cape St. Vincent in Portugal," an observation very close to the truth and exceptional for being made with the naked eye. Columbus was at 35° N, while Cape St. Vincent is at 37° N.

From that moment the Genoese had no doubts. He knew that the westernmost of the Azores, where he had been before conceiving the grand design, are on the same parallel as Cape St. Vincent, and the other islands lie a little to the north, so he headed east. On 10 February the two ships were at 31° N. Did Columbus wish to call at the Azores or not? He apparently wanted to miss them, well knowing that the Portuguese were there. On 11 February he had left Corvo and Flores behind. The next day he was south of Faial and Pico. Until that day he had been particularly fortunate. On 22 January it was so calm that "the Indians jumped into the sea to swim." The next day "the sea was always as calm as a river, infinite thanks be to God." On 1 February he notes, "Thanks be to God, the sea is always extremely calm"; the next day, "the sea is very placid, thanks be to God, and the temperature quite mild"; on the following, "the sea is very calm."

The sea began to make up on 12 February. Columbus noticed the air of the storm that would burst in the next two days. That night "lightning flashed three times to the northeast," a sign that a great storm would come from that or the opposite direction. At this point before a storm, calculations and reasoning are no longer valid. Forces that cannot be understood or molded come into play, the forces of nature. The storm that broke was one of the worst kind that can be encountered on the Atlantic.

We have no documentation, no reference, by Columbus or any of his contemporary chroniclers mentioning storms encountered earlier. Undoubtedly he had seen a good many in the Mediterranean and the Atlantic in his long maritime experience before the voyage of discovery. We do know that in this emergency he acted coolly and with skill. At first he ordered keeping the stormsail, with the topgallant before the wind and the rudder opposed to it. This procedure is chosen when the wind and sea reach such force that the usual sails can no longer be held nor the course maintained without peril. Keeping the stormsail means putting the ship nearly athwart the wind and leaving only enough sail for a little resistance so that the force of the wind against the sails and the hull makes the ship do nothing but drift a little sideways, scarcely advancing at all. The drifting creates a protective wake against which the waves break before reaching the ship.

The *Niña* continued to make leeway, but "the vehemence of the wind increased still more and the cross-action of the rough waves became even more terrible. The Admiral had until then kept only the topgallant, and that very low, so that the ship would rise above the waves, which were breaking on each other, and not founder." He realized that by keeping the stormsail they ran the risk of filling the *Niña* with water, for its bulwarks were quite low. He decided to scud before the wind, so he ordered the helmsman to keep the caravel's stern to the storm, letting the wind take the ship where it would. A ship scudding before the wind must keep some sail for handling and taking the waves on the stern or quarter and lessening the impact of the wind as much as possible. The design of the caravel lent itself well to this maneuver. While the caravel could not have lasted long with the stormsail, it was capable of withstanding the sea by scudding before the wind, for its high stern acted as protection.

Martín Alonso Pinzón, like a good sailor, scudded before the wind also. The two caravels had no other means of escape, and the storm separated them again. This time Pinzón certainly did not will the separation in any way. It would have been as much to his advantage as to Columbus's to stay close together in such dire straits. Only the fury of the tempest separated them, and it gave no sign of abating. Instead, despite the expedients that the ships' design and nautical art of the time allowed, the danger remained grave. "The danger was increased by the fact that the caravel lacked ballast—the consumption of food, water, and wine had greatly depleted its load." The Admiral had not provided the ships with ballast earlier because the weather in the islands was always ideal, and he had planned to take on ballast on the Isle of Women. But he did not go there and so made the crossing without ballast. The remedy now was to fill the empty wine and water barrels with seawater as soon as possible, "and in this manner the problem was corrected" (*Journal,* 14 February).

There was nothing more to be done with human power, so Columbus and the sailors turned to divine aid. They drew lots to see who would make a pilgrimage to the shrine of Santa Maria of Guadalupe, who would go to Santa Maria of Loreto, in the march of Ancona in the Papal States, and who would spend a night in vigil in the church of Santa Clara of Moguer. "Then the Admiral himself and all his people made a vow that, on their first landfall, they would go in their shirts in a procession to pray at a church dedicated to Our Lady."

Columbus feared not death but losing credit for the great discovery. "I wrote on a parchment, briefly as the time was short, how I had discovered the lands which I had promised to find, how many days it took and the route by which they were reached, the value of the countries, the nature of the inhabitants and how they were made vassals of Your Highnesses." The parchment was sealed, wrapped in waxed cloth, put in a cake of wax, and placed in a large barrel, which was sealed and thrown into the sea. The sailors believed that it was some kind of religious ritual and so were not afraid.

Another barrel with a parchment was tied to the top of the stern so that it would remain above the waves at the mercy of fate if the caravel should founder. This barrel survived with the *Niña*. The other, entrusted to the sea, no one ever retrieved. Even if the *Niña* had gone down with the Admiral, Vicente Yañez Pinzón, and the other sailors, there would still have been Martín Alonso Pinzón's *Pinta* to carry the great news to Europe. But in writing the account Columbus revealed his belief, with which we are already familiar: he and he alone was destined by Divine Providence to fulfill the great enterprise. He wrote his accounts so that the glory of bringing the news of his great achievement to the monarchs and the world would be his even if he died.

But he did not die. After sunset of 14 February "the sky began to clear toward the west." At sunrise the next day they sighted land. Some of the sailors believed it was Madeira, others the Rock of Sintra, near Lisbon. Columbus was certain he was near the Azores. He had no doubts on the matter, he just didn't know which island it was. They glimpsed another island to the northwest while they tacked to windward around the first. It turned out to be Santa Maria, while the one glimpsed was San Michele. Columbus had some trouble with the Portuguese on Santa Maria, and that justifies the hypothesis that, suspicious as always, he had meant to avoid the Azores and landed there only because of the storm.

The captain governor of the island very respectfully invited Columbus to disembark, but the Admiral refused to fall into a trap and would not leave the deck of the *Niña*. Ten of the crew landed to fulfill one of the vows made during the storm. The Portuguese imprisoned them, releasing them only when they realized the Admiral had decided to continue to Spain and denounce their abuse of power.

Columbus resumed the course for home on Sunday, 24 February. For three days the caravel, now alone, sailed quickly to the east with a calm sea. On 27 February they were troubled by contrary winds and high seas, which continued the next day but quieted down on 1 March. At sunset on Sunday, 3 March, when there already were "a few signs which indicated land was near, they found themselves near Lisbon," but another storm made up, so violent and sudden "it split all the sails." During the night the storm raged, perhaps worse than the preceding one. The sea was in a fury; the winds, blowing from every quarter, hurled the caravel toward the sky, while rain came down in sheets and lightning flashed on every side. Once again they sought divine aid, resulting in a new pilgrimage for the Admiral and vows of fasting on bread and water for the crew. Finally, in the first watch, land appeared.

It was the Rock of Sintra, at the mouths of the Tagus River. Columbus wanted to stop at the mouth of the estuary, at Cascais, but the raging storm forced him to enter the river. The people ashore spent the entire morning praying for the sailors in the endangered caravel. When the ship passed safely into the Tagus, all came down "to see them and express the greatest wonder that they had saved themselves from what seemed certain death." So ended the return crossing, more dramatic than the voyage out and equally important, for through errors, approximations, experiments, and storms, Columbus established the return route from America to Europe.

24 | *Mockery and Triumph*

O n 8 March 1493 King John II of Portugal received Columbus. Eight years ear-
lier the king had rejected the proposal of reaching the Indies by
sailing west. Whatever the king and the Discoverer said in their
conversations of 9 and 10 March is unknown but easily imagined.
The king was interested in knowing if vast new lands had really
been discovered or, as he hoped, just some remote Atlantic
archipelago like the Azores. Columbus dispelled any doubts,
showing him a sketch representing the Bahamas, Hispaniola, and
Cuba. The last, he said, "was so large that it was unknown
whether it was an island or a continent." Two Indians gave independent testimony, locating the islands on a table with large and
small beans. No doubt remained, only the hope that the lands
were to the south, in the area that the conventions with Spain
assigned to the Portuguese. No, Columbus lied, as he had in the
Journal, they lay at about 42° N, the latitude of Spanish Galicia.

There was nothing to be done. The success of the Genoese was
uncontestable, beyond appeal. The queen, staying at the monastery of St. Anthony, wanted to see him. On 11 March Columbus
visited there and showed the Indians to her, Duke Don Manuel,
and the marquis of Villa Real. It is said that John II struck his
breast and cried out, "O man of little wit! Why didn't you carry

out such an important undertaking?" He felt humiliated and dismayed. The irony of history humiliated not only him but his nation. A few years later Cabral would remedy it with the acquisition of Brazil, but the lost opportunity would hang over the ventures of the great nation for centuries.

At dawn on Friday, 15 March 1493, the *Niña* crossed the bar of Saltés, and at noon she entered the port of Palos. When the inhabitants of Palos saw the caravel that had left seven months before on a voyage from which most thought it would not return, they ran down to the pier to see the sailors, hug relatives, congratulate them, and get news of the portentous undertaking. Work stopped, shops closed, and bells pealed again and again. Everyone went with the Admiral and sailors to the main church and sang the Te Deum.

To further heighten the general enthusiasm, news came that another caravel was coming into port, Martín Alonso Pinzón's *Pinta*. On the afternoon of the same day he arrived from Bayona,[1] on the northwest coast of Spain, where he had completed the Atlantic crossing. What happened at this point between the Admiral and Pinzón is difficult to establish. We can be certain of only two facts: as soon as he had reached Bayona, Pinzón had sent a messenger to Ferdinand and Isabella, and a few days after arriving in Palos he died of a mysterious illness. With these two facts historians have indulged their fantasies, concocting opposing interpretations. It is, however, certain that Pinzón was already gravely ill and died before he could participate in the triumph in Barcelona—and he may not have participated in the celebration in Palos. It was a most sad and undeserved end, for he had contributed decisively to the organization of the voyage and had given undisputed proof of being an expert and courageous sailor.

Columbus stayed at least a week at La Rábida. From there he went to Seville, where on Easter, 7 April, or on the following Monday, he received the letter from the monarchs. Addressed "To Don Cristóbal Colón, their Admiral of the Ocean Sea, Viceroy and Governor of the islands which he discovered in the Indies," it was signed "I the King" and "I the Queen." His titles, then, were immediately bestowed; he did not even have to wait until he

[1]In Galicia, not to be confused with the French Bayonne on the Bay of Biscay.

exhibited the proofs of his discovery: the Indians, parrots, and gold masks.

He set out again, going from Seville to Córdoba and Valencia. The Admiral neglected nothing to make his entry into Barcelona impress the king, the courtiers, and the people. The Indians were reduced to six—one had died during the voyage and three were sick—but these six were impressive, their bodies painted and adorned with gold trinkets. The Spanish sailors brought the parrots, other animals, plants, and the strangest things gathered in the New Lands. The Admiral brought up the rear of the picturesque and lively procession.

Ferdinand and Isabella received the Discoverer in the royal palace, surrounded by the nobles and high dignitaries of the court. Columbus genuflected and asked the favor of kissing the monarchs' hands. The king and queen arose, extended their hands, and invited him to sit and tell the story of his voyage and discoveries. Sitting in the presence of the king was a sign of exceptional recognition. Columbus was moved to tears, but his voice, clear and sonorous, did not betray his emotion.

He spoke at length, presenting the gold ornaments, the animals, and the Indians, praising the greatness and beauty of the countries he had visited, of whose riches the monarchs could get only a faint idea from the things before them. He said he was certain he could bring fabulous treasures of gold, gems, and spices back to Spain if he were given more ample means for a second expedition. At the end of the audience, Ferdinand, Isabella, and the courtiers went to the palace chapel and raised a hymn of thanks to heaven, the Te Deum. When the ceremony was over, the king had the Admiral escorted to a sumptuous apartment and, for the whole time he stayed at court, overwhelmed him with courtesies and signs of favor.

Thereafter Pedro Gonzales de Mendoza, grand cardinal and primate of Spain, called the "second king," invited Columbus to his table and had him seated

> in the most eminent place, near himself, and had him served with a covered plate and had his food tasted for poison. That was the first time that his food was tasted and served in a covered plate, and from then on he was served with the solemnity and grandeur required by his title of Admiral.

So says Las Casas. As Salvador de Madariaga comments, "Having his food tasted was recognition of Columbus's rank, for only great men ran the risk of being poisoned." Thus, the foreigner of humble origins became one of the greatest men in Spain overnight, and the news of the great discovery spread throughout Europe.

25 | *The Second Voyage*

*I*t took Columbus seven years to convince the Catholic sovereigns and organize the first voyage of discovery. It took less than seven months for the second. The fleet for this expedition gathered at Cádiz because the port of Palos was not large enough. There were seventeen vessels: three *naos*, twelve square-rigged caravels, and two lateen caravels. Some of the caravels were very light and of shallow draught, suitable for navigating the treacherous soundings among the coral reefs and going up the rivers. The flagship—a new *Santa María*, nicknamed *Maria Galante*—was much larger than that wrecked in the bay of Cap Haitien on the first voyage. The new ship probably weighed around two hundred tons. The precise number of men who shipped is unknown. Historians agree that it was somewhere between twelve hundred and fourteen hundred, including the crews. The smaller figure is more probable. There were priests and friars, learned and unlearned, seamen and landsmen.

The route was again to the southwest for the Canaries. The fleet took six days and nights to reach the Grand Canary, where it stopped briefly during the day on 2 October and weighed anchor at midnight. On Saturday, 5 October, the armada was at San Sebastián, Gomera. Here the Admiral was received with lombard shots, flares, and fireworks. Beatriz de Bobadilla had not forgotten the idyll of the previous year and probably wanted to show the noblemen who courted her and contended for her favors that she had not been mistaken about the foreign captain when few had believed in him. The chroniclers do not say if the old knot was retied during the brief stay. They speak instead of the provisions that the Admiral shipped: seeds of oranges, lemons, citron, melons, and every kind of vegetable. They took on goats, sheep, and "eight sows at seventy maravedis each. . . . This was the seed," Las Casas would later write, "from which would come all those things which are today found here from Castile."

The crossing took twenty-one days, from 12 October to 2 November. It was disturbed by only one storm, which lasted four hours, on 26 October; otherwise, the sea was nearly always "as smooth as polished marble." The trades blew constantly and with greater force than on the preceding voyage. On the first voyage the ships stayed between 28° and 26° N until, after seeing the flight of birds, they descended to 24°; this time they descended to 16° just after departing, a zone where the trades are stronger.

Columbus took advantage of his experience from the first voyage, during which, as I have said many times, he had discovered not only America but also the routes between Europe and America. It is no wonder that the route perfected on the second voyage remained through the next four centuries—indeed remains today—the route recommended by nautical charts and indicated in directions to navigators of sailing vessels headed anywhere in the West Indies north of Barbados. The route after leaving Hierro, then, was no longer west but west by south.

They were at 16° N when they sighted land at dawn on Sunday, 3 November. "On Sunday," writes Michele da Cuneo, "we saw land, five unknown islands." Columbus named the first island, with its high mountains, Dominica, because it was sighted at dawn on Sunday. The island on which they landed he named after the flagship, Maria Galante (today given the French spelling, Marie Galante). He called the smallest, which they glimpsed to the northeast, Deseada ("Desired") because, being farthest to the east, it was closest to the Old World and therefore desired by the navigators who had crossed and would cross the ocean.

The small islands today called Les Saintes were named Todos los Santos by the Admiral on the morning of 4 November in honor of the celebration of All Saints three days earlier. The prettiest island he named Santa María de Guadalupe (today Guadeloupe), fulfilling his promise to the monks of the shrine where he had fulfilled the vow made during the terrible storm in the Atlantic. Our Lady of Guadalupe was one of the most celebrated madonnas of Spain and today has the most shrines devoted to her in the world thanks to the spread of her cult in the Americas. Even before the Mexican sanctuary was built in 1531, today more renowned than the Spanish shrine, Columbus, a devotee of the Madonna, contributed to that diffusion by giving her name to one of the world's loveliest islands.

Columbus did not find a port on the northeast coasts of Dominica. He sent a ship in search of one, but when it rejoined the fleet he had already found an anchorage protected from the dangers of the coral in a roadstead on the lee coast of Marie Galante. There he went ashore with the royal standard, took possession in the name of the monarchs, and had a cross erected and mass celebrated, the first in America since those in Greenland during the Norse colonization.

Nature in the Lesser Antilles displays an astonishing variety. The soil contributes to this variety, for on some islands it is calcareous and on others volcanic. The rain patterns, with their astounding variations, also play a part. Clouds come in from the Atlantic driven by the trades, rise over the high volcanic ranges, spread out, and cool. Rain falls abundantly, from eighty inches per year on the plains to over three hundred per year on the peaks. The high precipitation sustains great forests with gigantic trees, lianas, and sudden and varicolored blooming seasons.

Thus did Dominica and the volcanic massif on the western half of Guadeloupe appear to Columbus. In sharp contrast, the low, calcareous islands—La Désirade,[1] Les Saintes, and the eastern half of Guadeloupe—having no high points and so unable to stop the rain-bearing winds, grow thorn bushes in arid landscapes, at times steppes, with bare rocks and gray or brown cliffs scattered here and there among the cacti. Five, six, seven islands can be taken in at a glance—they offer stark contrasts, from virgin forest to desert. The strange thing is that these contrasts occur not only from one island to another but within a few miles of each other on the same

[1]The modern French name for the Castilian Deseada.

island. For example, the lee shore of Guadeloupe, along which the ships coasted on the morning of 4 November, is arid, while "three leagues" inland the sailors saw "a towering cliff, ending in a point, from which came" an enormous waterfall "so loud it could be-heard from the ships." Around it was an immense, enchanting forest. The peak was La Soufrière, one of the wonders of the Lesser Antilles.

Columbus does not say much about La Soufrière; he mentions only the beautiful waterfall. Don Ferdinand says that there the Spanish found aloe, mastic, sandalwood, ginger, incense, "some trees that, from their taste and odor seemed to be cinnamon," and a great deal of cotton. They also saw "kites, magpies, crows, pigeons, turtledoves, partridges, geese, and nightingales"—a hunt-er's paradise. Besides the "geese, similar to ours, there were numerous varicolored parrots, green, white, and red, as big as the common rooster, and squash and a certain fruit that looked like our green pinecones but much bigger. Inside was a melonlike pulp. It comes from a plant like the lily or aloe." He is describing the pineapple, another discovery Guadeloupe offered the Spanish dur-ing their fortunate stay in early November 1493. Don Ferdinand reports that cultivated pineapples were discovered later, better perhaps than the wild ones, but even the wild ones "smelled and tasted better" than the best melons of the Mediterranean.

Guadeloupe offered another new thing to the Spanish, the most important: contact with the Caribs, who were eaters of human flesh, cannibals. Concerning the first contact between Christians and Caribs (or Canibas or Cannibals as Columbus calls them at different times), it is necessary to proceed with caution because one cannot avoid the impression that Columbus's contemporaries do not adhere to facts. They seem to exaggerate and create details, making it difficult to avoid the suspicion that fantasy prevailed.

Columbus went ashore and visited some houses, which had been deserted. Many of the Carib men were absent. They had gone in ten canoes, led by the king, on one of their raids to procure slaves and restock their supply of human flesh, according to one of the Arawak women who fled to the ships. The few men who remained and their wives, along with the Carib wives of the absent men, were hiding in the forest. In the houses Columbus found a great deal of cotton, both spun and raw, and he noted that the looms for weaving it were different from those used in Europe. He also observed that the houses were better than almost any others they had seen on the first voyage and that they were well stocked with food, furniture, and weapons—bows and arrows. In the houses, he remarked, were "many heads of men hanging up and chests filled with bones of dead men." That is as much as Columbus actually saw. The rest comes either from the testimonies of other Spaniards or from the accounts of the Arawaks who escaped.

Las Casas clings to this last detail—the heads and the chests of bones—anxious as always to defend the natives. They were relics of ancestors, he asserts, preserved for religious reasons, not the remnants of banquets. This may be true for the heads. Peter Martyr, however, again gives us a detail difficult to reconcile with such a pious hypothesis: "They also found the head of a recently killed youth hanging from a beam and still covered with blood." A youth obviously cannot be an ancestor. In any case, wherever there is anthropophagy it is associated, to a greater or lesser degree, with magical or religious rites, so Las Casas's interpretation may be at least partly true as far as the human heads go. But as for the chests of bones, Peter Martyr's explanation seems more likely: "They take great care to preserve the human shinbones and arm bones to make arrowheads. Indeed, they make them of bone since they lack iron."

Having resolved the problem of the heads and bones, we must consider the most important one: Did the Caribs eat human flesh or not? The answer is yes, they did, and not just once in a while or as part of a rite. They ate it for nutrition. The accounts of Dr. Chanca, the fleet surgeon, and Michele da Cuneo are sufficient proofs. To these must be added the supporting testimonies of the explorers who followed them in the Lesser Antilles and on the facing shores of the South American mainland.

After the extended stay on Guadeloupe, Columbus weighed anchor and headed northwest. North of Guadeloupe is not open sea. After crossing the Guadeloupe Passage one comes to an island, also volcanic and consequently covered with vegetation. Columbus named it Santa Maria de Montserrat after the monastery near Barcelona, famous then as now not only in Spain but throughout the Catholic world. The name is appropriate, because the island emerges from the sea like a tall mountain. Today it is one of the gems of the Lesser Antilles. Colonized by the English in

the seventeenth century, it has a black population and is cultivated, but its beautiful forests are still intact. The name bestowed
by Columbus has remained, shortened to Montserrat.

From Montserrat to Puerto Rico stretches a chain of islands, all
pretty and very different from one another in size and shape. The
names Columbus gave them have changed but the enchantment of
their beauty has not: Redonda, Antigua, Nevis, St. Kitts, St. Eustatius, Saba, St.-Barthélemy, St.-Martin, Anguilla, Dog Island, St.
Croix, and, finally, the wonderful, unimaginable Virgin Islands.
The Admiral did not stop at all of them; he was preoccupied with
reaching La Navidad. He stopped for a day and a night on Puerto
Rico, the largest and finest of these islands. He did not allow
himself to be charmed by its beaches, forests, gulfs, and keys, the
thousand charms that entrance modern tourists.

The first Spanish empire in the American Mediterranean had
four great pillars: Hispaniola or Haiti, Cuba, Jamaica, and Puerto
Rico. Of these four large islands Puerto Rico, closest to Europe,
was the smallest but certainly not the least in natural beauty and
economic and agricultural resources. It was the only one Columbus neglected. Yet the inhabitants of Puerto Rico were not the evil
Caribs but enemies of the Caribs and therefore friends of the
Spanish. Their island did not deserve to be neglected by Columbus—that was due to one of the tricks of fate with which history is
filled. As chance would have it, the Discoverer found Puerto Rico
at the time he felt most strongly the summons to La Navidad and
the discoveries that would lead to the coveted goals of Cathay and
India.

A single day (19 November) was sufficient to run along the
northern coast of Puerto Rico. That evening Columbus sought a
bay and found one on the west coast, somewhere between Rincón
and the Rio Grande de Añasco. It is a good river for taking on
water and has ample space for anchoring, protected from the
trades and winds from the north. Resupplied with fresh water and
food—fish and game—the fleet left Puerto Rico at dawn, 22
November, and by nightfall was in sight of the eastern end of
Haiti.

Neither Columbus, Michele da Cuneo, Dr. Chanca, Peter Martyr, Don Ferdinand, Las Casas, nor Nicolò Syllacio mentions the
significance, in the overall picture of the great discovery, of the
numerous series of islands, from Dominica to Puerto Rico, dis-

covered between 3 and 20 November 1493. The Lesser Antilles are not coralline and flat like the Bahamas. They are volcanic and often mountainous, some of their peaks being quite high. All the islands were inhabited and often cultivated. The Lesser Antilles confirmed for Columbus the unpleasant fact that the New Lands had "bad" people besides the "good" Tainos of the first voyage. The Genoese had anticipated that, but only from reports. Now he had proven it.

The Lesser Antilles showed the sailors of the seventeen ships unparalleled natural beauty. But what had the hundred islands of the Lesser Antilles told Columbus about geography? Specifically, what did they tell him about maritime geography, for which he had a sixth sense? If one adds to the hundred islands and islets of the Virgins the others they had coasted along or seen from Dominica to Puerto Rico, the total comes to 130 or 140. This archipelago was very different from those known previously in the Atlantic, the Azores, Canaries, and Cape Verde Islands. Columbus realized now that the great lands discovered during the first voyage, Cuba and Hispaniola, had a halo of islands from south to northeast: the Bahamas from north to southeast, and the Lesser Antilles to the south.

Such a chain of islands had to be a sign, an outpost, of a nearby continent, and Columbus kept hearing indications of terra firma, vague hints constantly repeated by many of the natives he had taken aboard. And where did those ferocious Caribs come from if not from the continent? Thus, even the minor but still important discovery of the Lesser Antilles and Puerto Rico helped confirm Columbus's great error. He thought he had reached Asia, that he had sailed through the halo of islands which—as he had read in Marco Polo—Christendom knew was the eastern outpost of the Asian mainland.

26 | Tragedy

On 28 November Columbus reached La Navidad and saw the tragedy that he had perhaps sensed in the preceding days. The thirty-nine colonists were all dead, their houses and fort burned. It is difficult to say how the tragedy occurred. Dr. Chanca says that "the little that could be understood from the Indians and their equivocal explanations all confused our minds, so that *until now* it has not been possible to know the truth about the death of our people." "Until now": the whole truth was not known then, nor is it today.

Nevertheless, certain facts stand out. There seems to be no doubt that the first disturbances at La Navidad were caused not by the Indians but by the Spaniards among themselves over women and gold and probably other, more trivial matters. One must use imagination to re-create the setting of this first adventure of Europeans in the newly discovered lands. Thirty-nine men, neither criminals nor saints, often buffeted by storms at sea, were used to living far from their families and fulfilling their sexual desires with the women they met in their ports of call. Here they found as many women as they could want, and all were free. But life would be too easy if mutual respect and free love went hand in hand; that never has been nor will be. These Indians were not prostitutes, simply available, but even if they had been a man can fall in love with a prostitute, as historical and modern accounts demonstrate. Hence one man's claim to exclusive possession of a woman was contested by another.

Less easy to obtain was gold; coveted and fought over, gold, and the secret of obtaining it, was jealously guarded. When a group managed to find some, fights would inevitably break out over dividing it. And the climate? Months and seasons passed, but the temperature was always the same, the humidity always high. Rain fell hard, seasons changed, trees flourished, but the climate did not change. In a little over ten months there was not one day of a good, cold, Castilian winter, not a day of a good, hot, dry Andalusian summer.

Particularly noteworthy is the fact that eleven men had died recently, killed no earlier than the end of September 1493, nine months after the founding of the colony. That is an indication that the atmosphere grew heavier with time and that the climate undoubtedly influenced the Europeans' nervous systems. The Spaniards were by nature bold, overbearing, and touchy, and the climate exaggerated their defects and depressed them. Good sailors, they adapted to work on land with difficulty, and then only if forced. Here they did not have to be coerced, for the Indians of Guacanagarí's nearby village were an inexhaustible source of manual labor to be exploited.

In addition, the leader of the Spanish could not make them do anything nor lead them. Diego de Arana had no experience as a commander. Columbus had chosen him because he trusted him as a relative. Napoleon did the same thing centuries later. The greatest Genoese and Corsican in history are a pair in their loyalty to family. Both put relatives in positions of authority whenever they could (even when they should not have), giving them the greatest privileges. One can understand his naming of Arana on the first voyage as marshall of the fleet, whose duty was overseeing the supply of fresh water for the entire fleet, a delicate position demanding diligence but not genius or personality. One cannot, however, understand naming him commander of La Navidad. He was loyal and discharged his duties, but he did not control his companions' quarreling or bridle their greed and lust in dealing with the Indians, who had proven themselves genuine friends.

To what level of debauchery the colonists of La Navidad descended can be sensed in a short but telling passage in the accounts by Don Ferdinand and Las Casas: "Since one of the dead men had misinformed Guacanagarí regarding matters of our faith, saying that the law of the Christians was vain, the Admiral had to defend it himself." It does not take much to imagine what happened. Precisely because he considered himself a friend of the Admiral and his men, which he was, Guacanagarí could not help being scandalized by the Spaniards' behavior, for as the months passed it grew worse and more arrogant. Obviously, he expressed his surprise, observing that that kind of behavior did not match what Columbus had told him about their intentions and those of the Spanish monarchs, not to mention about their religion, God, Christ, and the Madonna. The answers were blasphemies, sarcasm, mockery.

In this situation, relations between the Europeans and Indians were bound to deteriorate. How can the Indians' just reaction be criticized? Caonabó came down from the mountains and put an end to that infamous behavior, killing the white survivors and setting fire to their village and fort. Caonabó was one of the two Carib caciques, a Haitian Carib who had abandoned cannibalism but not yet lost the Caribs' courage and warlike qualities. In this episode Caonabó was the avenger, not in a vendetta but a just revenge, the logical punishment of the severe God of the Old Testament.

It seems unlikely that Guacanagarí opposed Caonabó, nor is it likely that he summoned him, for we know that relations between the Taino and Carib caciques were not friendly. Guacanagarí saw the developments leading to the tragic events but could not stop them, and he may even have tried to help the Spaniards, which would explain Dr. Chanca's statement: "Indeed, their enemies did many things to Guacanagarí's Tainos." But it might also be that when Caonabó's Caribs came down from the mountains to destroy La Navidad they molested and injured the Tainos even though the Tainos were not allied with the whites nor defending them. The traditional hostility between the two caciquedoms and the aid that Guacanagarí had given the strangers after the shipwreck easily explain any conflicts between Taino and Carib.

The most probable hypothesis is that Guacanagarí remained neutral in the episode of La Navidad and that his statements and those of his subjects to Columbus contained half-truths and deception prompted by fear of retribution. That fear was not un-founded. Indeed, Father Boil wanted him taken prisoner, and the other Spaniards shared that view. It is understandable that the hidalgos and sailors held that view, but that Father Boil, sent to convert the infidels, maintained it too is not edifying.

In any case, it is instructive to report in its entirety the reasoning Las Casas attributes to Columbus for leaving Guacanagarí free: imprisoning the cacique would not resuscitate the dead Christians nor send them to heaven, if they were not there already. If what Guacanagarí said was true, Columbus adds, it would have been a great injustice to imprison him, and all the Indians would have felt rancor and hatred toward the Christians and would have considered the Admiral himself ungrateful for the great assistance they had given him on the first voyage and the risk Guacanagarí had run in defending the Christians. The monarchs had sent him to colonize, and it was necessary to avoid anything that would impede that goal, anything that would cause conflict rather than concord between the two peoples. Even greater would have been the damage to "our holy faith, which was closest to the hearts of the Catholic sovereigns." This fine lesson from a layman to a priest concludes the tragic history of La Navidad.

No sign of the settlement remains. Built of wood, it burned completely. Its thirty-nine inhabitants, all dead, left no account, written or oral. Even the site itself is hard to identify. The best recent studies have identified the site of Guacanagarí's village and that of the later Spanish city of Puerto Real. Yet something did remain, and still does: children were born from the amorous liaisons and violent rapes of those ten months, children of Spaniards and Indians. Some must have been born before that inauspicious late November when Columbus discovered the tragedy of his first colony. Many others were in the swelling wombs of the pregnant Indians, children of a tragedy. They were the first children of a union that through many other tragedies would ultimately prevail, the union of the Indian peoples and the culture of Christian Europe, a union that the Spanish, despite many errors and not a few cruelties, achieved—unlike the Anglo-Saxons.

Let us return to Columbus. His first reaction is not clear. He apparently was unmoved, even cold—at least outwardly. He ordered his men to search for the gold that the dead men might have buried and to look for a more suitable site for a colony. Whatever the effect of this tragedy on his soul, at least for the moment Columbus hid it; secrecy was one of his most conspicuous traits. But the shock must have been traumatic. It is easy to imagine the reactions of the twelve hundred men who had enthusiastically volunteered for the second adventure. Granted, they had seen many novelties and new peoples, among them not only the docile Tainos, so glorified by Columbus in Spain, but also the fierce, human-eating Caribs. Nevertheless, they had left Spain not to satisfy curiosity but to get rich, to inhabit lands as yet uninhabited or inhabited by gentle and cowardly people, the kind easily subdued and exploited.

Something very different had happened instead, and at the hands not of the cannibals of Guadeloupe but of the Indians of Hispaniola, whom Columbus had guaranteed were the meekest people on earth. The houses were burnt and the well, which should have been full of gold, was empty, as empty as the hollow eye socket in a white man's corpse. That was what Columbus had to show the dismayed and disappointed Spaniards.

From this point Columbus's star began to decline. Here he was in a hostile land, in unhealthy forests, with twelve hundred men to lead, he who was born to command at sea, who could express his genius as a true leader and inspirer of men only at sea. There was nothing to do but turn back. But why go back along the east coast? Columbus knew very well that west of where he had founded La Navidad was the best port on the entire north coast of Haiti, the present-day Cap Haitien. He must have known that from the first voyage. In any case, on this occasion he used two caravels to explore the coast around La Navidad, one going to the east, the other to the west.

There is no doubt that Cap Haitien was the best site suggested by nature because of its low humidity compared with the plain to the east, because of the protection of the steep mountain behind it, and because of the fine port protected by two, sometimes three coral reefs. It was a site especially suitable for a European settlement and would become, a few centuries later, the "Paris of the Caribbean." But Columbus chose not to use it "because it was far from the gold mine." The gold mine would surely be found inland, east of the mouth of the Yaque del Norte that ran under Monte

Cristi; the Genoese had already determined that on the first voyage. So he chose not to settle at Cap Haitien and turned back, turning his prow to the east.

Columbus remembered two sites east of La Navidad that would be suitable for a city because they were good ports: Bahía de Gracias, today Luperón, and Puerto Plata, at the foot of Monte Plata. The former is the port where the *Pinta* stayed sixteen days; there Martín Alonso Pinzón had collected some gold, so it seemed an ideal goal. "The entrance," writes Columbus in the *Journal* of the first voyage, "is narrow, for there is a bank with only two fathoms of water over it; however, inside is a good port, enclosed and well protected." But "it has much fog" and is infested with teredos, which had caused extensive damage to the *Pinta,* so Columbus did not consider it. What about Puerto Plata? Today it is the most populous and best-known city on the northern coast of the Dominican Republic. It has enjoyed that status for a long time, first as a military base against the filibusters and later during the Caribbean wars. The great mariner's sharp eye had spotted the advantages of Puerto Plata. Why did Columbus not found a new colony there? Because, to put it bluntly, he could no longer allay his men's anxiety. Perhaps for the first time since he had formulated his design for the great discovery, Columbus made a mistake, not out of obstinacy or pride, not out of avarice, ambition, or even religious fanaticism. It would appear to be—but we shall see that it was not—a mistake typical of those who cannot brook the least delay. The winds contributed to this mistake, the trades that on so many other occasions had been Columbus's best ally.

One has only to try venturing east along the northern coast of Haiti and the Dominican Republic in a sailboat to appreciate the difficulties of navigating against the trades. Nevertheless, in January 1493 the *Niña* had taken seven days to make the passage from La Navidad to Puerto Plata. Now, slightly over ten months later, Columbus left La Navidad on 7 December and made Monte Cristi the next day. He left again, or rather tried to leave, on the ninth. It took until 2 January to reach the place where he would found Isabela. Let us consider for a moment the distances:

- From La Navidad to Monte Cristi is thirty modern miles (thirty-eight Mediterranean miles).

- From Monte Cristi to Isabela is thirty-three modern miles (forty-two Mediterranean miles).
- From Isabela to Puerto Plata is twenty-six modern miles (thirty-two Mediterranean miles).

Twenty-five days to go thirty-three miles! A little over a mile per day if the ships had sailed without interruption, but it is easy to imagine how long and how often they were becalmed, probably one or two whole weeks.

There is no mention of this veritable torture by Columbus, for he stopped writing in the *Journal*. The only evidence is Dr. Chanca's laconic but forceful testimony: "The wind was so contrary that we had more difficulty going thirty leagues in those conditions than we had in the whole passage from Castile." Chanca, a doctor rather than a sailor, confuses leagues with miles. It was not thirty leagues, which would have been 120 miles. It was actually a little over 42 miles according to Columbus's calculations, measured in Mediterranean miles.

What did the crews, hidalgos, soldiers, colonists, and horses do? They were always aboard ship, obviously. They did not go ashore, because it is not easy to get near the beach from outside the coral reef. Some boats may have landed to fetch water, and the men probably caught good fish. But horses do not eat fish, and twenty-five days for the men was a hopeless eternity in a hot, humid climate so different from Europe's. The sailors were worn out from constantly making sail, and nine times out of ten that task was fruitless. The others were inactive, unable to exercise except on a crowded deck, unable to swim except for quick dips because the sea was teeming with sharks.

This was another disaster after that of La Navidad, for only Columbus knew, from his experience the year before, that it was an unusual situation that could be overcome. Puerto Plata was nearby, less than a day's sail away if only they had a good wind. But the wind did not come. So how would they arrive in Puerto Plata? With the horses dead? With hundreds of men in revolt?

Columbus had to give in, had to stop, had to go ashore at last and found the new city, the promised colony. But where should he choose the site? He had already rejected the plain at the mouth of the Yaque del Norte; the water in the gulf there is a muddy soup.

After it, the first stretch of plain on the coast is at the mouth of the Bajabonico. Today it empties into the sea a good mile farther west; then it lapped the knoll, about twenty feet high, right on the sea. There the Admiral went ashore and, making a decision as hasty as it was necessary, founded the new colony. He did not name it La Nueva Navidad; even the failed colony's name was to disappear from memory. He named it La Isabela, after the queen who had sustained, aided, and protected him. Thus, a double misfortune gave birth to the first city of the New World.

27 | *The Gold Mine*

*L*a Isabela was founded on 2 January 1494. The 6 January, the feast of Epiphany, saw the first high mass in the New World. Father Boil—a Catalan, Benedictine, and papal nuncio—officiated. Concelebrants were the Franciscan fathers Juan de la Duela and Juan de Tisín, the Hieronymite Father Román Pane, four secular priests, and five Franciscan friars from the monastery of Montserrat in Catalonia. Mass was celebrated in an improvised chapel decorated with gorgeous crimson hangings given for that purpose by Queen Isabella the Catholic, who had taken them from the royal chapel.

On 2 February the church was already finished; it consisted of a parsonage and sanctuary surrounded by a stone wall to protect it from anticipated attacks by the natives. Other public buildings were also built of stone; only private dwellings were made of wood and straw. By 24 April 1494, according to the documents, La Isabela already had *regidores* ("notaries public"), an *alcalde mayor* and *alcaldes ordinarios* ("mayor" and "aldermen"), and *alguaciles* ("overseers of water supplies"). It was the first *cabildo* ("municipality") in America.

On 10 March 1496, when Columbus left for Spain, ending his second voyage of discovery, he named his brothers Bartholomew and Diego governor general and lieutenant governor respectively. The transfer of power took place at La Isabela and included the investiture of Francisco Roldán as *alcalde mayor* of the municipality. The quarrels between Roldán and Bartholomew and later between Roldán and the Admiral would contribute to the decay of La Isabela. In the last years of the fifteenth century, the new city of Santo Domingo on the southern coast of Hispaniola began acquiring ever greater importance. But neither fratricidal struggles nor competition from Santo Domingo fully explain the rapid decline of La Isabela. In 1499 the city was already dying. A year later the stone buildings were mute, sad witnesses of a bygone era. La Isabela disappeared without the honor of a dramatic event, either man-made or natural.

The first city Columbus built, the first Spanish municipality, the first root of the Latin American world—so many firsts for La Isabela. And there is one more—it was the first to die, within the space of six years. It was not reborn. Belief that the place was haunted spread so soon and so rapidly that Las Casas recounted hearing it a few years later: the colonists who had died there walked again, wandering through the ruined houses, ceremoniously greeting those who ventured into the abandoned streets, and then dissolving into powder when anyone tried to hug them, shake their hand, or touch them in any way.

Stories that the place was haunted were not the only factor preventing La Isabela's rebirth. The northern coast of Hispaniola, more than the southern, suffered from the recurrent raids of filibusters and the effects of wars among the European powers. La Isabela today is not a municipality nor a district, not even an *aldea* or *pueblo* ("village"). There are only the little houses on the hill, inhabited by the six hundred natives who fish, farm, and earn a little money from the infrequent tourists interested in visiting the source of the Latin American empire, an empire extinct politically but culturally very much alive and well. But La Isabela was not reborn primarily because it did not have a port. What could have possessed Columbus not to pick a good port? He was not born to found cities, but as an outstanding mariner he was the best judge of ports. There can be only one reason: the trying experience on which I have dwelt for so long. The torment of making only thirty-three miles in twenty-five days forced Columbus into making a poor choice. It was poor not because the hill of La Isabela is unattractive or unappealing but because the bay is neither an adequate port nor protected from the winds.

The high mass of the Epiphany was scarcely over before the Admiral ordered Alonso de Hojeda and Ginés de Gorvalán into the interior in search of the gold mines. After crossing the Cordillera Setentrional ("Northern Range"), they went down into the Vega Real, the extensive plain where ran "a big stream, wider and bigger than that at Seville," as Michele da Cuneo describes the Rio Yaque del Norte, which Columbus had named Rio del Oro the year before because of the abundance of gold dust collected from it. Many rivers come from the mountains of the Cibao and flow into the Rio Yaque from the left. As Peter Martyr writes,

> In the sands of these rivers the Indians accompanying the Spaniards gathered gold by scooping out sand with their hands to a depth of about a foot and a half. From the bottom of the hole they scoop up sand in their left hand and pick out the gold with their right hand, and just that easily they put nuggets in our hands. Many said they saw a number of nuggets the size of a chickpea. I myself later saw a raw nugget like a river rock that weighed nine ounces; Hojeda had found it himself.

Michele da Cuneo assures us that among the gold specimens presented to the Admiral were three pieces worth eight, fifteen, and twenty-two castellanos (about $165, $300, and $450 respectively in 1987 dollars). Cuneo's estimates, like those of every good Ligurian on the subject of gold or money, are not exaggerated but cautious and prudent.

So there *was* gold! There *were* mines! As Cuneo writes, "The Admiral and all the rest of us, caring no longer for spices but only for this blessed gold, held a great celebration." Columbus regained his confidence and decided to send twelve of the seventeen ships back to Spain. It would have been better if he could have sent barrels of gold instead of specimens, but specimens were proof that he had not been carried away by fantasy in his account of the first voyage. Along with specimens Columbus also sent Gorvalán, one of the commanders of the expedition, back to Spain. With the other, Hojeda, Columbus left for the Cibao to verify personally the existence of the mines.

It was an important expedition. The first inland march, it would serve as a model for the conquistadors, from Balboa to Cortés, Pizarro, Orellana, and so many others until all passable routes in the hemisphere between 40° N and 50° S were known. It was the first time since the beginning of the discovery that Columbus went more than a few miles from the sea, and this was as far as he went inland. His destination, of which I will speak shortly, was nearly forty miles as the crow flies from La Isabela.

Five hundred men went on the expedition, divided into ranks, "as is customary when they go to war, with trumpets playing and banners unfurled." They carried muskets, and when entering or leaving villages they sounded the trumpets and fired volleys so the Indians "could see the Christians' power." It appears, however, that the Indians were more astonished by the horses. Besides the infantry, Columbus brought cavalry with him and "equipment for building a fort so that the province of the Cibao could be kept peaceful, and the Spaniards should be safe from any insult or injury after gathering gold." The sad experience of La Navidad had taught the Admiral to take precautions.

Columbus left on 12 March 1494, fording the Bajabonico, the river from which La Isabela drew its water. He then went up the left side of a tributary of the Bajabonico. The present road from the sea to the pleasant locality of Los Hidalgos largely follows the same route. Immediately south of Los Hidalgos the road rises to 1,640 feet at the pass; to the west is a 2,700-foot peak. In the southeast rises the Cordillera Setentrional, whose sharp, jagged peaks reach 4,100 feet. Today the pass has a good asphalt road. Then there was perhaps a *camino,* a modest trail beaten out by the Indians and continually obstructed by the luxuriant and over-whelming vegetation that bursts out after every rain.

Beyond the pass a fabulous panorama opened before the Span-iards. So it is today at any time of year, but especially during March and April, when the rains have made every part of the countryside green, flowers are in bloom everywhere, and the air is soft and fresh. It is the panorama of the Vega Real, the royal plain. So Columbus named it, and with reason the name has survived down through the centuries, for among the countless wonders of the Caribbean one rarely sees a plain as wide, rich, and serene bounded by such lush, beautiful mountains. Here is the description by Las Casas, who saw it a few decades after the Discoverer:

It is eighty leagues long, and from high up the mountain where the Admiral and his men stood one can see twenty or thirty leagues, from one side to the other. It is so fresh, green, and free from obstacles, so multicolored with bright hues, so beautiful that right away they thought they had wandered into a corner of paradise.

The army began the descent "with great rejoicing and cheerfulness," for after seeing the unrivaled panorama of the Vega Real they were passing through enchanting forests. The forests are still alluring and flourishing today, although the native trees have been supplanted by imports from tropical Asia and Africa, primarily coconuts but also breadfruit trees, bananas, peppers, nutmegs, and many others. The joy that seized the five hundred men of the Columbian army captures the modern-day traveler who reaches these splendid regions of the Dominican Republic.

Michele da Cuneo, Don Ferdinand, and Las Casas do not agree as to the course of events after the expedition left the Vega Real. They agree, however, on the army's eventual destination, an area today called Fortaleza, a little southwest of the town of Jánico on a great slope that divides the watershed of the Rio Bao from that of the Rio Jánico.

From Jánico one can go part of the way in a vehicle and then must walk or ride a mule. As Don Ferdinand noted then, large areas are still treeless, but along the banks of the Jánico and Bao are dense forests. The Bao carries a large volume of water even in the dry seasons. It is turbulent and hemmed in by the lush mountains. It is a stirring spectacle and must have impressed the Spaniards, especially those who had not gone ashore on Guadeloupe. The forests in this part of the Cordillera Central are darker than those of the Cordillera Setentrional and just as fascinating.

Nothing, however, was as fascinating as gold. The Admiral collected ten kilograms of gold from the Indians and realized that the Cibao was not like the Bahamas, coastal Hispaniola, nor Guinea, where gold was used in trade just as it was in Genoa. Here gold was found in its native state; here were mines. Gold is still found there, not in the Cibao but nearby. The Dominican Republic reported gold production of 11,240 kilograms in 1983, a substantial quantity.

This was the second great discovery Columbus had yearned for since 12 October 1492, when he had seen a Taino with a gold nose ring. He was now high-spirited and confident. He laid out the plan of the fortress, superintended the start of its construction, and decided to leave a troop of cavalry—because horses terrified the Indians—and fifty men under the command of Mosén Pedro Margarite (or Margarit). After digging ditches and building palisades, they garrisoned the fort, making a safe refuge and center for mining.

Columbus realized the Cibao was not Cipango. But Cipango interested him less now. The second voyage had given him many reassurances: the New Lands had numerous previously unknown plants, including many spices, marvelous forests, plains far more fertile than any in Europe, abundant rain and many rivers, enchanting seas both inside and outside the coral reefs, and plentiful, delicious seafood and turtles. In short, the New Lands had all of God's bounty, including gold, enough to enrich the Spanish Crown and all of Spain. What was left to discover? India, the object of the grand design. Yet reaching India required finding the mainland. The Cibao was not Cipango, but that no longer worried Columbus. The problem was finding the mainland, Cathay, in order to reach India at last.

28 | Exploration of Cuba and Jamaica and Misfortunes at La Isabela

From 24 April to 29 September 1494 Columbus explored the southern coast of Cuba with three caravels, discovered Jamaica, and returned along the southern coast of Hispaniola, doubling the eastern end of the island. In the course of this exploration, on 12 June, he summoned the royal notary and ordered him to interrogate the captains, pilots, and sailors of the three caravels and have them swear that Cuba was the beginning of the Indies—the Asian mainland. If anyone was of another opinion, the Admiral would convince him of his error. Anyone who signed the statement and later contradicted it would be fined ten thousand maravedis and have his tongue cut out. Forty-two men—captains, pilots, and sailors, Juan de la Cosa among them—swore they had never seen or heard of an island extending 335 leagues from east to west (Cuba is in fact longer than England [though it is smaller] or any other European island); therefore this land had to be part of the mainland. If they had continued they would have soon met "civilized and intelligent people who knew the world." Thus did they swear and sign.

This exercise seems strange today, and it provoked derision and mockery from Columbus's detractors. It had, however, been done before by other explorers. Bartolomeu Dias did the same thing after rounding the Cape of Good Hope and being certain he was on the route to the Indies, only to have the crew force him to turn back. Columbus was well aware of the incident; what he did, then, was not peculiar for the times. Having the procedure rigorously notarized helps explain a sudden decision: Columbus deliberately lied. Knowing full well he was lying, he wanted to make it official, to legalize this falsehood and compromise those involved with him in one of the most important episodes of the great discovery.

Effort is necessary to understand fully and, if possible, to penetrate Columbus's state of mind during that fateful June 1494. He was now certain that the New Lands were not another of the many archipelagoes scattered throughout the Atlantic by the medieval imagination and by cartographers. Columbus told Peter Martyr after the second voyage that he had nearly reached the Golden Chersonese (the Malay Peninsula). If he was convinced he had reached, or almost reached, the Golden Chersonese, Columbus was equally convinced he was near India. Between the Golden Chersonese and India lay, according to medieval geography (correct on this point), a relatively short stretch of sea, the Bay of Bengal.

Columbus told Andrés Bernáldez that, hoping Cuba was an Asian peninsula, he had at the beginning of June 1494 considered passing it, crossing the Indian Ocean, and returning to Spain east to west, either by sailing around the Cape of Good Hope or by disembarking in the Red Sea, going overland through Jerusalem, and then sailing from Jaffa to Cádiz. It was an ambitious plan, anticipating Magellan. Did Columbus really think he could realize it? Yes. Did he think he could realize it on this occasion? No. He knew he could not carry it out with three ill-equipped caravels. But he thought of it. And he believed, he hoped, he was coasting along the Malay Peninsula. There he would return and finally realize his unfulfilled dream: reaching India and circumnavigating the globe. But on 11 June the fundamental premise of his plan fell apart when Columbus learned from the Indians that Cuba was an island. He would have to accept the sad reality that Cuba was not the Malay Peninsula. That day he reached Bahía Cortés, less than one hundred miles from Cape Corrientes ("Currents"), the southwestern tip of Cuba.

Historians are fond of saying that with a little perseverance Columbus could have determined that Cuba is an island, and they give free rein to their imagination about what would have happened next. After a brief crossing he would have reached Yucatán, or, if he had continued coasting the island, the Gulf Stream would have borne the caravels within sight of the Florida Keys, and from there he could have easily reached another part of the mainland, Florida. The conclusions based on these *ifs* are obviously varied. However, there is surprising agreement—compared with the arguments over so many other aspects of Columbus's life—that Columbus could have proven Cuba to be an island. I do not agree. He quit coasting Cuba not only because of fatigue, lack of provisions, grumbling of the crews, and the poor condition of the ships but above all because he did not *want* to ascertain whether Cuba was an island. He knew from his Indian guides that he was near the western end of Cuba, and he absolutely did not want to acknowledge by his own experience that it was not the Malay Peninsula, as he had believed until then. He was convinced that there was mainland, so convinced that even if Cuba and all the other lands discovered until then turned out to be islands they would have to be a kind of crown to the mainland. That is why he demanded the oath. He forced hidalgos, officials, and sailors to swear that Cuba was a peninsula, not to avoid the accusation that he had turned back prematurely but to allay the suspicion that those islands were an enormous archipelago far from Asia.

This interpretation is close to Madariaga's, except that Madariaga sees the incident as another of the many proofs of Columbus's folly. There is no need, however, to consider Columbus a fool to explain his psychology, in this as in so other many cases a complex, contradictory blend of trite medieval beliefs and anticipations of Renaissance and modern ideas. The modern man shows in Columbus's acuity and unfailing observation of every experience. From that acuity and spirit of observation Columbus formed an idea that turned out to be correct: the discovered islands suggested a nearby continent. The medieval man shows, however, when he tries to document not the experiential truth but his intuitions, when intuition and falsehood are made one, when signs are transformed into proofs, interpretations of facts into facts themselves, and intuition into reality. When the Genoese returned to La Isabela on 29 September he was well aware—despite the mendacious oaths—that he had not yet found the mainland, much less India.

Another disappointment awaited him at La Isabela. Many hundred—actually nearly a thousand—Spaniards had settled at La Isabela at the beginning of January, spreading out from there as far as San Tomaso. All were men: sailors, settlers, hidalgos, priests, and friars. Others, including women and children, had come from Europe on later voyages and joined them. The first arrivals had spent eleven months in the New Lands, nine in the northern part of Hispaniola with La Isabela as their base. No one had a precise understanding of these lands yet. Whether or not they were the eastern outposts of Asia, they were a new world, new in climate, sea, land, flora, fauna, and people.

To begin with the climate, eleven months were sufficient to prove that the New Lands did not have European seasons. In Europe it is cold in winter and hot in summer; in the Caribbean the heat varies only slightly throughout the year, decreasing in winter but never going below 68°F. The median temperature at La Isabela is 73°F in January and 80°F in July. There is no autumn or winter. Plants sprout in every month, myriads of flowers open at the first rays of the sun after a violent rainstorm, and meadows and hills are always green. Here and there during the dry months there are patches of yellow or gray away from the rivers, but as soon as the rains come they are green again in a few days.

The prodigious fecundity of the newly discovered lands impressed contemporary historians. Here is Don Ferdinand's account:

> When the Admiral returned from the Cibao to La Isabela on 29 March he found some of the melons already ripe, although barely two months had passed since planting. Similarly, the watermelons were ready after twenty days, and a local wild vine produced good, round grapes when tended. The next day, 30 March, a farmer harvested wheat he had planted at the end of January, and chickpeas were bigger than the seeds that had been planted. Everything sprouted within three days after planting, and within twenty-five days it was ready to eat. The roots of the trees send out shoots in seven days, and the vine cuttings put out leaves within seven days. So does the sugar cane.

Michele da Cuneo gives more details about new plants and fruits discovered on Hispaniola, including roots "quite big and of

167

many types, very white, from which they make bread." He adds
that because many seeds had been brought from Spain, he was
able to report which ones did well and which did not. Those that
did well, indeed very well, were watermelons and other varieties of
melon, squash, and radishes; among those that did poorly were
onions, various types of lettuce, and leeks. Wheat, chickpeas, and
fava beans grew rapidly but just as quickly wilted and dried out, so
they had to be harvested quickly to avoid being burned in the
extreme heat. Overall, then, in soil fertility and agricultural potential the balance was clearly positive.

But there was another matter, health, the physical condition of
the settlers. In this respect the balance was not just negative, it was
disastrous. On his return from the Cibao, Columbus had found
many sick men at La Isabela; on 28 September, after exploring
Cuba and Jamaica for five months, he found La Isabela reduced to
a hospital, and many more graves in the first Christian cemetery in
the New Lands. Why? In particular, why did the second voyage
have such a different effect on the men's health from that of the
first?

The primary explanation lies in the calendar. The first stay in
America took place between 12 October 1492 and 14 January
1493 according to the Julian calendar, or between 22 October and
24 January in the Gregorian calendar used today. In contrast, the
first period of the second voyage—to stay for the moment at the
point we have reached in our account—took place between 4
November 1493 and 29 September 1494 (14 November 1493 and
9 October 1494). Although the Caribbean has no real change of
seasons, from June through August the heat is very humid, op-
pressive, and stressful. The stay in America on the first voyage was
completed outside those months, in the best possible season for
those accustomed to the Mediterranean climate.

A second explanation for the difference in the consequences of
the two voyages is that the participants in the first were few (less
than one hundred), they were all sailors (most were used to living
in diverse climates), and they all lived the whole time aboard ship.
Except for those who remained at La Navidad and the few explorers sent into the interior of Cuba in search of the Great Khan, the
crews of the *Santa María, Pinta,* and *Niña* never slept ashore. The
food aboard ship was what they were used to, the standard diet of
Mediterranean sailors: hardtack or sea biscuit, olive oil, vinegar,

wine, garlic, olives, and salt meat. They did not scorn the native fish, seafood, birds, and other game, but those were supplemental foods. The basic elements in the Mediterranean sailor's diet were always available on the first voyage. In particular, there is no indication they ever lacked hardtack, oil, or wine.

On the second voyage things were completely different. It was quite impossible to provide twelve hundred people with hardtack, oil, and wine for eleven months and more. What remained of the hardtack and salt meat brought from Spain or Gomera putrefied from the humidity and heat, and the wine turned sour. Those who settled at La Isabela had to get used to cassava bread. We know how it was prepared—grated, minced, or made into flour—but it always came from tubers: yams, sweet potatoes, or *yuca*. They do not have as much protein as wheat does.

In the sea off La Isabela was an abundance of fish, mollusks, and crustaceans, but many of the hidalgos and farmers were not used to seafood. And how could they season them? Besides the shortage of grains and wine, fats were scarce. And vegetables and fruits? All kinds grow in the lands bathed by the Bajabonico and Yaque del Norte rivers, but they were unfamiliar to the Spanish. The stomach is the human organ most accustomed to routine, and it becomes most resentful if its regimen is radically modified. As a result the men went hungry and wasted away. Five hen's eggs were rationed to five convalescents, and ten ounces of cooked chickpeas had to suffice for eighteen sick men.

Despite all this, the earth could produce good grain if it was harvested on time. But someone had to cultivate it. The Admiral ordered everyone to work, even the hidalgos, which caused grumbling and resentment. He ordered them to build water mills to harness the power of the Bajabonico. But they did not feel like working; the hidalgos were offended at being forced to do manual labor, and even the farmers, hardy Andalusian peasants, felt debilitated by the climate. They not only did not want to work but could not.

As the years and decades passed, the whites adapted to the hot, humid climate, found adequate remedies, and effectively integrated the fruits, fish, and other products of the New World with the basic elements of the European diet. They learned to prevent tropical diseases through hygiene and medicine and developed a life-style that was more than tolerable, even pleasant, in the basically healthy environment of Haiti and the Dominican Republic, Cuba, Jamaica, Puerto Rico, and the Lesser Antilles.

In short, they resolved all of the European's environmental problems—except adjusting to work. Work in the fields, on plantations, in construction—the colonists could not adapt to manual labor in such a hot, humid climate. The tragic consequences would soon be felt. Here I will point out that, despite the Admiral's explicit orders, the people of La Isabela were unwilling or unable to work, and so they could not solve the problem of securing food. The time came when the daily ration consisted "of a plate of grain that had to be ground in a hand mill (many ate it boiled) and a slice of rancid bacon or moldy cheese with some fava beans or chickpeas." So Las Casas tells us, adding that, "as for wine, it was as if none existed in the world." To survive, the Spanish ate *iutias,* the barkless dogs, and *mohuys,* a kind of rabbit smaller than those of Europe. They grew accustomed to eating iguanas and other reptiles. With these animals and fish they satisfied their need for meat, but there were no substitutes for oil and wine. Cassava and *yuca* were a barely passable substitute for bread. The settlers' wasting away and hunger were accompanied by the tropical illnesses common in that climate.

The weakened, undernourished settlers easily fell victim to various diseases. In this period—between January and September 1494—the *buba* ("pustule") appeared. Was it syphilis? According to Las Casas and Oviedo it was, and it must have been carried to Europe—again, according to Oviedo—by the men who return to Spain with Captain Antonio de Torres in February 1494. According to Ruy Díaz de Isla, the Spanish doctor who wrote a book on the subject in 1539, syphilis arrived in Europe after the first voyage, from the Indians who infected the prostitutes of Barcelona in 1493. According to other scholars there was an endemic form of syphilis in both Europe and America before the great discovery. It seems certain, however, that the *buba* was syphilis. Whatever caused the explosion of this venereal disease in Europe, there is no doubt that the *buba* spread in La Isabela because the Spaniards frequently raped Indian women.

This brings us to the subject of the Indians' sexual customs before the arrival of the Europeans and the impact of the sailors and Spanish settlers on the Tainos' sexual behavior. The Tainos everywhere, on the Bahamas, Cuba, and Hispaniola, had quite free habits. They practiced anal intercourse, and the women were promiscuous. The debauchery of Anacaona, Caonabó's wife, after she was widowed became so wild and unrestrained that she rivaled Semiramis. There was, however, a limit: no one had relations with his mother, daughters, or sisters; incest was abhorred by all. There were modest women, but even those who were not openly lustful "easily gave in to the Christians, never denying themselves."

The first known sexual episode is that reported by Michele da Cuneo. It occurred in mid-November 1493 in the Bay of St. Croix in the Lesser Antilles:

> On the boat I took a most beautiful Cannibal woman, whom the Admiral gave me. When I had her in my cabin, she being naked as is their custom, I felt the desire to take pleasure with her and wanted to carry out my will. She did not want me, though, and scratched me with her nails to the point that I wished I had never begun. To tell you how it ended, I took a piece of rope and thrashed her soundly, and she raised such dreadful cries you would not have believed it. In the end we came to an agreement in such a way that I can assure you she seemed trained in a school for whores.

The ending has a Boccaccian flavor. More dramatic than Boccaccian were the incidents at La Navidad, where the men's jealousy about women was among the causes of the tragedy. While it is certain that some Spaniards quarreled and fought among themselves, even killing each other over women, the Indians apparently retaliated more for the Spaniards' arrogance, raids, and depredations than for specific problems over women. The Indian women were so clearly available that males did not take offense. Deceived by this freedom, the settlers took it for granted and recognized no limits, not even respecting the wives and daughters of the caciques.

Just as they abused the women, the settlers abused the naïve hospitality of the Indians, who offered whatever they possessed. Diego Columbus, whom Christopher left in command of La Isabela and the entire island, could not maintain control. Contemporaries say he was more suited for the cloister than politics.

Whatever the cause, when the Admiral returned he found a dreadful situation: famine, disease, sexual excesses, and no hope of any kind of meaningful relationship with the Indians.

The question naturally arises, How could things have changed so radically from the first encounter in the Bahamas to this interaction of the second voyage? The Caribbean islands seemed, then as now, to be a terrestrial paradise. All is beautiful. But even good things take getting used to. It is fine to fall asleep swinging in a hammock, yet how many Europeans, workers or professionals, would readily trade their beds for hammocks? The taste of pineapple, papaya, and avocado is fine, but if you give them to Italian or Spanish soldiers accustomed to apples, pears, and oranges, the exotic fruits end up in the latrine. Swimming in the sea off La Isabela is wonderful. I have enjoyed that pleasure more than once, but the hidalgos and peasants of those times had absolutely no desire to swim in the sea. These are just three examples showing how the terrestrial paradise turned into purgatory for the Spanish.

Also recalling purgatory—if not hell itself—was the hurricane that struck La Isabela at an unknown date, probably in the autumn of 1495. "Such a furious wind was unleashed from the northeast," writes Peter Martyr, "that its equal is not remembered." No one could have recalled such a thing, for nothing like it had been known in Europe. The word *huracán* is Mayan and means "the one with a single foot," referring to the god of the storm. The Spanish adopted the name for the kind of cyclonic storm that is more destructive than an earthquake. In the autumn of 1495 a hurricane uprooted the gigantic trees in the valley of the Bajabonico, snapped moorings, and—without becoming a fullfledged storm—sank two, perhaps three, ships anchored in the bay of La Isabela. "An awesome miracle," comments Peter Martyr. It was not a miraculous event but another novelty among the many of the great discovery, one that would make even more difficult the Europeans' encounter with the New World.

29 | War and Slavery

N ot only was acclimatizing proving difficult, but the developing relationship between whites and Indians, begun so idyllically, was turning sour and acrimonious. Thus, the colony was in critical condition at the end of September 1494.

Before leaving for Cuba and Jamaica, Columbus, as viceroy, had ordered a canal built from the Bajabonico to the center of town, to supplement the well water and power a mill. Everyone was to work, but—as already noted—the hidalgos, according to Las Casas, "felt that manual labor was a misfortune equal to death or worse, especially since they were not eating well." The other settlers may have been willing to work but could not because of the climate and poor nutrition, so Columbus, Las Casas also reports, "had to enforce his will with violence." Oviedo is more specific: "He had some men hanged, others whipped, and became more severe and rigorous than usual." Father Boil, the apostolic vicar, accused him of being too severe. Thus began a tragicomic duel between Father Boil's spiritual power and Columbus's temporal power. Father Boil interdicted the viceroy and suspended the sacraments. The viceroy responded by cutting off the priest's food, already strictly rationed. Hunger forced Father Boil to capitulate.

Such proceedings did not encourage respect for authority nor promote the orderly development of the colony. Neither did Columbus's other errors help. A great sailor, he was no politician. One error was granting supreme power to the inept Don Diego during his long absence; another was putting Margarite in charge of exploring the Vega Real. In sending that expedition Columbus was under the illusion that he was solving several problems at once: completing the exploration of the island, keeping several hundred men occupied, avoiding a strain on provisions at La Isabela, and getting the men accustomed to the natives' food. Instead, Margarite's men swept through the Vega Real, living off the natives and committing every outrage imaginable.

Before the Admiral returned, Margarite and Father Boil had decided to go back to Spain with the caravels that had brought Columbus's brother Bartholomew and the new settlers. They intended to tell the sovereigns that that damned Genoese foreigner had deceived them with promises of gold, pearls, and spices, yet all they had found were hunger, sickness, suffering, and the Indians' hatred. When the Admiral came back from exploring Cuba and Jamaica, the crimes committed by the settlers at La Navidad were being repeated on a much larger scale at La Isabela. In groups of two or three the Spaniards were roving the Vega Real and nearby hills, violating women, carrying some of them off, and forcing the men into slave labor.

The Admiral did, however, have the comfort of seeing Bartholomew again, who had gone to England when it seemed that Spain definitely would not sponsor the grand project. Bartholomew had experienced various vicissitudes—pirates, a long stay in London as a mapmaker, and a journey through France—until he heard the news of the great discovery, whereupon he returned to the Spanish court. The Catholic sovereigns received him favorably, granted him the title of *don,* and gave him command of three caravels furnished with provisions for Hispaniola.

Bartholomew's presence in the New World was an unexpected boon. His temperament was unlike Diego's. Columbus had an enormous sense of family, throughout his life entrusting the most delicate tasks to relatives. He had done so with Diego de Arana and Don Diego. Now he immediately gave Bartholomew the title of *adelantado.* That was a mistake and technically an abuse. The monarchs were displeased, for only they, not the viceroy, could confer titles of such high rank. But it was also a mistake in judgment, for it offended Spanish pride. The hidalgos and caballeros could accept the foreign Discoverer because he had had the good fortune to find new lands for the Spanish Crown. But why should this other Genoese be given authority over the rightful representatives of the Spanish nation?

Growing discontent among the settlers increased, and instead of getting better, matters grew worse. As so often happens, when problems build up until they seem insoluble those in power go to war to solve them. That was the case on Hispaniola at the end of 1494 and beginning of 1495. In March 1495 open warfare broke out between the Indians and Spaniards, but Columbus did not deliberately choose it—he simply did not know how to use political power. Aboard ship he held a captain's power, wielding it with skill, audacity, and the quickest imagination. But political power and power at sea are altogether different, and Columbus was not familiar with politics. Consequently, the theory that he wanted war, that he deliberately chose the worst means in the hope of solving all his problems with violence, must be rejected. In fact, a guerrilla war was already going on before the Admiral returned from his long naval exploration. He was dragged into war by circumstance—his own mistakes and those of the men who assisted him and fear that the Indians would profit from the Spaniards' weakness.

As early as January 1494, in composing the memorandum that Antonio de Torres was to take to the monarchs, Columbus had observed that the Indians were "simple and without malice," but he wondered whether they might change and destroy everything, men and provisions. "An Indian," Columbus continues, "could easily set fire to the houses because they are always coming and going, day and night, and so we keep guards in the surrounding area, for the city is open and defenseless." The monarchs noted in the margin "it was good," that is, he did well to post guards. There was also Caonabó, "very bad and very bold." For fear of him, Columbus explained, he could not risk venturing inland to collect more gold. Beside this passage the monarchs again noted "it was good."

The first pages of the memorandum Columbus sent with Torres

are dated 30 January 1494; they clearly reveal the fear that gripped the Spanish at La Isabela and Columbus himself. Those fears were justified, considering how many were sick. Because of the scarcity of food, especially fresh meat, many of the sick could not get well, and if the diseases had continued unchecked the Indians would have taken advantage of the opportunity to attack La Isabela.

If the memorandum reflects Columbus's state of mind before leaving to explore Cuba and Jamaica, we can imagine what it must have been seven months later, when nothing had been done to lessen the fears, while the risks and dangers had increased. During the Admiral's absence, the Indians had given more than one clear sign that they could respond, that they knew they could fight back against the outrages of the settlers. Another, ulterior motive for Columbus's move toward war should not be forgotten: his foreigner's complex, the awareness that anything he did to defend the Indians and punish the Spanish would be interpreted by the Spanish in nationalistic terms. Thinking that he would not guarantee the interests and rights of the subjects of his adopted country, they would portray him to the monarchs in a critical light.

Whatever the reason, rather than punishing the hidalgos and dishonest settlers, Columbus placed all the blame on the Indians, adopting Father Boil's harsh policy, which he had rejected six months before. As a result the Spanish captured fifteen hundred Indian men, women, and children and herded them together at La Isabela. It was a true concentration camp of people bound for slavery. Columbus had thought of slavery the moment he discovered the Caribs in the Lesser Antilles. The Caribs were mortal enemies of the Tainos, who had proved docile, obedient, faithful subjects. Enslaving the Caribs, fierce and pitiless eaters of human flesh, had seemed legitimate and politically expedient to Columbus. He had suggested it to Ferdinand and Isabella in the memorandum sent with Antonio de Torres. The monarchs, who had made approving notes by the other paragraphs of the letter, expressly forbade the proposed traffic in slaves, writing, "This project is to be set aside."

Their reply arrived quickly in Hispaniola, in autumn 1494. Antonio de Torres brought four caravels with a badly needed cargo of food and tools and a letter from the monarchs dated 16

August. Ferdinand and Isabella, after consulting with their coun-selors over the Admiral's memorandum of the preceding February, approved most of his suggestions and actions. They wanted better reports on the climate of the New Lands, because that was most important for would-be immigrants. The negotiations with Por-tugal were going so well that the monarchs proposed beginning a monthly packet between Spain and Hispaniola. They added that a new, definitive line of demarcation with Portugal was to be es-tablished as soon as possible, and so they invited the Admiral to return and give them his counsel. However, "if your return should cause difficulties or in any way prejudice your immediate affairs, select your brother or someone else who is knowledgeable, in-struct him either orally or on paper as to your thinking on the matter, and send him back with the first caravels that can be spared."

Thus was Columbus given a chance to escape his problems. He could have interpreted the letter as an order to return to Spain, left Bartholomew in command, and personally refuted the calumnies of Margarite and Father Boil, who would arrive at court shortly. That easy solution he rejected, choosing instead to stay and bear the burden of the first severe colonial problems of modern history. He would not return to Spain. But what could he send to the monarchs with Torres's caravels? In March he had sent a letter promising huge gold specimens, new plants, and the usual varicol-ored parrots. There were still plenty of parrots, but the Admiral could not keep sending them. Nor could he send gold, because the specimens had already arrived, and at San Tomaso they had not yet collected enough to send. Every Spaniard had his own personal stash hidden in his clothes or buried, but not even a barrelful had been gathered for the Crown. The Spanish merchants did not value any of the spices and tropical essences sent earlier. The cotton goods were easy to sell but brought little profit. He had to send something to Europe that would repay expenses and counter the base suggestions already being made that the Indies be aban-doned completely. The only merchandise left was slaves, so he collected a cargo of them.

And so, after having proclaimed over and over that the Tainos were generous, docile, and defenseless, that they wanted to be-come good subjects and good Christians, Columbus now decided

177

to send them to the slave market in Seville. I have said that fifteen hundred Indians had been captured and were being held at La Isabela. Of these, the five hundred "best men and women" were loaded into the holds of the four caravels. The citizens of La Isabela then chose as many of the rest as they wanted. Some four hundred remained, many of them women with children at the breast. These "were given permission to go where they would," as Michele da Cuneo says. The women, "being afraid we would recapture them, dropped their children so they could flee unencumbered and ran as if possessed. They were so desperate they went seven or eight days' journey from La Isabela, crossing mountains and quite large rivers."

The four caravels, under the command of Antonio de Torres, left on 24 February 1495. On board were Michele da Cuneo and Diego Columbus, the latter to represent the Admiral and defend his decisions at court against the calumnies of Boil and Margarite. "When we arrived in Spanish waters," recounts Michele da Cuneo, "about two hundred Indians died, I believe because the air was colder than they were used to. They were thrown into the sea. Soon afterward we arrived in Cádiz, where we unloaded the slaves, all more or less sick. They are not used to hard labor, suffer from the cold, and do not live long." Don Juan de Fonseca put the survivors up for sale in Seville. Bernáldez says they "were naked as they were born, and no more embarrassed than wild animals. They were not a good buy because they all died since the country did not suit them."

The slaves had embarked on 17 February. Forty days later, on 27 March, occurred the first large, pitched battle between Europeans and native Americans. But first we must discover what led to it. Unlike Guacanagarí, Caonabó was strong, brave, and warlike. He ruled the mountains in the center of the island down to the southern coast. Despite his bellicosity, Caonabó had received two Franciscan missionaries, Giovanni Borgognone and Juan de Tisín, who converted and baptized some of the natives. When Margarite and his men resorted to violence and outright brigandage, Caonabó expelled the missionaries and asked the other caciques to ally themselves with him. Three did so, but Guacanagarí refused even when threatened, whereupon Caonabó invaded his territory, destroying many villages and killing the inhabitants. Guacanagarí saved his life by fleeing.

A vassal to Cacique Guarionex, who ruled the territory around La Isabela, had surrounded and killed ten Spaniards quartered near the Rio Yaque and then burned a large shed that served as a hospital. Forty sick Spanish soldiers died in the fire. Caonabó gathered his warriors and camped near Fort San Tomaso, hoping to surprise the garrison and repeat the tragedy of La Navidad. But Alonso de Hojeda, clearly an outstanding soldier, kept fifty men inside the fortress and was careful to keep an eye on his sentinels, who were always posted, and sent patrols into the woods every night. Realizing the impossibility of scaling the fortress because of its deep moat and the river, Caonabó tried to starve the Spanish. He occupied the surrounding forests, controlled the trails, and placed many warriors where he thought the Spaniards would have to go in search of food. Hojeda did not lose heart. He shortened rations and mounted surprise raids from time to time, slaughtering the Indians. The siege lasted an entire month. His forces depleted by battle, the discomfort of sleeping outside, and sickness, Caonabó finally withdrew, turning his attention to La Isabela.

Before attacking he went through the woods and walked around the town walls at night, searching for the weakest points. He was even so bold as to enter La Isabela in daylight, feigning friendship toward the Spanish. Discovering that La Isabela had no soldiers and that most of the settlers were sick, their morale sapped by dissension, he decided to try to destroy the settlement. But Guacanagarí saved Columbus and the Spanish for the second time. He went to the Admiral, in bed with arthritis, and revealed the plot by the other caciques. Columbus congratulated himself for defending Guacanagarí when his men had wanted to condemn Guacanagarí as a traitor and prepared for the emergency. He sent a small force against the tribes besieging a fort in the interior, defeated them, pursued them into their own lands, and subjugated them. But his most warlike and dangerous enemy, Caonabó, remained. Letting him recover after Hojeda had forced him to retreat was the same as giving him the field for new and desperate reprisals.

Hojeda's boldness and extraordinary courage solved the problem. He proposed capturing Caonabó in his refuge and volunteered to bring him back to La Isabela. Columbus granted him permission to try, and Hojeda left with nine of the bravest caballeros and showy gifts to entice Caonabó. After traveling over sixty leagues, he came to Caonabó's village. Seeing such a small band of

Spaniards, Caonabó suspected nothing and received Hojeda cour-
teously, whose exceptional courage on the battlefield he had
admired. He accepted the gifts and asked the reason for the visit.
Hojeda replied by inviting him to La Isabela, where Caonabó
could personally work out a peace pact with the Admiral, and
promised to work on getting him the church bell. When Caonabó
had explored La Isabela earlier, he had been amazed that the
Angelus called all the Spaniards to church, believing that the bell
had the power to make them obey. Afterwards, he had many times
expressed the desire to carry the bell into the mountains and had
said he would give most anything for it. Hojeda knew of his desire.
Caonabó could not resist the promise of the bell and agreed to go
to La Isabela, but not alone. He was accompanied by a large band
of Indians armed with bows and arrows.

After marching for several days, the group stopped near the Rio
Yaque, where Hojeda carried out his bold plan. Taking Caonabó
aside as if to tell him a secret, Hojeda took two pairs of shackles
from a sack and showed them to him. Caonabó admired their
brightness and asked what they were for. Hojeda replied that they
were the ornaments the Spanish monarchs put on their hands and
feet on formal occasions and proposed that Caonabó present
himself to his people wearing those bracelets and seated on a
horse. At the thought of the surprise he would give his people and
the fame that would be his from riding a fierce beast, as the
Indians believed the horse to be, Caonabó agreed. The Indians ran
around in amazement on seeing their chief adorned with such
brilliant circlets, but they held back from the snorting, pawing
horse. Hojeda turned it in ever-wider circles, creating an open
space as the warriors gradually fell back in fear and amazement.
When he got near the forest he suddenly prodded the horse toward
the Indians, who broke the circle. He made the horse do a slow
caracole and then spurred it into a gallop as soon as the trees
provided cover. His caballeros joined him at full speed and bound
Caonabó with stout ropes. They then rapidly set out for La
Isabela.

Caonabó's capture stirred up surprise and fear but did not put
an end to hostilities. His brother and two other caciques prepared
for revenge. They advanced quickly against La Isabela with a
horde of men. Contemporary historians clearly exaggerate in
speaking of 100,000 warriors, but there were several thousand.

On 24 March 1495 the Admiral left La Isabela with his brother Bartholomew, two hundred infantrymen, and twenty caballeros, armed with crossbows, harquebuses, lances, and swords. Accompanying them were five hundred Indian warriors commanded by Guacanagarí. The two armies met in the Vega Real. Bartholomew Columbus, whom Christopher had placed in command, divided the Spanish in two, placing one part in the open and the other in the woods, and ordered them to surprise the enemy. The Indians, protected in the rear by the mountains, were marching in five groups and preparing to attack when gunfire erupted from the forests on all sides. Many Indians fell, and confusion and terror spread everywhere. The cavalry, under Hojeda, attacked the center and broke through, creating terrible carnage with their swords. The Indians were thrown into confusion and fled. At this point, says Las Casas, the Spaniards used

> their other frightening weapon after the horses: twenty hunting greyhounds. They were unleashed and fell on the Indians at the cry of *Tómalo!* ["Get them!"]. Within an hour they had preyed on one hundred of them. As the Indians were used to going completely naked, it is easy to imagine what the fierce greyhounds did, urged to bite naked bodies and skin much more delicate than that of the wild boars they were used to. . . . This tactic, begun here and invented by the devil, spread throughout these Indies and will end when there is no more land nor people to subjugate and destroy in this part of the world.

It was the first of many "barbarous inventions discovered, applied, and spread for the total destruction of the Indian people."

What a change from the idyllic encounter two years earlier on San Salvador! The battle of the Vega Real marked the decisive turning point in the tragic fate of the Tainos of Haiti. The caciques submitted promptly and unconditionally. To consolidate his victory, Columbus made a triumphal march through the interior, where he oversaw the construction of three new fortresses. Hojeda secured the lines of communication with his cavalry. "The region," writes Don Ferdinand, "remained so peaceful from that time on that a Christian could go wherever he wished alone without fear of disturbance. The Indians themselves conducted him where he pleased, carrying him on their shoulders like pack horses." The entire island was pacified, but at what cost!

Another abuse was now added to the trade in slaves sent to Spain: the tribute system. Every Indian fourteen years old and above had to provide enough gold dust to fill a Flemish hawk's bell every three months. Where there was no gold they could provide an arroba (twenty-five pounds) of spun or woven cotton every three months. When he submitted the tribute each Indian received a stamped brass or copper token to wear around his neck indicating he had paid his obligation.

Guarionex was the only cacique who could meet the first installment of tribute, perhaps exacting from his subjects the mite that had not yet been plundered. The gold necklaces that had so impressed Columbus were in fact the work of whole generations. When the tribute system began, the Spanish had already taken all or nearly all of the Indians' gold. They could obtain more only by washing the sand and gravel of the riverbeds or by an even more laborious and complicated procedure, removing the vegetation from the land and digging until they found gold in the alluvium. The second method was impractical with the Indians' tools. One must realize that to turn the soil for cultivating corn and *yuca* they had only the *coa,* a hardwood stick with a fire-hardened point. The other method, washing sand, takes a tremendous amount of time and requires uncommon patience. The gains are usually modest and unpredictable. Sometimes a person would find a large nugget, but usually the Indians could not produce the amount required. For these reasons, when delivering the first installment of tribute, Guarionex suggested this change to Columbus: he would provide enough *yuca* to feed the entire Spanish population, which in his opinion had more need of food than minerals. The Admiral would not hear of it. He did cut the tribute in half, but even that amount was exorbitant.

Another fatal political—not to mention moral—error resulted from the tribute system. The Indians abandoned their villages and fled to the mountains en masse. The Spanish hunted them down with dogs, while privation and disease decimated those who managed to escape. Hundreds of the poor wretches committed suicide, poisoning themselves with manioc. War, slavery, genocide—the string of tragedies occurred within the space of a few years. By some estimates about 350,000 Tainos lived on Hispaniola when the Spanish arrived. By 1508 there were 60,000, and in 1548 Oviedo estimated that no more than 500 survived on the whole island.

When the errors and crimes—for which Christopher and Bartholomew Columbus were personally responsible—of the first stages of colonization are emphasized, as here, we must not forget the context in which they occurred. Even in the most appalling aspect of the encounter, the sending of slaves to Seville, one must consider the time in which it was done, however repugnant the practice appears today. That is not to say that Columbus was justified because he was merely following the customs of his time. Alessandro Manzoni, commenting on some of Cardinal Federico Borromeo's attitudes toward persecuting and condemning witches, observed, "He who wishes to defend him in this matter uses the excuse that is so common, 'they were errors of his time, not his.' This excuse, when applied after examining the facts, has some, perhaps much, validity. But when applied blindly, as it usually is, it means nothing."

Such an excuse means nothing in Columbus's case. True, not only he but other Genoese, Portuguese, and Florentines, his predecessors and contemporaries, had trafficked and were trafficking in slaves. However, his behavior was unlike theirs because of the developing relationship with the Indians during the first voyage and, until that point, the second also. We should not forget that on 14 October 1492, writing his first thoughts about the new peoples in the *Journal,* he had added this: "If Your Highnesses should order them all carried off to Castile or held as captives on their own island, it could easily be done." *Captives* means slaves, though it is only a hint. The Admiral behaved magnanimously on the first voyage, treating the Indians well, committing no offenses, punishing the outrages of the sailors, and showing some condescension. He definitely considered them inferior—the idea of equality was not congenial to him—but inferior in the sense that children are inferior to adults. He considered them naïve and innocent and treated them accordingly; he continued to do so during the first part of the second voyage. Very different was his behavior toward the cannibals. When the Admiral first thought of taking slaves in the New Lands he was thinking of the wild and fierce Caribs, eaters of human flesh, the bitter enemies of the friendly Tainos. He felt they deserved the harshest punishment, so slavery was appropriate.

Now, however, when at La Isabela he suddenly decided to send slaves to market at Seville, he chose Taino men, women, and children. It is not easy to judge this decision or determine how Columbus came to it. Could he have thought that the Tainos had no right to the respect every human being deserves because they were not baptized? Could he have held—as someone would later try to prove—that the natives did not have an immortal soul like the Europeans? What the Admiral had written and was writing on the subject in the *Journal* and memoranda shows that he did not hold those views, so such answers cannot explain the despicable undertaking.

Another explanation is possible. Until then relations between the Indians and Christians were humane, friendly, and peaceful. Now, since his return to La Isabela, there was war. In the fifteenth century slavery was the traditional, unavoidable result of every war fought outside Christendom. That standard, valid in the relations between Christians and Muslims, he applied to the relations between the Christian Spaniards and the non-Christian Tainos when war broke out between them.

Such considerations explain but do not exonerate. It is more than strange, indeed absurd, that in the last century some French and Genoese historians seriously proposed canonizing Columbus. Some went so far as to suggest that he married Beatriz de Arana and that Ferdinand was therefore legitimate. Even if his personal life were impeccable, however, a man responsible for even some of the crimes perpetrated at La Isabela in 1494 could have no claim to sainthood. Columbus's character was complex. Episodes on the first and second voyages brought out his contradictions, revealing a man open to Christian love and at the same time intent on amassing riches and power for himself and his monarchs. If these human contradictions allow us to remain sympathetic to Columbus for his profound religious faith, problematic political decisions, violent passions, and mystical enthusiasms, they are the contradictions that deny Columbus, matchless sailor that he was, the status of a saint or statesman.

30 | *Humiliating Return to Spain*

On 10 March 1496 the admiral departed for Spain. There he had to defend himself against the accusations of Father Boil, Margarite, and so many others who, disillusioned or sick, had abandoned the Indies to return to their homeland.

When he left on the return voyage, the Admiral charged Bartholomew with building a new capital. Bartholomew went to the southern coast and selected an excellent natural port at the mouth of a river in an exceptionally fertile region bathed by many streams, their sands rich with gold. He named the new settlement Santo Domingo in memory of their father, Domenico. By contrast, Christopher always used names honoring Christianity or Spain. He broke that habit only once, when he named Saona, and that, as he made clear, was to honor Michele da Cuneo, his friend from Savona, not himself or his family. His foreign origin had to be forgotten and his deference to his adopted land total. Bartholomew had no such scruples and wanted to memorialize their father in naming the new capital. Christopher sometimes called it La Isabela Nueva. While the population of old Isabela was declining until the city was completely abandoned, the new one quickly flowered and prospered; it was a true capital. Philip II called it the "ladder, port, and key to all the Indies."

This return crossing turned out to be exceptionally long, ending 11 June in the Bay of Cádiz. With Columbus were 225 Christians and a few survivors among the thirty Indians who had embarked at La Isabela. It is difficult to understand how two little ships, which as a rule carried two dozen sailors, could hold so many people, but that indicates the strength of many Spaniards' desire to leave the Antilles. People who had emigrated in search of the paradise described by Columbus were now returning, their faces and emaciated bodies marked by long suffering.

This time Bernáldez saw the Admiral of the Ocean Sea, Viceroy and Governor of the Indies, "dressed in clothes the color of those worn by observant Franciscans, with the sackcloth habit and cord of St. Francis in fulfillment of a vow." He did wear the cord in fulfillment of a vow, but the habit was the usual sailor's clothes, made of burlap and easily confused with the Franciscan habit. It was, however, modest apparel, appropriate for a crewman but not for an officer and admiral. Nevertheless, hoping to impress when he went to visit the monarchs, he placed a gold chain weighing six hundred castellanos on the neck of Caonabó's son.

The visit to the monarchs was also very different from that after the first voyage. Columbus notified them of his arrival as soon as he disembarked at Cádiz and went to Seville to await their summons. It was a long wait. Boil and Margarite had been plotting at court for months, and now Aguado had joined them with a dossier of denunciations and testimonies. On the subject of Columbus's relations with the Catholic sovereigns, some historians try to contrast Ferdinand's attitude with Isabella's, making him suspicious, intolerant, and hostile while she was sensitive, sympathetic, and admiring. No reliable evidence supports that position.

There is, however, a sound hypothesis that Columbus had more enemies among the Catalans than among the Castilians. Some have even spoken of the Catalan clique at court, not only because of the people involved but because the enterprise of the great discovery was becoming the exclusive achievement of Castilians: "*Por Castilla y por León nuevo mundo halló Colón*" ("Through Castile and León Columbus discovered a new world"). But if Margarite and Father Boil were Catalans, the very hostile Aguado was a Castilian from Seville, as was the goldsmith Zedo. The latter, punished and sent home by the Admiral, had spread the rumor that the nuggets and jewels from Hispaniola were a base alloy. That charge was easily proved a lie, but calumny rides the wind, and not only Zedo's but those of others spread as well. By now the Genoese had lost the support of public opinion. The monarchs still showed esteem and gratitude to him, as is clear from their letter of 12 July 1496, written from Almazán. Courteous and benevolent, it nevertheless postpones the audience. In August Columbus received another, particularly significant letter. In it Isabella sought his counsel on the best course for the ships leaving from the Bay of Biscay with Princess Juana and her entourage, taking her to Flanders to be married to Archduke Philip of Austria. The queen still respected his maritime skill. He made his suggestions immediately, and Isabella's response of 18 August is kind and grateful.

In the fall the monarchs were at Burgos, where they would celebrate another wedding, that of Crown Prince Don Juan to Princess Margaret, daughter of the Holy Roman Emperor Maximilian. There Columbus finally received an audience. The monarchs showed him their affectionate goodwill, rejecting the accusations and calumnies of Father Boil, Margarite, and Aguado. The criticisms, some of which were not without foundation, had not yet destroyed their gratitude and trust. The enemies and detractors had one satisfaction: the withholding of recognition for Bartholomew's title of *adelantado*. Granting that title was not Columbus's privilege but the monarchs'; they would confer it the following year, on 22 July 1497, ignoring the fact that Columbus had bestowed it earlier.

At the first audience in Burgos, Columbus requested ships and supplies for a third voyage. He was pursuing his *idée fixe,* the goal he had not yet reached, India. He had to reach it. They began talking about the third voyage in the fall of 1496, but Columbus faced difficulties and problems far more serious than those surrounding the preparations for the second voyage. In the end his tenacity overcame all obstacles, and on 30 May 1498 he sailed on the third voyage of discovery.

31 | The Treaty of Tordesillas, Ferrer, Vespucci, and the Preparation for the Third Voyage

Columbus would make the crossing of the third voyage much farther to the south. Following the discoveries of Columbus's first voyage and in anticipation of future discoveries, on 7 June 1494 the Treaty of Tordesillas between Spain and Portugal was signed, establishing a line of possession in the Atlantic between east and west. Earlier divisions had always been drawn between north and south.

Columbus proposed that the line be established 100 leagues (about 300 nautical miles) west of the Azores. The pope, in the bull *Inter caetera* (3 May 1493), accepted in its entirety Columbus's proposals made on behalf of Spain. But Portugal protested, and—without Columbus's advice, because he was in the New Lands—Queen Isabella, willful and stubborn as always, did not intend to miss a chance for reconciliation with Spain's Iberian neighbor. And so Spain and Portugal agreed to move the line 270 leagues west, making it 370 leagues west of the Cape Verde Islands. All islands discovered east of that meridian, even by Spanish ships, would belong to Portugal; those discovered west of it, even if discovered by Portuguese ships, would belong to Spain.

The many consequences of the treaty could be the subject of an entire volume. I will mention only that, on the one hand, it did not settle the dispute over discovered lands, which soon became more heated than ever, while on the other hand the simple shifting of the line west from 100 to 370 leagues forced Spain to recognize Portugal's right to Brazil. I would like to stress that an immediate result of the Treaty of Tordesillas was that Columbus's third voyage could begin in a new atmosphere, one of peace. His nagging preoccupations on the first two voyages were gone. Then the Spanish ships could not put in at Madeira, Porto Santo, or the Cape Verde Islands. For the third voyage the accord made these islands available as stations for resting and resupplying.

However, the accord between Portugal and Spain simply made possible Columbus's choice of a new route; it did not determine it. Something else, ignored by most Columbus scholars, influenced Columbus. I am referring to the theories of a Catalan cosmographer, Jaime Ferrer, and to his correspondence with Columbus. Ferrer's influence on the Columbian discoveries cannot be compared with Toscanelli's, but it is significant enough to merit more than a hint or vague reference. Jaime Ferrer was born about 1445 at Vidreras, not far from Blanes in the Catalan province of Girona. When very young he was taken to Naples, where a Juan Ferrer was the royal treasurer and Ippolito Ferrer the King's jeweler. They were probably related to Jaime. Jaime Ferrer was not self-taught. Earning the title of lapidary (jeweler) required study, and the learning Ferrer exhibited in cosmography, in turn dependent on knowledge of mathematics and astronomy, would be hard to explain without the equivalent of a university education today.

Extant documents make it clear that Jaime Ferrer was at the royal palace in Naples as early as 1466. In 1469 he was treasurer on board the ships sent to Catalonia to aid the king of Aragon; in the royal memorandum of appointment his name appears in the Italian form, Giacomo. Soon he took up the calling of lapidary again, going to Cairo, Damascus, Rhodes, Jaffa, Beirut, Venice, and Rome to buy precious stones. He enjoyed the trust of Ferdinand I of Naples and was involved in transporting artillery to Abruzzo and purchasing wine and gunpowder for the fleet. In 1488 he was in the service of Queen Giovanna. He had by this time acquired a considerable fortune and was more than a jeweler: he was a counselor entrusted with delicate missions. That same year, he left Naples with Ambassador Giovanni Galiano. At Genoa he saw the relic of the Holy Basin in the rich and splendid cathedral chapel, recently built through renewed interest in crusades. He reached Spain and probably settled there, living in Blanes, a charming town on the east coast of Catalonia about forty miles from Barcelona. At Barcelona, which he visited frequently, he probably witnessed Columbus's triumphal return in April 1493.

We are certain that Ferrer was a cosmographer known and valued at court, evident from a letter to him, dated 23 August 1493, by the Cardinal Mendoza, primate of Spain:

> To Jaime Ferrer, our especial friend. We desire to speak with you about certain courses of action, and therefore we request you, when you see this our letter, to come here to Barcelona, bringing your globe and other instruments you may have pertaining to cosmography.

From the letter one can deduce that Ferrer had previous contacts with Cardinal Mendoza. It also reveals a quite lively interest by the "second king" in cosmographic subjects, an interest undoubtedly due to Columbus's Atlantic discoveries.

Interest also grew at court with the Treaty of Tordesillas. Some considered the treaty a diplomatic success, others a capitulation to the Portuguese. The monarchs were troubled. They invited Ferrer to court to give an enlightened opinion on the matter that was beginning to bother them, the real results of the Treaty of Tordesillas. Ferrer indicated two methods, theoretical and practical, for determining the much-discussed line and showed sincere appreciation of Columbus and his accomplishments. After hearing Ferrer's judgment, Isabella suggested that he write directly to the Admiral. Ferrer's letter, dated 5 August 1495, merits thorough discussion.

Ferrer says, "Our Lady the Queen has ordered me to write you of my propositions and ideas." He agrees with Columbus that the discovered lands are Asia, where, he says, St. Thomas the Apostle is buried. This opinion confirms that Columbus's error was more than validated by the science of the time, no matter how unjustified by experience, as has already been discussed. Not just Toscanelli but the whole cosmographic science of the time was responsible. Ferrer continues as follows:

> I maintain that beyond the equator are choice and valuable things, such as precious stones, gold, spices, and drugs. I say

so from my great experience in the Levant, from Cairo to Damascus. A conviction I developed from many Indians, Arabs, and Ethiopians was that most precious things come from the hottest regions, where the inhabitants are black or dark brown. Therefore, in my opinion, until Your Grace finds such people you will not find an abundance of riches. I know very well that you know all this since you have more awareness asleep than I have awake. Nevertheless, Your Grace will take good care so that God will be served and our monarchs satisfied.

The letter is addressed *"Al muy magnífico y spetable Señor Almirante de las Indias. En la gran Isla de Cibau."* We do not know whether it reached Columbus on Hispaniola or when he returned to Spain. Because the queen was the intermediary in the correspondence, we can be sure not only that the letter arrived at its destination but also that the Catalan cosmographer and the Admiral met and understood each other. They did so because they shared a rigorously Catholic and mystical conception of the world, the cosmographic theory that located Asia beyond the Atlantic, a passion for geography, and a strong interest in precious stones. Finally, the long years Ferrer had spent in Italy gave him something in common with the Genoa-born Admiral, reducing the barriers that divided peoples and cultures despite their common Christian roots.

The two men, then, met, understood, and influenced each other. Columbus was already stubbornly convinced that Cuba, Hispaniola, and Jamaica were Asia; Ferrer reinforced that conviction. Columbus had always wanted to find gold and precious stones in Asia; Ferrer, a lapidary, as he emphasized in his letters, helped feed that desire. Columbus had always harbored the thought that the greatest riches of the Orient were in India, that is, south of Cuba and Hispaniola. Ferrer confirmed that by citing the testimony of the Indians, Arabs, and Ethiopians he had met in Cairo and Damascus, the two great gateways to the Orient east of Chios, that other gateway, which had excited the first dreams in the young Christopher.

Ferrer's confirmation was decisive. Hadn't Columbus perhaps already thought of leaving from the Cape Verde Islands when he presented his project to King John? He had left from the Canaries on the first and second crossings to avoid trouble with the Portuguese. Now the Treaty of Tordesillas removed his concerns, enabling him to call at the Cape Verde Islands and from there sail southwest, as Las Casas says, "to the south of the equinoctial line. The Admiral says that below that parallel are found more gold and things of value." Jaime Ferrer, the Catalan cosmographer and jeweler overlooked far too long in Columbian historiography, had made the same suggestion in nearly the same words.

There is no doubt that Jaime Ferrer had a significant influence on the planning of the third voyage. We cannot be as certain about Amerigo Vespucci's influence. It is well to speak of him, however, because he too was involved in the preparations for the expedition and because, Vespucci being the other leading protagonist in the events that would change the course of history, it is advisable to establish the truth about the relationship between the two navigators.

First, few people besides Columbus scholars know that Columbus and Vespucci not only knew each other but were friends. As early as 1492, if not before, Vespucci was Gianotti Berardi's right arm. We know about the financial relationship, not to mention friendship, between Berardi and Columbus, so it is obvious that Vespucci was also involved to some extent since his employer, Berardi, and other shipowners, probably including the Ibarras, were organizing the fleet for the second voyage.

In 1495 Berardi died, naming Vespucci the executor of his will and head of his firm. That is when we find Columbus and Vespucci at each other's side in the preparations for the third voyage of the great discovery. We find them sharing financial interests (those established between Columbus and Berardi), impelled by the same passion (a need to discover, an avid curiosity about new things), and bound by mutual respect and friendship. A letter dated 5 February 1505 from the Admiral to his son Diego is incontrovertible evidence of friendship and respect:

> Amerigo Vespucci has always behaved properly toward me; he is a very honest man. . . . Now he is going to court on my behalf with a great desire to help me, determined to do everything possible for me. . . . See that you profit by working with him, because he will translate his words into deeds and do everything, even operating secretly so as not to arouse suspi-

cion. I told him everything that could be useful in my cause and informed him of the treatment I have received and still receive.

Columbus is moody and suspicious toward the court—as usual, and with justification—but trusting and grateful toward Vespucci. His feelings frustrate any attempt to find rivalry or hostility between the two great navigators.

The Admiral of the Ocean Sea and the manager of the Florentine firm both felt driven to make discoveries. It is difficult to know if Vespucci caught the passion for navigation and discovery from Columbus or if it grew on its own in his ardent spirit, fed by the feverish atmosphere after Easter 1493 in Seville, the Spanish gateway to the Atlantic and point of departure from Europe for the New Lands beyond the Ocean. Both Vespucci's position—overseeing the furnishing and outfitting of the ships and providing maps and instruments for the Atlantic voyages—and continuing news about the marvels of the New Lands may have stimulated his desire for the maritime career that would be so brilliant.

Vespucci made two expeditions that decisively affected the discovery of the continents named for him. There are conflicting opinions on the first, which went to Guyana in 1499, commanded by Hojeda. According to some, Hojeda and Juan de la Cosa took two ships to the north while Vespucci took two others south and reached the mouth of the Amazon River. That is only speculation. There is no doubt about the second expedition, in 1501. Vespucci reached the coast of Brazil at the equator and followed it beyond 32° S, probably as far as 50° S.

Twelve years would pass before Balboa crossed the Isthmus of Panama and Europeans realized that another ocean lay between the New Lands and Asia. Nevertheless, Vespucci coasted a continent to a latitude farther south than had ever been reached before—farther south than the Cape of Good Hope, rounded by Bartolomeu Dias—yet he found none of the signs that should have proved it was Asia. Thus, his voyage started the realization that the New Lands were a continental mass completely independent of Asia. Columbus sensed as much but blocked the thought, and so Vespucci received the glory, not unfairly.

We are concerned here with the preparation for Columbus's third voyage. The gratitude Columbus shows in his letter of 1505 assures us that Vespucci fulfilled his obligations for finances and organization. But it is not unrealistic to suggest that he did something more; namely, that he contributed to Columbus's choice of the new southern route. There are no documents to this effect, but our earlier considerations support the hypothesis that before facing the Atlantic Vespucci was aware of what Jaime Ferrer had written to Columbus: "Beyond the equator are choice and valuable things, such as precious stones, gold, spices, and drugs. . . . Most things of exceptional value come from the hottest regions." We may suppose that since 1496, when he was managing the ship chandlery firm, Vespucci had had in mind a course of action he would follow without deviation in his voyages and that he may have shared his thoughts with his friend Columbus, helping point him to the new route that Ferrer suggested and the Treaty of Tordesillas now permitted.

32 | "Another World"

August 1498 is another key moment in the great discovery: Columbus reached a large continent to the south, opposite Africa and not Africa, Asia, or, obviously, Europe. It is not a parched, arid, uninhabitable land but pleasant and beautiful, fertile, lush, and populated, with an abundance of water. The water, the great river flowing from the south, indicates beyond doubt that it is a real, true continent. It is, then, a fourth continent, the existence of which the Old World and the Middle Ages, Christendom, Islam, India, and China had been unaware. A fourth continent, absolutely unknown, whose inhabitants in turn were ignorant of the existence of the other three.

In August 1498, then, occurred the most profound upheaval in the science of cosmography. As happened with the most momentous encounter in history between peoples, that of 1492, so too the greatest revolution in geography would scarcely reveal itself, would be only partially recognized and unveiled by Columbus.

In stark contrast with his behavior at San Salvador, Columbus was timid and uneasy in Venezuelan waters. He seemed to react negatively to the fabulous news, as if wishing to refute the discovery, which was clear and indisputable, right in front of his eyes.

His observations and references overlap in confused, often contradictory ways. Confusion, uncertainty, and perplexity came from two related causes. The first involves Columbus's personality. I have already said that Columbus belonged to both the modern era and the Middle Ages. He was modern when he studied the diversity of nature. He was medieval when he moved, or tried to move, from experience to dogma, when from empirical facts he tried to deduce laws and general principles, when from particulars he sought to rise to the universal. In geography, especially nautical science, Columbus, although self-taught, was an expert. Even with the limitations of his time and of the instruments available to him he had a formidable grasp of modern methods. But when he moved from particulars to general geography he immediately revealed he was handicapped by preconceptions from the Middle Ages, proving himself thoroughly medieval when venturing into cosmography, philosophy, and theology.

The other cause of some of the confusion and contradiction at this key moment in the great discovery was Columbus's physical condition. He had not been well when he left Seville. Gout was beginning to afflict him; it would plague him terribly on the fourth voyage. In addition, the torrid climate of the Cape Verde Islands and the eight days of calm in mid-Atlantic near the equator had given him severe ophthalmia. He was responsible for the course and normally trusted no one else, always relying solely on his own vision, which was exceptionally keen and accurate. Thus, he ruined his sight by constantly gazing over the prow at the horizon, in the morning, with the sun over his shoulder but the light intense and burning; in the afternoon, when the westward course made him gaze directly into the sun; and even in the moonless nights, when only starlight brightened the dark waves sheared by the keel.

Columbus's eyes were swollen, weeping, and bloodshot. When he reached land he could not see all he should have. He could not see details that would have helped him better understand the place, could not make the observations that on the other two voyages he had personally verified and investigated. He did not even write the *Journal* but probably dictated it, or perhaps it was transcribed from what he said. Much of what was recorded came not from his own experience but from that of others.

The scene for the great discovery of August 1498 was the Gulf of Paria. I have crossed and recrossed the Gulf by boat, airplane, and helicopter, stopping at various points on the coasts and going some distance up the main channel and the most important smaller ones. Only with the aid of topographic charts from the Venezuelan Military Geographic Institute and suggestions from local experts—mayors, boatswains, and fishermen—was I able to form a clear picture of the geography of the area. As a result I can appreciate the immense difficulty for the Spanish sailors and their Admiral in trying to determine whether they had really reached the mainland. I can also appreciate how that situation could so confuse Columbus, leading to a profusion of hypotheses and considerations in the *Journal*, some of them to the point, some fantastic, many contradictory.

Here are the phases and dates of the process by which Columbus, after his first contact with the South American mainland, became aware that he really had discovered a continent.

Wednesday, 1 August 1498: For the first time the sailors on the three ships see South America. No one imagines it is a continent. Columbus names it Isla Sancta ("Holy Island").

Saturday, 4 August: The three ships anchor at the edge of the Paria Peninsula, on the coast of the mainland, but all believe the peninsula an island. Columbus names it Isla de Gracia ("Island of Grace") in honor of the mother of Monsignor Geraldini, a staunch supporter of his at the Spanish court.

Monday, 6 August: The Spanish take possession at Güiria, but no one thinks he is on the mainland, much less a new continent. The Admiral does not even leave the ship. Captain Pedro de Terreros is convinced he is taking possession of an island.

Wednesday, 8 August: The ships anchor before a large Indian village near Irapa. There are many encounters between Columbus and the Indians. Their culture is superior to that of the Tainos of Hispaniola, Cuba, and Jamaica, but the Admiral seems not to realize it. The water is muddy and brackish. Columbus continues to believe Paria is an island.

Saturday, 11 August: A caravel sent ahead to explore returns. The sailors are convinced that the fresh water comes from an enormous river and that therefore "those lands, which seemed to be islands, were all one continental mass." Columbus cannot believe it because "he has never heard tell" of such a mass of fresh

197

water carried even by the largest rivers on earth, the Nile, the Euphrates, and the Ganges. In any case, he cannot continue because of the shallows, so he turns back.

Sunday, 12 August: After coasting the southern shores of the Paria Peninsula, which he still considers an island, Columbus anchors at the northeastern point of Venezuela.

Monday, 13 August: The ships begin to sail along the northern coast of Paria, from east to west. Columbus hopes to reach the western end of Paria, which he still believes is an island. As Las Casas comments, "The reason driving him on was that he had not seen lands extensive enough to produce rivers that large, *'unless,'* says the Admiral, *'this is terra firma.'* These are his words" (emphasis added). Only on 13 August, then, did the suspicion that it was a continent finally begin to take root in Columbus's mind.

Tuesday, 14 August: "Yesterday and today the Admiral proceeded thirty or forty leagues. He verified that the northern coast extended farther west than did the southern one, so the gulf south of Paria did not have an outlet to the north. Thus he realized that a land so large was not an island but a continent" (Las Casas). Experience prevails over false science at last. Science was wrong about the size of the other great rivers, which Columbus had not seen and so could not know how much water they carry at their mouths, a volume difficult for a European to comprehend. On 13 and 14 August his three ships went twice as far on the northern coast as they had inside the gulf south of the peninsula, and there was no sign of a channel leading from north to south.

Columbus's estimate is correct: the gulf penetrates south of Paria Peninsula over 55 miles; when he decided to abandon the coast and head north on 15 August, he had sailed 110 miles along the northern Venezuelan coast, and he could see another 55 miles to the west. There could no longer be any doubt that Paria was terra firma. The fresh water in the gulf, as the sailors had said, came from an enormous river to the southwest. But what large Asian river could possibly flow north and empty into the sea near the equator? None. Therefore, the land could not be Asia.

Was it then a fourth continent? Columbus did not dare say so. He did not dare set himself against medieval cosmography and the geographic wisdom of his time. However, he was now certain. With a rapid about-face typical of geniuses, he went from disbelief to doubt to certainty. On the evening of 14 August and the morning of 15 August, his ship running swiftly on a calm sea, he wrote or dictated in his cabin, as if he were standing before the monarchs, the first account of the great news: "I believe that this is a most extensive mainland, which no one knew about until today. I am strongly led to believe this by the river which is so large and the fresh water in the sea." Columbus would meditate on this important news during the following nights and days.

17 August 1498: By evening the ships have run thirty-seven leagues. Columbus has meditated, and his imagination suggests a hypothesis: Could it not be a vast land south of the equator which he saw, the source of the mass of water? Could it be that the earthly paradise, which medieval doctrine located in the east, was in the southern hemisphere? Here is the passage in Las Casas: "He says the land he reached is a large mainland, or the place of the earthly paradise, *'because everyone says,'* he says, *'that it is at the end of the Orient, and this is it,'* he says." The italics are mine; the quotation marks and the repeated *he says* are Las Casas's, used to give full credit for the hypothesis to its author, Columbus.

It is a hypothesis, not a categorical assertion. There is no need to confuse or associate Columbus's hypothesis with that of Dante, who located purgatory in the southern hemisphere on a mountain emerging from the Dark Sea. While Dante's poetic imagination infuses into the terrestrial reality of the Ocean the transcendent mystery of the beyond, Columbus is not referring to the paradise of the other world but to the earthly paradise, whose existence was assumed since ancient times. But why did Columbus not consider the simplest and most immediate explanation, that this would have to be a fourth continent, instead of resorting to hypotheses provided by medieval culture? Because the dominant geographical conception of the second half of the fifteenth century ruled out the existence of a fourth continent.

The depth of Columbus's desire not to stray far from cosmographic orthodoxy clearly emerges from his letter to Ferdinand and Isabella of 7 July 1503, in which he speaks of "the site of the earthly paradise, which Holy Church approves." The last clause explains what lay behind the difficulty and hesitation he exhibited in the face of the reality of a fourth continent. The earthly paradise found certain support in Church doctrine, but there was no room in the accepted cosmography of the Middle Ages for a fourth continent. The bond between cosmography and theology was exceedingly tight, and so Columbus was making sure he would not be charged with heresy.

That he was uncertain, that he had doubts is clear from his own words: "If instead this water does not come from the terrestrial paradise it comes from a vast land in the southern hemisphere, of which until now we have had no knowledge." Taking up this theme again in the letter of 1503 to the Catholic sovereigns, he would write as follows: "Your Highnesses possess here another world." What is "another world" if not a fourth continent?

33 | A Mysterious Intuition

O n the night of 16 August Columbus sailed from Venezuela—Margarita Island to be precise—for Hispaniola. Even though in waters new to him, with his sixth sense for things maritime he accurately calculated the correct route to the northwest. That night the compass needles suddenly declined a point and a half to the west, some of them two points. The Admiral also noticed, writes Las Casas, that at this latitude Polaris was 14° above the horizon when the Guards were two and a half hours past the head.[1] They reached that point at 6:30 P.M., a bit too early to be observed, especially by a man suffering from ophthalmia. If we accept the observation, Columbus should have been at latitude 15°N. At nightfall on 16 August, however, the fleet was near 13°N. Columbus's error would therefore have been minimal, no more than two degrees, perhaps less.

Why did the needles not decline to the northwest until that moment? Columbus compared this observation with the one he had made in the doldrums on the same voyage, when he had found a deviation of five degrees in the polestar. On earlier voyages, made in latitudes much farther north, he had found a deviation of two and a half degrees. As a result of this inference, Columbus

[1]See Samuel Eliot Morison, *Admiral of the Ocean Sea* (Boston: 1942), 169–70.

hypothesized that the earth was not a perfect sphere. As he wrote to the monarchs,

> I have always read that the world, land and water, is spherical; the authority and experience of Ptolemy and all the others demonstrate that. Now, however, I have perceived a great deformity, and I have discovered that it is not round, as is written, but rather shaped like a pear, very round except for the stem end, which is a bit raised, or like a ball with one spot like a woman's breast. That stem end would be the highest and closest to heaven and it would be found under the equinoctial line, in this Ocean Sea at the limit of the Orient.
>
> In crossing the north-south line that passes one hundred leagues west of the Azores the ships are raised gently toward heaven, and so there is a more temperate climate. The compass needle varies a point due to the mildness of the climate, and the farther one goes to the northwest the more the ships are raised. The closer it is to the equinoctial line the higher one goes up and the greater the difference between Polaris and the Guards in the circle they describe.

For a long time these ideas seemed bizarre, the fruit of a naïve imagination, early science fiction. It was only in the twentieth century that research in geodetic studies and evidence from satellites gave unexpected support to Columbus.

On 29 December 1958 J. A. O'Keefe and A. Eckels, astronomers at the Harvard College Observatory, disclosed that, in the light of information from the *Vanguard* satellite received at Goddard Space Center, the traditional conception of the earth's shape had to be revised: it is shaped like a pear, with high points at the equator. This news was fully confirmed on 19 June 1959.[2]

How Columbus realized it in 1498 is a fascinating mystery. In his time there were still many who believed the earth was flat, while scientists and scholars all held that it was perfectly spherical. No one—learned, cultivated, or ignorant—doubted that the sun revolved around the earth. Was it intuition? Presentiment? Lucky imagination coinciding with reality, a reality that would be scientifically confirmed only centuries later? It is certain that, strictly

[2]See J. A. O'Keefe, A. Eckels, and R. K. Squires, "The Gravitational Field of the Earth," *Astronomical Journal* 64(1959): 245–53.

speaking, a scientific discovery cannot be attributed to Columbus. Only exact measurements since his time have produced evidence that the earth is not a perfect sphere and the equator is not a circle but an ellipse.

The polar crushing or flattening is very slight $(1/298)$,[3] imperceptible to the eye and even with the instruments available to Columbus. Equally small and indeterminable, both by sight and the instruments of Columbus's time, are the other anomalies in the earth's surface, its pear shape and the ellipticity of the equator. How Columbus reached this insight is, then, nearly unfathomable. Similarly, he was the first to realize that ocean currents flowing from east to west erode land from the western shore of the Ocean, explaining the many islands there. Columbus observed the strength of the currents and concluded that a strong current from east to west had cut the island of Trinidad off from the mainland and formed many little islands from what were originally inlets and jutting rocks along the mainland. He came to this conclusion on emerging from the Gulf of Paria and sailing into the Caribbean Sea, with its many islands. "I am certain," he wrote, "that the waters of the sea direct their course from east to west, following the heavens, and that in this area, when they pass by, they have a greater velocity." In a primitive way he has described the phenomenon exactly. Following Ptolemy, Columbus attributed the direction and force of that current to inertia resulting from the apparent movement of the heavens; today we explain it in the same way, substituting terrestrial rotation for celestial.

---

[3] $s = (a-b)/a$, where a and b are equatorial and polar semiaxes, respectively, of the ellipsoid (the polar semiaxis is the shorter of the two).

34 | Coup d'État at Santo Domingo

On 31 August 1498 the three ships reached Santo Domingo, the new center of the colony on Hispaniola. The Spaniards had split into two factions, and the situation was explosive. For all practical purposes the island had two governors. Those in both camps were fed by the Indians under their control. Bartholomew's group governed the central and southern part of Hispaniola, and the rebels, led by Francisco Roldán, held the west, which included Yaragua, Behechio's region.

Columbus had obtained a reaffirmation of the monarchs' trust at court. He could not allow the situation to degenerate further; to do so would prevent him from realizing the ambitious plans for colonizing the island that he and the monarchs had worked out. On the other hand, crushing the rebellion was difficult if not impossible, for it was not feasible to engage the rebels in battle. That sad truth was well understood by the commander of the fortress of Bonao, or Concepción, in the interior, Miguel de Ballester, who had remained faithful to the Columbuses. He urged an agreement with Roldán that would allow as many to return to Castile as wanted to go.

But Roldán demanded much more. After long negotiations between Ballester and the rebel leaders, they agreed on a set of conditions. There was little time and the interests of the Crown were in jeopardy, so Columbus had no choice but to allow Ballester to settle the differences "in whatever way" he could, which meant accepting the entire package of demands. He confirmed Roldán in the title of *alcalde mayor* of Hispaniola and paid back wages to the rebels who had not worked. Those who did not want to stay on the island had permission to leave at the first opportunity. This was at the end of 1498.

The most important aspect of the agreement between Columbus and Roldán—a peace that smells of complicity—is that it sanctioned what would form the basis of Spanish colonial policy in America. Columbus had arrived in Hispaniola with a letter patent from the monarchs, dated 22 July 1497, authorizing him to divide the land among the colonists—land, not Indians. Now, however, he was committed to distributing not so much land—which the colonists had already taken possession of, with or without official title—as the Indians' labor. The Indians were now reduced to the status of serfs in medieval Europe. That kind of servitude was not approved by the Crown, which would have wanted to consider the Indians free vassals. But the system begun at this time continued; Don Nicolás de Ovando, who in 1501 became governor of Hispaniola, obtained legal recognition for it in 1503. It is the *encomienda* ("commission") system, which spread throughout the Antilles and the Caribbean mainland. Cortés introduced it into New Spain (Mexico), where the Indian villages kept their lands, at least in principle, but paid a large tribute in money and products to the *encomendero* ("colonist" or "master"). The institution of the *encomienda,* clearly inspired by the Middle Ages, had its roots in the practice of the military orders of medieval Spain.

These developments merit comment. Columbus, a man halfway between the Middle Ages and the Renaissance, held economic ideas looking more toward the Middle Ages. In Genoa, Portugal, Valencia, and Catalonia, mercantilism, or nascent capitalism, was already flourishing. Columbus was a typical mercantilist, dealing in percentages, shares, interest, and profits with the monarchs of Spain and their ministers, with his Genoese compatriots, with Florentines, and converted Jews. In 1499–1500 at Santo Domingo, when he had to choose a politico-economic system for the New Lands, Columbus was caught between his internal quarrels with the colonists and the first Castilian conquistadors. Lacking political skills equal to his maritime abilities, he felt constrained to institute the familiar *encomienda,* the "medieval inheritance," as the Mexican historian Weckmann Muñoz calls it. The *encomendero* had and would have for centuries in the Spanish American empire the same rights over his Indian laborers as feudal lords of the Middle Ages exercised over their serfs. The Indians were not slaves that could be sold—as they were in the Portuguese, English, and Dutch colonies, already capitalistic or mercantilistic—but serfs tied to the land. The institution was morally worse than slavery. It was a return to the past, not a step toward the modern age, when the disgraceful institution of slavery would be abolished.

Malcontents with access to the royal ears depicted him as a tyrant. Peter Martyr reports that the three Columbus brothers, especially Bartholomew, were accused of being "unjust men, cruel enemies and shedders of Spanish blood" always ready "to torture, hang, and decapitate."

Don Ferdinand recalls bitterly how, in the summer of 1500, over fifty colonists who had returned to Spain went to the court in the Alhambra, shouting out that Their Highnesses and the Admiral had not paid them:

> Their impudence was so great that, if the Catholic king went out, all would surround him, crying "Pay! Pay!" . . . And if by chance my brother and I, who were pages to the Most Serene Queen, passed them, they cried out to heaven and harassed us, saying "There are the sons of the Admiral of the Gnats, who found lands of vanity and deception to be the sorrow and grave of Castilian gentlemen." They added other wicked things, and we carefully avoided going near them.

It was not easy for the monarchs, thousands of miles from the new possessions, to reach a decision. Columbus, both judge and accused, was not capable of deciding who was right and who wrong. A chief investigator was needed, and they chose Francisco de Bobadilla, knight of the Order of Calatrava. They ordered him to punish the culprits in the rebellion and to take command of the island from Columbus.

Their motive was as precise as it was simple: Columbus was an obstacle to Spanish expansion in the New Lands, an obstacle created by the unlimited privileges they had granted him at Santa Fe and his equally unlimited egoism. If the Capitulations had remained in force, the Crown would have found it impossible to authorize legitimately any new explorations on its own behalf in the increasingly vast regions that were opening up for profitable investment. In 1499 bankers and merchants in Seville were considering joint ventures with the Crown if it could give them a lucrative share in the profits of future expeditions and consequent discoveries. Four expeditions were being prepared for the continent and the Antilles. It was practically impossible to carry out voyages without stopping, both coming and going, at Hispaniola, which, in the plans the Crown had developed with Columbus himself, was becoming the supply center as well as stopover and staging area for all exploration and conquest. Santo Domingo was the only port capable of giving logistic support to all undertakings in the Indies. If Columbus remained in command of Hispaniola, absolute viceroy "of all lands discovered and to be discovered," none of those undertakings could be carried out without his assent. And considering his personality, he probably would not have consented often.

Some of the concessions already made to Hojeda and Pero Alonso Niño and to Vicente Yáñez Pinzón and Juan de la Cosa violated the original contract between Columbus and the Crown. The fact that these authorizations were sent with Francisco de Bobadilla's credentials reveals the monarchs' intentions. I will discuss these concessions and those of the resultant expeditions below, and we will see how essential they are for understanding the episode of Santo Domingo, which ended with Columbus's arrest and return to Spain in irons.

This dramatic episode had a tremendous repercussion. The protagonist, the hero, of the grand discovery in chains! The man who gave Spain dominion over nearly half the world imprisoned! One immediately feels indignation, criticizing and condemning Francisco de Bobadilla, the villain in this drama of bleak, sad scenes. Such an interpretation is too simplistic. Historians bent on justifying Bobadilla's actions stress the cruelties under the three Columbuses. "At various points in the city, gibbets stood, always with their human cluster hanging down. . . . Bobadilla first saw Santo Domingo just after two men had been hanged.

Five more awaited hanging the next day." Everyone accused Columbus and his brothers of treason. "He wanted to give the island to Genoa," says Bernáldez. Years later the Hieronymite friars would write that the ills of Hispaniola stemmed from Columbus's time, who discovered it "to fulfill some agreements he had with Genoa."

The fact that Columbus was a foreigner of humble origin is significant. Less weight should be given to the charge of cruelty, because Ovando, who succeeded Bobadilla, acted with greater severity than did Columbus toward both the Indians and the colonists. Oviedo says that anyone who governed Hispaniola then would have had to have been "angelic and superhuman" to do a good job. Las Casas defends Columbus and rejects most of the charges; he even tries to justify the Spanish. He observes that the three brothers did not display the modesty and discretion they should have as foreigners and that they placed themselves in the wrong by distributing the supplies sent from Spain unequally, using them to reward friends and punish enemies. In explaining Bobadilla's harshness, Las Casas gives particular weight to Diego's refusal to surrender the fortress. Diego offended the monarchs' envoy by rudely telling him his brother's powers and warrants were "better and more guaranteed."

One could probe at length the causes and wrongs of this complex and dramatic episode, but that path does not seem to be the correct one for reaching an unbiased judgment. Francisco de Bobadilla does not seem to have been a depraved, malicious tyrant. Oviedo says he was "an old knight, a very honest and religious man." Bobadilla used force to remove Columbus and his brothers from the government of the island because he had no choice. In the fact of the obstinacy of the Columbus brothers, imprisoning them was a necessary step in making the enterprise of the grand discovery produce concrete results for the benefit of Spain. The benefit of Spain is the only key to the whole episode. As mentioned, it was necessary to cancel the Capitulations of Santa Fe, by which the administration and revenues of the New Lands would have been divided in a limited partnership between the monarchs and the Columbus family. It was necessary to substitute for this strange partnership the state alone, represented by the Crown alone.

Bobadilla put Columbus in prison and sent him to Spain in irons for the same reason that he succeeded him in the government of Hispaniola, the linchpin of the New Lands: he was a representative of the state, a functionary of the monarchs. It was a true coup d'état, and coups are always the same, whether in the fifteenth century or the twentieth: they are conducted by force. Francisco de Bobadilla was, in his own way, a servant of the state. If anything, one should ask whether the state—personified in the monarchs, and in this episode especially by Ferdinand—could not have used some other means to bring about the new regime in the discovered lands, could not have worked with Columbus, recognizing how very much it owed him for the outstanding services he had rendered. But history is not made of *ifs*, and history records that Columbus tried in vain to resist. He had no popular support on Hispaniola; and his enemies supported Bobadilla, hoping to gain for themselves his offices. At the beginning of October 1500, Columbus left Santo Domingo in chains. He would return only in death. It had been a coup, but the following incident shows the Spanish were not as cruel and wicked toward the Genoese as some would have it. No sooner had the ship Columbus was on, *La Gorda*, left port than the captain, evidently on orders from Bobadilla himself, offered to unchain Columbus. Columbus refused; he had been put in chains in the name of the monarchs and so he would stay until Isabella and Ferdinand personally ordered their removal. The crossing was swift and without incident. Sometime between 20 and 25 November 1500, *La Gorda* entered the port of Cádiz. It is mere legend that on the return Columbus was often mocked and mistreated. Neither Alonso de Vallejo nor Andrea Martín, owner of *La Gorda*, nor the other men on board were disrespectful to the Admiral in the least. On the contrary, they treated him and his two brothers, also prisoners, with the greatest respect.

As soon as they landed at Cádiz, Columbus, still voluntarily in chains, wrote a long letter to Doña Juana de Torres, former nurse to the Infante Don Juan, an intimate of Queen Isabella, and the sister of Antonio de Torres, second-in-command on the second voyage. Doña Juana was a friend and protector of Columbus from the time he came to court seeking approval from the monarchs for his grand design. The letter, filled with profound melancholy, is disorganized, a medley of indignation, resignation, wounded self-esteem, pride, and evangelical humility. Its tone, however, is genuinely sincere. It is the cry of one who is aware of having rendered services to Spain and Christianity for which adequate recompense does not exist, the lament of a soul exasperated by injustice but still able to trust fully in Divine Providence, whose aid for the innocent oppressed by evil must come only in time.

The old and faithful friend had influence with the queen, and the monarchs ordered that the Columbus brothers be set free immediately. At the same time, the queen sent a letter to the Admiral, also signed by the king, deploring the injuries suffered by his person and dignity. She went on to say that the royal orders had not been interpreted according to the intentions with which they had been made. Columbus was invited to go as soon as possible to Granada with his brothers, where they would be received in a formal public audience. The Columbuses were sent two thousand gold ducats so they could buy suitable clothes.

On 17 December 1500 Christopher, Bartholomew, and Diego Columbus presented themselves at court, in the Alhambra in Granada. The Queen granted them a special audience. According to legend Isabella was the tenacious and faithful protector of the Genoese whereas King Ferdinand was a treacherous simulator, essentially an enemy. That portrayal has a grain of truth in it. In the private audience Columbus apparently fell on his knees and burst into a flood of tears, to which Isabella added hers. On this occasion Columbus had at least two consolations for his wounded pride. The most important was to see the voluminous legal proceedings against him destroyed before his eyes, so there would be no more talk about it. The second was the clear royal intention to revoke Bobadilla's power as governor and recall him to Spain.

The monarchs would not, however, reinstate Columbus, naming an interim governor instead. It was good that the Admiral, after the emotional upheavals he had endured, could rest and try to regain his health. And with the passage of time discontent among the colonists would die down. Thus, Bobadilla was recalled, but Columbus was not reinstated in his rights, privileges, and offices in the lands he had discovered. Everything, then, would not be as it was before 1500. A coup had taken place on Hispaniola, and since it promoted the interests of the Spanish state the monarchs could not disavow it. No matter how great her esteem, affection, and even gratitude for the foreign Discoverer, Isabella's first duty was to carry out her responsibilities as queen, and the interests of the state did not permit a return to the bizarre joint ownership established by the Capitulations of Santa Fe.

Meanwhile, the Catholic monarchs were absorbed by much more pressing matters: war with the Turks, in which Venice was involved, and struggles with the French over the Kingdom of Naples. Time passed, bringing new and enervating delays. The Columbian route, which the monarchs had been bound to keep secret to secure the monopoly to the Crown and Columbus and his heirs, became public knowledge. I have already said that some people who had accompanied the Genoese on his voyages— Vicente Yáñez Pinzón, Pero Alonso Niño, Juan de la Cosa, and Alonso de Hojeda—requested and obtained royal permission to carry out voyages at their own expense for the transatlantic lands. Among the major consequences of the coup of October 1500 at Santo Domingo was the elimination of any debts these men might have owed Columbus for their undertakings. This argument supports my interpretation of Columbus's arrest. It was not an adventure or incident but a real coup d'état in which the interests of the Spanish state prevailed against the claims of Columbus and his family.

The voyages that were enlarging and completing the grand discovery were not minor excursions. Every season they were proving the discovery more important and significant, filled with consequences for Spain, especially considering the great activities of the Portuguese and even the new initiatives of the English. Columbus's claims grew increasingly out-of-date. The coup of 1500 denied those claims in a brutal but politically understandable way. It had to be done to void every remaining right.

In drawing up the Capitulations at Santa Fe, the monarchs had been thinking of Cathay, Cipango, and especially India, territories vast but organized in independent states with their own sovereigns, political structures, and commercial organizations. Making business arrangements under those expectations made granting a 10 percent share to the leader of the voyage and the discoveries very understandable. But no one, including Columbus, foresaw at the time the Capitulations were drawn up that new lands completely lacking efficient economic organizations and effective political structures would be discovered. The result was not simple business but outright annexation. Nor is the objection valid that the offices of admiral, viceroy, and governor were promised in perpetuity; the granting of these offices presupposed, among other things, the capacity to exercise them, something Columbus could not demonstrate even on the single island of Hispaniola.

Columbus retained his titles but not their powers. On 3 September 1501 the monarchs named Don Nicolás de Ovando governor and supreme justice of the islands and mainland of the Indies, except for certain parts of the mainland that were placed under Vicente Yáñez Pinzón and Alonso de Hojeda. The titles of viceroy and admiral were not conferred on Ovando, but his appointment signified the definitive break in the powers and privileges of the Discoverer. The only concessions Columbus obtained were an order to Bobadilla to furnish an inventory of his property and the right to send someone he trusted to Hispaniola in Ovando's fleet to collect his share of the profits from trade and gold mining. Columbus designated his faithful captain, Alonso Sánchez de Carvajal, who discharged his mission skillfully, scrupulously, and efficiently.

Ovando left Cádiz on 13 February 1502. At this point Columbus would have been wiser if he had been content with the goods he had acquired and renounced his rights in exchange for a secure and dignified position, perhaps a large pension and a castle, which the Catholic monarchs would have offered him in their recently conquered realm of Granada. But Columbus was not the man to do so; had that been his nature he would not have discovered America.

35 | To Complete the Uncompleted: The Fourth Voyage

*C*olumbus did not retire to a castle and enjoy the wealth he had acquired. His mind and heart had no room for anyplace except the world he had discovered. He was haunted by the thought that he had not completely realized his dream, his original plan. Now he was obsessed with completing the uncompleted, with reaching India at last. And so Columbus thought of undertaking the final discovery, a new exploration of the sea, no longer new, that bathed the islands and mainland beyond the Atlantic. He had seen terra firma beyond the Atlantic south of the equator, a beautiful, huge continent. And there was terra firma beyond the Atlantic north of the equator also; the Tainos of Hispaniola, Jamaica, and Cuba had spoken of it, and they were not lying. Now news had reached Spain that another Ligurian, a naturalized Englishman named John Cabot, had discovered terra firma on the latitude of France. If all these lands really belonged to the eastern edge of Asia—as was still believed—there had to be a passage to the Indian Ocean somewhere.

Europeans had known for some time that there was a strait on the extreme southeastern edge of Asia. It is the Strait of Cattigara (today the Strait of Malacca) between the Malay Peninsula and Sumatra, the shortest, in fact the only, maritime route for ships passing from the South China Sea (which we know today is part of the Pacific Ocean) to the Bay of Bengal and the Indian Ocean. The strait leading to India had to be somewhere. That was always the enigma, the vexing question now sharper than ever. The fourth voyage would not be undertaken to discover new lands. It had to have a single goal: discovering the strait between the sea of Cathay and the Indian Ocean and reaching India.

An important new development gave the project great political interest: the Portuguese had reached India by sailing east. In early September 1499 Vasco da Gama's small fleet, which had left two years before, reentered the Tagus. It had reached Calicut, India, the famous spice market. Although long, the route was open and promising. As a result the Columbian enterprise was discredited because it had not succeeded in the alluring plan of finding a short, easy route to the west and reaching India before the Portuguese. Nevertheless, Columbus did not give up. He wrote to the pope, asking for priests to teach the Gospel to the Indians, hoping that His Holiness could persuade the Catholic sovereigns to furnish the ships he needed. But Alexander VI had other things in mind. Columbus then composed a brief treatise on the art of navigation in the form of a letter to the monarchs. His purpose was to convince the monarchs to trust him and give him ships.

He did not succeed by these indirect methods. He succeeded only when he decided to set forth his plan for a new voyage in detail. He did so in a memorandum dated 26 February 1502, now unfortunately lost. It is easy, however, to imagine what it contained: a proposal to search for the strait leading from the sea of Cathay, which Columbus identified with the Caribbean Sea, to the Indian Ocean. The monarchs responded immediately and positively. On the one hand they were delighted to have the opportunity to rid themselves of a man who by now was a burden; on the other hand they thought that probably only someone as clever as Columbus could help them reach those Indies that the Portuguese had already reached. Thus, on 14 March 1502 the monarchs gave clear assent to Columbus's fourth voyage. In a courteous and flattering letter, they said his imprisonment had saddened them; they wanted and needed him always to be treated honorably, his privileges intact and, if necessary, confirmed so that he and his heirs could enjoy them freely. However—this was not said explicitly but it was clearly implied—Columbus could not, for the moment, exercise the functions that ought to have derived from his privileges.

In the letter the monarchs do not mention the basic purpose of the voyage, the search for the passage to India. But an accompanying letter—entrusted to Columbus and addressed to Vasco da Gama, "captain of the Most Serene King of Portugal, our son," then undertaking a second voyage to India—said explicitly that the Almirante Cristóbal Colón was headed for that same country by going west, "and it is possible that you will meet on the way." There is, then, no doubt that the monarchs had given their assent to a project to find the strait and return to Spain by da Gama's route.

To avoid new and predictable conflicts, the Admiral was prohibited from landing at Hispaniola on the outward leg of the voyage. Only if the voyage proved unsuccessful and Columbus should have to return the way he came was he authorized to stop at Hispaniola, and then only "if it seems necessary to do so." From this condition it follows (historians have not paid sufficient attention to this point) that the plan—if it did not fail, if the Admiral was not forced to return by way of Hispaniola—was not merely to find the passage to India but to circumnavigate the globe. Nothing less!

Preparations for the fourth voyage proceeded with unusual speed, and on 9 May 1502 a small fleet of four caravels sailed from Cádiz. There were 150 men, among them the Admiral's younger son, Ferdinand, thirteen years old, and Bartholomew Columbus, the *adelantado*. Diego Columbus, disgusted by the events on Hispaniola, had chosen the religious life and stayed in Spain. The crossing was the fastest of the eight Columbus made. After only sixteen days he arrived at St. Lucia in the Lesser Antilles, on 15 June. From there he went to Matinino (Martinique), where the crews went ashore to wash clothes, rest, and resupply the galley with water, wood, and food. The four ships sailed three days later. Coasting the arc of the Lesser Antilles, they found themselves on 24 June off the southern coast of Puerto Rico. On 29 June they were off Santo Domingo. Columbus knew of the monarchs' prohibition against landing on Hispaniola, but he used the excuse that he needed to trade a ship that had proven slow and poorly masted. It was a typical case of *force majeure,* what sailors call a forced stop. Several ships were available at Santo Domingo. If the Admiral could not trade the ship, he would buy or charter another with his own money.

So far I have followed the version of the voyage furnished by Don Ferdinand and Las Casas. One cannot, however, escape the suspicion that the Genoese exaggerated the problem so he could set foot in what was now the capital of the New Lands, lands which "by the will of God and by sweating blood he had conquered for Spain." There was another reason for his desire to stop at Santo Domingo: he had already sensed the hurricane that was approaching. Of that I will speak in the last chapter, which treats of the maritime genius of the Genoese. For now we are concerned with 29 June. On that day Columbus gave the order to stop, without putting out anchors, a league outside the port of Santo Domingo. He sent ashore the faithful Pedro de Terreros, who on the third voyage was sent ashore at Paria, on the mainland, to take possession for the Catholic sovereigns when the Admiral was sick with gout and ophthalmia.

Terreros returned with a rude reply. The king's order was that Columbus was not to land on Hispaniola, and Ovando had no intention of contravening it. Columbus was outraged. Nevertheless, learning from Terreros that most of the thirty-two ships that had come with Ovando were in port, ready to sail for Spain with a great shipment of gold, he sent a message that their departure should be delayed for at least eight days because a tremendous storm was about to break. Being unable to enter the well-protected mouth of the Ozama River, the port of Santo Domingo, Columbus was anxious to find another refuge for his four caravels a few miles west along the coast, in a place protected from the north and west.

All four of his ships survived the storm, and Columbus put out to sea again. He intended to go into the unexplored area of the Caribbean Sea, certain that to the west he would find the mainland and that by coasting it he would at last discover the strait to the Indian Ocean and the Indies. Cuba no longer interested him, nor did Jamaica. However, on 17 July, in a flat calm, the current carried the ships south-southeast to the eastern edge of Jamaica, within view of the splendid Blue Mountains. From there the southeast wind and the equatorial current drove the ships northwest.

But on 27 July the wind began to blow from the northeast, and the ships made 360 miles in three days, when a sailor saw a beautiful green mountain. It was Guanaja Island, in the Gulf of Honduras. The British pirates who settled the island from the seventeenth to the nineteenth century built their capital on pilings in the lagoon to guard against attack. There the population still lives.

Today the town of Guanaja looks like a miniature Venice, its wooden houses a typical Creole-English style of architecture. On the island itself there are no dwellings, only the cemetery, to which family and friends take their dead in a procession of boats. So it is today and so it was in the time of the pirates. When the Spanish came on their punitive raids, the pirates put their women, children, valuables, and food into boats and took the channel to the northern coast, to the Playa de los Soldados. On its west side a slope well suited for a prolonged defense rises over thirteen hundred feet, with woods, grottoes, caves, coves, springs, and fruit trees.

Bartholomew Columbus landed here on 31 July 1502. Apparently the Admiral, suffering from gout, remained aboard ship. That same day a great canoe carved from a log of colossal dimensions arrived in the bay where the Spanish ships were anchored. Long as a galley and eight feet wide, it had a shelter of matting amidships to protect women, children, and goods from seawater and rain. Over forty people were aboard, twenty-five men plus women and children, as Don Ferdinand says in the *Historie.* Its cargo included cotton mantels and big sleeveless shirts with strange, brightly colored designs; loincloths in showy colors like those of Granada; wooden swords, both edges set with flint or obsidian sharp as steel; axes and bells, razors and knives of copper; bars and forges for working copper; and hatchets of bright yellow stone with wooden handles. These products clearly came from a culture more advanced than anything Columbus had discovered on his previous voyages. The food on the canoe was the same as that of the Arawak—corn, *yuca,* yams, and sweet potatoes—but a novelty was a fermented beverage with a flavor like English beer. And there was, above all, an abundance of nuts, "cacao almonds," which the men of the large boat used as money in trading with the Indians of the village.

The size and distinctive finish of the canoe, the quantity of the products, the woven textiles, the craftsmanship of the copper, stone, and wood, the use of money as a medium of exchange—all these things gave a glimpse of a culture very different from those encountered previously. The Discoverer had finally found signs of a great civilization. The men, women, and children in the large canoe were Mayas, Chontal Mayas to be precise. They lived in the southeastern corner of Campeche Bay, which separates Yucatán from the rest of Mexico. Accustomed to easily finding their way in a labyrinth of waterways and swamps, the Chontal Mayas were expert canoeists. As a result the Aztecs called the Mayas' territory *Acallan* ("Land of Canoes").

They worked the waters of the Yucatán Peninsula. Their goods came overland from the plateaus of Mexico to the ports of Tabasco, one of the Mexican states still inhabited by the Mayas. There they loaded the great canoes in which they plied the coasts of Yucatán, going south to north on the west coast and north to south on the east until they reached the beaches of Mopan (today southern Belize), Guatemala, and Honduras. Here the Chontal Mayas had trading posts, one of which was the village on the Playa de los Soldados, Guanaja Island. The Chontal Mayas brought their goods here and traded primarily for cacao from mainland Honduras.

The copper articles in the large canoe probably came from central Mexico. The textiles were products of the Yucatán, obtained through bartering along the way. But if all these goods indicated, as Columbus realized, "wealth, civilization, and industry" until then unknown, cacao, or better, cacao almond nuts, deserves separate discussion. Did Columbus realize the importance of the discovery of cacao? Apparently not. Corn, peppers, sweet potatoes, manioc, pineapple, and so many other plants Columbus may be said to have discovered, but not cacao, for he did not realize its importance. Neither he nor his companions on the fourth voyage brought any news of it to Christendom. That came only with the Spanish conquest of Mexico several years later.

Columbus was tempted to modify his plans and follow the people in the canoe. Had he done so he would have reached Yucatán, where he would have seen its monuments and discovered Mexican civilization, which, together with that of Peru, was for at least three centuries the major attraction of the Americas. He did not do what historians believe he should have done. He thought that he could easily visit the country whence those people came later, using the trades to reach it from Cuba. For now he was intent on finding the passage to the Indian Ocean, which he could do only by going farther south. In clear weather one can see the coast of the mainland from Guanaja Island. Along that coast Columbus would have to pursue his course if he wanted to find the passage to India he wished for so ardently. Consequently, he limited himself to obtaining the goods that the Mayas had aboard, trading the usual little bells, small mirrors, and other worthless objects. Struck by the modesty of the women, who unlike those previously encountered were entirely clothed and even had their faces covered like the Muslims of Granada, the Genoese ordered his men to respect them. He forcibly detained the commander of the boat, an old man named Giumbe. Renamed Juan Pérez, his quick intelligence made him a very useful interpreter.

In the second week of August 1502, after many islands large and small, Columbus finally reached the North American mainland. The people wore colored sleeveless shirts and "small cloths over their private parts." But the most significant detail was the close-fitting jerkins, or jackets, of thickly padded cotton, "armor of cotton wool" as Don Ferdinand called them. These jerkins—not seen on the three previous voyages, either on Caribbean islands or in Venezuela—were the same as those carried and traded by the men on the great canoe at Guanaja. They are the sign of an advanced civilization, the Mayan, that extended for a considerable distance in the territory of the present-day Republic of Honduras—Copán is one of the major Mayan archaeological sites—halfway to the Atlantic coast of Honduras. The borderline, according to Don Ferdinand, between Mayan culture and the barbarians was the area of Punta Caxinas, today Cape Honduras and Trujillo.

On Sunday, 14 August 1502, the ships anchored at the mouth of a large river. The Admiral was sick. Bartholomew went ashore "with the banners and captains and many crewmen to hear mass." The following Wednesday, 17 August, the Spanish formally took possession in the name of the Catholic monarchs. This time the Discoverer knew it was not an island but mainland. Thus, it was in Honduras that Spain received, thanks to Christopher and Bartholomew Columbus, its fundamental claim to all of Central America. After taking possession the Spanish left, turning their prows east. They should have sailed along the coast as far as a cape where—as Giumbe had said and other Indians confirmed—the coast turns south. Doing so should not have been difficult, but for the second time Columbus had to confront one of the most tortured coastings in maritime history. For the second time, but under entirely different circumstances. While in December 1493 they were becalmed north of Haiti, the coasting along Honduras in August–September 1502 was torturous for the opposite reason: an interminable succession of storms. It took twenty-six or twenty-eight days to go 170 miles.

Only on 12 September did the ships reach the point where the coast falls off sharply to the south for hundreds of miles. It is still called Capo Gracias a Dios ("Cape Thanks Be to God"), a name justified only by the Discoverer's experience. He thanked God because the storms and contrary winds finally ended and the coast turned south at last. To the south he had intended to go when he had decided not to follow the Mayan canoe on its return trip. To the south must be found the coveted goal: the strait.

Rounding Cape Gracias a Dios, the caravels tacked along the Atlantic coast of what is today Nicaragua. They followed the coast, crossing the present-day border between Nicaragua and Costa Rica. On 25 September they reached the Atlantic coast of mountainous Costa Rica, an area the Indians called Cariai. Here, in the protection of a sunny island covered with palms and myrobalans, they stopped. Columbus named the island La Huerta ("The Orchard") and decided to stay for some time to repair the ships and rest the men. The port of Limón is Costa Rica's outlet and Atlantic market. In the bay of Limón lies the island Columbus called La Huerta. It was called Uva ("Grape") or Uvita for centuries, but in 1985 its Columbian name was restored.

As at Guanaja, Columbus had come to the threshold of an advanced society. On the plateaus—today the center of one of the most progressive nations in the New World—flowered a remarkable civilization, one of the Middle American cultures that in the fifteenth century had reached a level of technological sophistication that suggests equally developed social structures and intellectual advancement. Here, for the first time on American soil, they found a large wooden building and sepulchers of careful workmanship. His comment is significant: "These Indians were more intelligent than any others in those areas."

All this is important for the history of the great discovery but not so important for Columbus's biography. He wrote to the monarchs: "On the hill I saw a sepulcher big as a house, all carved, and I heard tell of other excellent works of art." Only two lines, yet he devotes ten lines to a fight between a pig (really a peccary or boar) and a spider monkey. The discovery of signs of the most advanced culture encountered so far in the New Lands aroused no emotion in the Genoese because he persisted in believing he was in Asia, and it would not be strange to find signs of civilization in Asia. Marco Polo had found many more and much better civilizations, and so would he. If the new discoveries led to anything it was the opposite of what modern historians would expect. Columbus interpreted these signs as further confirmation that he was in Asia, and so they reinforced his decision to continue along the coast in order to finally reach the strait that would lead to the Bay of Bengal and India.

36 | *Chiriquí: The Shattered Dream*

O n reaching Laguna de Chiriquí, Columbus felt he had found the strait at last.
Cerabora Bay was not yet open sea leading to another part of the
continent, not yet the Bay of Bengal. But there were clear signs that
straits led from it, and the Indians indicated with word and ges-
ture, translated by two interpreters picked up in Cariai, that to the
west lay the sea. Columbus felt more joy than hope; he could taste
his triumph after all the anxious anticipation.

Making even more joyous and triumphant those fatiguing days
was the added discovery that on Cerabora Island (Isla de Colón
today) was gold, very pure gold, eighteen karat and higher. It was
not just gold that they found. Don Ferdinand and Las Casas say
that "in the channel they caught innumerable fish, and ashore
many animals" as well as gathering a great quantity "of edibles,"
including iguanas, corn, and fruit.

Columbus's caravels sailed on 8 October in search of the strait
that would bring them to the other ocean. They found it, probably
from the indications of the local natives. In fact, they found two
channels, Sunwood and Split Hill. The first was—or at least it is
today—long, narrow, and deep but choked with mangroves; Split
Hill is wider and more open. Don Ferdinand says that "the ships
went between the islets as if they were going down streets. The

channels were so narrow that the fronds of the trees brushed the ships' rigging." The English names were bestowed by blacks from Jamaica, or perhaps by pirates in the seventeenth century. Cerabora Bay, now called Bahía de Almirante, with its labyrinth of islands, would become an ideal hideout for pirates.

Split Hill Channel is ten to forty feet deep, according to the local fishermen. From Bahía de Almirante it runs north to southwest. It has some sandbanks that are not dangerous because they are clearly visible on the right, or the mainland, side. The channel is deep and passable on the left, or island, side, which is higher, covered with dense, high vegetation and has a steep cliff. Extensive research gave me the same sensations Columbus must have felt five centuries ago, for it has changed little. Some of the mangrove thickets are probably different, and the water is probably deeper or shallower in places. According to my pilot, Split Hill Channel was not as wide a few years ago at its southwestern end. Where today there is a sandbank once was a tongue of land covered, as usual, with mangroves. The surrounding area is the same. Time and civilization have not changed the two lagoons and their splendid environs. The only new items are coconuts and mangoes, but they are lost in the thick, tangled vegetation that beckons with the magic of the Caribbean.

Sailing among the islets and mangroves along the southern edge of Bahía de Almirante and finally entering Split Hill Channel gives one the impression of having definitely left the open sea and of advancing toward the unknown. But suddenly, beyond the broken hill, beyond the tall trees and low mangroves, appears another, broad lagoon. Today it is called Laguna de Chiriquí. It is about fifteen miles wide and thirty long, its water turquoise and salty as the ocean. Deep green mountains surround it, the dark green characteristic of the tops of a tropical forest. The mountains are the Cordillera Central, whose tallest peak is 11,400 feet. But one can rarely see the peaks because of thick clouds. In October, the month Columbus was there, the weather is usually better than during the rest of the year. The average annual rainfall for the period 1920–1980 is 100 inches. It has been as high as 146 (in 1950) and 155 (1970). The wettest month is December (13 inches average) and the driest, if one can call it that since the humidity is always so high, September (4 inches average).

One could say that Columbus was fortunate to reach there in

good weather. But even if it was perfectly clear he would not have realized that it is only a lagoon. Today we know it is, open on the east and closed on the west, but Columbus could not help but be fooled by the fact that while the waters of Bahía de Almirante are calm, these of Laguna de Chiriquí are agitated and as salty as the ocean. At ebb tide the waves move from west to east, giving the impression that there is a connection with the sea not only to the east but also to the west. For a few days—or hours—Columbus hoped that he had found the passage to India. That was on 8 October 1502. Ten years earlier almost to the day he had seen the first sure signs of land beyond the Atlantic.

Columbus spent at least two days, perhaps three, exploring the shores of the lagoon with the boats, in search of a strait between the mountains glimpsed to the west and south. That the lagoon was not the Indian Ocean Columbus the expert sailor must have realized immediately. But couldn't there be a passage between those mountains leading to the Indian Ocean? Columbus had had experience with other nearly impervious passages: in the Mediterranean, the Strait of Messina, the straits between the islands of the Aegean, and that between Chios and the mainland; in the Caribbean, those between the Virgin Islands, so close to one another, the treacherous waters separating Trinidad from Venezuela, the Boca traversed two days before, and Split Hill Channel, which he had just crossed. Less than twenty years later Magellan, having reached from a wide entrance the bay today called Punta Arenas ("Sandy Point"), would find the most famous strait in the world between two walls of mountains.

The mouths of the five rivers that empty into the lagoon—Uyama, Róbalo, Guarumo, Guariviara, and Cricamola—were explored one by one. Only a day or two later, on 10 or 11 October, hope was extinguished. There was no alternative but to return to the open sea, toward which the great lagoon offers two calm outlets. Disappointment was sharp, bitter, and complete. The Admiral abandoned the main goal of the fourth voyage.

Here is a decisive period, one which brought a sudden change in his strategic plan. It lasted ten days, from 6 to 16 October 1502. Before now, no Columbus scholar was able to fix precisely the time of this important turning point in Columbus's thinking, simply because it cannot be done without personally examining the sites of these events. Only by direct research could I understand what happened between 5 and 16 October 1502 and what could have been going on, in those decisive days, in the minds of Columbus and the pilots of the four caravels.

The strait by which he could pass into the Bay of Bengal and so reach India was not there—or at least he could not find it. Therefore, the main goal of the voyage vanished. From 16 October until 6 January 1503 they spent days, weeks, and months in a wearisome traversing back and forth along the Atlantic coast of Panama. For by now Columbus was thinking only of gold; he wanted to found a colony in the richest part of the New Lands, as close as possible to the mines. He had found the most gold near Veragua between 20 and 25 October. There he would return. Why had he not stopped there at the end of October?

37 | Veragua: Gold and Coca

Veragua is one of the most important—
and least known—episodes in the great
Columbian enterprise. Veragua is the region of Panama overlook-
ing the Golfo de los Mosquitos ("Gulf of Mosquitoes"). Many
large rivers empty into it from the wild and impenetrable Cordillera (Cerro Santiago rises 9,272 feet). The Republic of Panama
has changed its administrative districts: Veragua is no longer only
on the Atlantic coast, as it was in Columbus's time, but extends
beyond the Cordillera to the Pacific. When I speak of Veragua I
am referring only to the region Columbus knew by that name. In
1536 Vicereine Doña Maria de Colón y Toledo, on behalf of her
son, Don Luis Colón, the Discoverer's grandson, renounced the
titles and privileges Columbus never ceased to boast of in the
"Spanish Indies." In return Emperor Charles V created Don Luis
duke of Veragua and granted him the territory.

Veragua is important for a single, indisputable reason: the
abundance of gold. In the last ten days of October 1502, the
Spaniards found much more gold there than in the Cibao of
Hispaniola: nineteen mirrors at Guaiga and another nineteen at
Cateva (near the present-day Santa Catalina). In addition, five
villages around Cobrava, near the mouth of the Rio Veraguas, all

traded gold. At first the Spaniards found plenty of gold everywhere, then no more: none at Puerto Gordo ("Fat Port") nor Portobelo ("Beautiful Port") nor Puerto de los Escribanos ("Port of the Notaries"). The information from an Indian interpreter captured in Cariai was precise: the gold region began at Laguna de Chiriquí and ended at Rio Belén, so named by Columbus because he reached it on 6 January, the Feast of the Epiphany, after the troubled wanderings along the Costa de los Contrastes ("Coast of Contrasts"). *Betlém* ("Bethlehem") was later contracted to *Belén*. About four miles west of Belén, the Rio Veraguas empties into the sea.

Gold—a lot of it—explains why Columbus chose Belén as the site for a colony, a new one to surpass that on Hispaniola, which had been taken from him. The choice would be condemned by pitying historians. "An inauspicious place," Morison calls it. Bradford agrees: "There has never been any successful European settlement in this area. . . . Columbus was a paranoiac." True, Columbus was no longer the man he was on the first voyage. He was sick as well as tired, incoherent, and contradictory. However, he was not crazy, and certainly not in choosing Veragua. First of all, there was gold, a great deal of it. "One thing I dare say," he writes, "and I have many witnesses: I saw more evidence of gold in the first two days at Veragua than on Hispaniola in four years." Nor is Belén as unpleasant as historians who have never been there make it. In fair weather Belén is a lovely corner of the Caribbean. Waves from the Atlantic roar ceaselessly over the coral reef that leaves only a gap in front of the sandy beach. Here is the river bar, also named Belén. Some two hundred yards from the mouth of the river a lagoon opens up, sheltered from the winds and protected on both sides by easily defensible hills.

At its center the lagoon has a depth of about thirty feet; over twenty ships the size of Columbus's caravels could easily anchor there. Sharks come into the lagoon from the sea; though dangerous, their flesh is tasty. Lobsters also inhabit the lagoon. From the lagoon I went seven and a half miles up the river, with its innumerable bends, through tropical forest, which owes its luxuriance to the burning kiss it receives nearly every day from the sun and to tremendous rains, among the most generous on earth. There are few birds but many flowers and many types of trees—tall, medium, and small—with their many kinds of fruit and aromas. One could go considerably farther than seven and a half miles in a pirogue, as far as the rapids and waterfalls in the Cordillera.

The density of the population in Columbus's time proves that the land was not unpleasant then, as it is not now. The population has almost disappeared primarily because this northwestern edge of Panama has remained cut off from the great currents of trade, far from the points of contact between the mining and agricultural regions of the New World and the Old World. It has not been trampled by the peoples who came from far off to absorb the American civilizations into their own. It has remained cut off even after independence, because it was the most peripheral and hard-to-reach area in the Republic of Colombia, later the Republic of Panama.

The heavy and continuous rains protected Belén and Veragua from invasion by the whites, who did not even try to transplant blacks there. Instead, they took the many Indians who used to cultivate the land and moved them elsewhere. By the middle of this century, the village of Belén was reduced to 50 inhabitants, and the main valley and the valleys of its tributaries became deserted. With the advent of the airplane and the completion of projects by PROESA (Projectos especiales del Atlantico, begun by President Torrijos of Panama), the village today has 120 inhabitants. A little uphill from it is another village, Ciudad de Romero, with about four hundred Salvadoran refugees. Columbus scholars formed a negative judgment on Belén not because of the rain but because they simply had not seen it.

On 7 January Columbus sent Diego Méndez in a launch to the mouth of the Rio Veraguas, about four miles from Belén. Méndez took soundings and found there was not enough water for the ships. He rowed into the interior, traded with the Indians, and brought twenty gold mirrors back to the Admiral. The fame of the infinite riches of the mines of Veragua was not false. Since the Rio Belén had been sounded, two caravels entered it on 9 January. The next day the other two came in at high tide and anchored in the large lagoon. The ruler of the area with the gold mines was a powerful cacique, Quibian. The Admiral decided to come to an agreement with him and sent his brother Bartholomew to pay him a visit. Quibian met him wearing a crown, a large plaque on his neck, and rings on his legs and arms, all of thick gold. The reception was excellent and the trade profitable. The next day Quibian "came to the ships to visit the Admiral and they talked for a little over an hour. Then the Admiral gave him a few gifts, and the sailors traded a few bells for a good deal of gold. Without any more ceremony Quibian returned the way he came." So reports Don Ferdinand, but Diego Méndez says that at one point in the conversation the cacique scowled, looked around suspiciously, and, excusing himself, returned to his village; the unfamiliar ships and weapons had made him diffident.

In the meantime, the sea had changed again for the worse. Columbus thought he was safe inside the bar when, on 24 January, a storm dumped a tremendous amount of rain in the Cordillera, which the thousands of streams carried into the river. Before the sailors realized what was happening the Belén flooded, tearing a caravel loose from one of the anchors and smashing it into another caravel. The first sustained heavy damage, including a broken mast. The other ships, dragged furiously here and there, brushing first one bank then the other, were in danger of being broken into matchsticks. With heroic efforts the sailors managed to secure and anchor them. Over the next few days the waters receded, but the sand brought by the river and the waves of the sea made a bar at the mouth, trapping the fleet inside.

When good weather returned, the Admiral sent Bartholomew in a launch with about seventy men to explore the interior and find the gold mines. Quibian was troubled and resorted to cunning. He offered Bartholomew some guides but secretly told them to lead the foreigners into the territory of Cacique Urira, his enemy. The guides did so, taking the Spaniards on a long, tortuous journey, in the course of which they forded the same river some forty times. At last they reached a place where veins of gold appeared here and there on top of the ground among the stones and moss. Beside themselves with joy, the Spaniards gathered as much as they could.

It appears that on this occasion Bartholomew reached a peak or pass of the Cordillera. The peak could have been Cerro Negro (4,980 feet), on the eastern slopes of which lie the springs of the Rio Veraguas. In any case, inquiries I made there revealed that from no pass or peak in that part of the isthmus can both oceans be seen even on a clear day. It was not, then, tricks by the guides that prevented Columbus's brother from being the first European to see the greatest ocean from America—Marco Polo and other explorers had already seen it from Asia. The guides pointed Bartholomew not south but west. There, twenty days' journey away, beyond the western horizon, he would find many gold mines. Bartholomew was delighted with the news, coming as it did in addition to the gold seen with his own eyes and gathered by his men. Nevertheless, he was aware that the guides were using tricks to lead him far from their cacique's territory, and that is why he wanted to scout Quibian's territory also before returning to the ships. There he found more gold. No place was richer than the area of Veragua.

Bartholomew explored between Monday, 6 February, and Saturday, 11 February, or Sunday, 12 February. On Thursday, 16 February, he commanded a new exploring party. According to Don Ferdinand,

> Bartholomew went into the country with fifty-nine men; a sea boat took another fourteen. In the morning of 17 February they reached Rio Urira, which lies seven leagues west of Belén. A league farther on the cacique, accompanied by twenty people, received him. He presented much food, and they traded some gold mirrors. The cacique and his dignitaries kept putting a dry grass in their mouths and chewing it, and sometimes they put on themselves a certain powder they carried with the grass. It seemed a very nasty thing. . . . When they eat they always chew a certain grass, which we think is the reason their teeth are so decayed and rotten.

The grass was coca. Scholars agree it originated in South America; they disagree only on the exact place of origin. Some hold that it comes from areas bordering on the Caribbean, others that it is from the Amazon and was taken into the Andes along the river system. *Coca* means "tree" in the Aymara language. It is curious that a grass *(hierba)* should be called a tree, the grass par excellence. Today the Aymara live in the Andes of Bolivia and Peru, as they did in the Columbian era. Notable and widespread pre-Columbian art depicts coca chewing and coca lime containers. These artifacts, however, are found only in central Colombia, Ecuador, Peru, and Bolivia; none has been found on the isthmus of Panama. But contacts between Central and South America were innumerable. In addition, meso-American archaeology has brought to light several small containers that the Danish archaeologist Olaf Holm is inclined to identify as *eliptas,* a Quechua word for coca lime containers.

Coca, then, or a drug closely related to it, was the grass chewed by the Indians of Veragua whom Bartholomew met on 17 February 1503. The young Don Ferdinand sensed that it was "a very nasty thing." That seems a premonition of the scourge those leaves and powders would become for mankind. Unlike his nephew, Bartholomew was not preoccupied with the grass the natives chewed and their powders. He returned, on Thursday, 24 February, to the bar at Belén laden with "much gold," according to Las Casas, who says that the land was most fertile and rich with fruit; there were extensive fields of corn, and gold was found at every step, so many were the necklaces that the Indians wore.

There was no longer any reason to hesitate. The Admiral decided to found a new colony, Santa María de Belén, to be governed by Bartholomew. Don Ferdinand says it was "on the riverbank, a lombard's shot from the mouth, beyond a ditch that lies on the right as one enters the river, in whose mouth rises a hill." The place is clearly identifiable today because nothing has changed. The hill is covered with thick forest on the left, west of the mouth. Between the hill and the rise, which is part of the inland mountain range, a small ravine still comes into the west bank of the river at the end of the lagoon. The ravine carries a brook of crystal-clear fresh water. Along it is a footpath with steps cut into the rock here and there; Columbus's sailors could have cut them with their picks.

On the slope above the ravine, the Spanish built eight wooden houses and thatched them with palm fronds. Ten men lived in each. Another, larger building held the European provisions: oil, legumes, cheese, vinegar, garlic, and so forth. Because there were plenty of fish in the sea, the colony would be well fed. The Admiral left a ship for his brother and prepared to depart with the three other caravels, waiting for the rains so he could cross the bar. He hoped to reach Spain quickly and send the colony more men and supplies.

At this point Quibian, realizing that the foreigners intended to establish themselves in his territory, resolved to kill them and burn their houses and ships. But knowing the superiority of the Spanish forces, he continued to feign friendship, accepting with apparent satisfaction the Admiral's gifts. Meanwhile, under the pretext of going to war with a cacique who had recently wounded him in the arm, he gathered his forces. Over a thousand warriors camped with him on the coast near the colony. It was war, the second in America between the Spanish and Indians during the early Columbian era. The first had taken place on Haiti.

The Admiral immediately saw to arming of the ships and reinforcing the colony's defenses. But Diego Méndez and Bartholomew persuaded him not to give their enemies time, to surprise them with the bold stroke of kidnapping Quibian. Bartholomew and Méndez, with eighty well-armed men, went to the village of Veragua in the launches. They captured Quibian along with about fifty relatives and retainers, chained them, and took them to the launches. While the current carried the boat downstream, Quibian began to complain. His guard was moved by the cacique's complaints and loosened his bonds, holding on to the end of the rope. When the Spaniard was looking away, Quibian jumped into the water and disappeared. The guard could not hold on to the rope for fear of being pulled in and had to let go.

Everyone thought Quibian was dead, but though his hands and feet were tied he had swum under water and reached the bank. He reached his village and waited for his revenge. The opportunity came when the river rose and the Admiral decided to depart with the three caravels, leaving, as expected, eighty men and a caravel with Bartholomew and Méndez. The three other caravels crossed the bar and waited beyond the coral reef for a favorable wind. Columbus sent the *Bermuda*'s boat ashore, commanded by Diego Tristan, with eleven men to fetch water. At the same time sixty men from the small garrison left the colony in launches to say farewell to their companions. Only twenty remained with Bartholomew and Méndez to guard the houses. On 6 April 1503 Quibian and four hundred men armed with arrows, spears, and clubs came out of the jungle and suddenly surrounded the Spanish village.

This battle and those that followed were the bloodiest fought during the period of Columbus's voyages. With the first volley of arrows seven Spaniards were wounded, one fatally. Throwing aside their bows, the Indians attacked with clubs and spears; the

Spanish, wearing armor and carrying shields, waited for them. Nineteen Indians fell, wounded with swords and lances; the rest retreated into the woods, where they unleashed a shower of arrows. Bartholomew, with a javelin wound in the chest and supported by a handful of companions, fought back with the crossbow. The first engagement lasted three hours. Then the boat Columbus had dispatched from the *Bermuda* arrived. From shore Diego Méndez signaled to Tristan to turn back, but he ignored the warning, crossed the lagoon, and ascended the river to a pure spring that ran into the river. On both banks, hidden by the thick forest, the Indians followed. At the spring they surrounded the launch and fell on the Spaniards. Wounded and bleeding, Tristan was trying to retreat when a javelin struck him in the right eye, and he fell dead in the bottom of the boat. All the others were killed except for one man who let himself fall into the river when he was wounded. Swimming underwater, he managed to reach the Spanish camp and tell them of the disaster.

That evening the sixty men who had gone to say good-bye to the fleet returned to the village. They heard the tragic outcome of the battle and saw the horribly mutilated corpses of their companions come floating down the river, crows and vultures feeding on them. Since they were so few and some were wounded, the Spaniards decided to get in the boats the Admiral had left and rejoin the fleet, but the bar had closed the river once again; not even a launch could cross to the open sea.

The bad weather lasted ten days, and when Tristan did not return the Admiral grew afraid for him. He was hoping the Indians would not attack the colony because of fifty hostages he was holding on the ships. Every evening he had them locked below and a great chain put on the hatch, on which several sailors slept. One night the Spanish forgot the chain and had spread their straw pallets on the hatch as usual. The prisoners made a great mound of ballast stones under it and, climbing on one another's shoulders, lifted the hatch, overturning the sleepers. Some managed to jump into the sea. The others were recaptured and locked up again with the chain. During the night the remaining prisoners, including the women, gathered the ropes in the hold and hanged themselves from the deck beams. They had to keep their knees bent while they strangled, for there was not enough room to hang free.

The corpses alarmed Columbus. During the ten days of bad weather he had heard nothing from the colony, and his hope that the men ashore would be safe because he held hostages was eroded, for he now had none. The Admiral began to wonder what had happened. Pedro de Ledesma offered to swim ashore if a boat would take him as far as the coral reef. Taking off his clothes, he jumped in and swam, managed to avoid the coral, and reached the redoubt Bartholomew had built on the beach. He was greeted with shouts of joy as well as protest: the men were ready to face the stormy sea in the tattered ship that had been left them rather than stay in the inauspicious land of Veragua. Thus, the attempt to found a colony here failed miserably. The historian, however, cannot forget the episode at Veragua, memorable because it epitomizes one of the most significant periods of the great discovery.

From Guanaja Island to Honduras, Nicaragua, Costa Rica, and finally to Panama: tacking endlessly from west to east and east to west, Columbus discovered all of Central America during his fourth voyage. It would be a grave historiographical error to neglect or simply underestimate its importance. Veragua represents not only gold and coca but the isthmus between North and South America. When Balboa crossed the isthmus nine years later and told Christendom of a new ocean, he was simply harvesting the fruit of Columbus's obstinacy and determination in the last important episode of the great discovery. Often forgotten by historians, the name of Veragua has remained inscribed in indelible letters over the centuries: Columbus's direct descendants still bear the title duke of Veragua.

38 | *Santa Gloria*

*E*aster fell on 16 April in 1503. That night Columbus left Belén with three caravels, all of them riddled with worms, veritable sieves. "The crews manned the pumps and used pots as well as other containers, but they could not keep up with the water that entered through the holes bored by the teredos," Méndez relates in his will. The caravels had only one boat among them. Added to the suffering, toil, and fears of the new voyage was the memory of the dramatic events ashore, of their dead companions and defeats. All this caused some dissension.

At Portobelo the Admiral had to abandon another caravel "because of the quantity of water she let in," the hull being completely perforated by the teredos. The two remaining were little better, but dividing the men from the abandoned ship between the two caravels provided more arms for pumping and bailing out water, back-breaking tasks that had to be done day and night. From Portobelo Columbus tacked along the Atlantic coast of Panama. Then on 1 May 1503, near Cape Tiburón, the two caravels left the mainland. The ships were now headed north, and they should have come to the southern coast of Jamaica. But the constant trade wind from the northeast must have blown them off course. The two caravels were in bad shape, but even if they had been sound they could not have avoided going off course, because the wind and currents combined made it impossible to tack successfully. They fell off to the west, and on 10 May were in view of Little Cayman and Cayman Brac instead of Jamaica. Don Ferdinand says the islands were "covered with turtles, and the surrounding sea was filled with them too, so they looked like little rocks." Columbus named the islands Las Tortugas ("The Turtles"). They were the last places he discovered and named.

Jamaica lay more than a hundred miles to the southeast. They did not stop, and on the evening of 12 May were among the islands of the Jardínes de la Reina ("The Queen's Gardens"), explored on the second voyage. Here, ten leagues from Cuba (which Columbus still called the "province of Mangi, which is part of Cathay"), they anchored between two cays. That night a new storm came up. They touched the coast of Cuba and set a course for Hispaniola. They were sailing against the wind, but the water in the ships continued to rise. On the night of 22/23 June it rose so high "that they could do nothing to bring it down, and it nearly reached the deck." On 24 June the two caravels managed with great luck to reach a Jamaican port that Columbus had named Puerto Bueno in 1494. Today it is called Dry Harbor because it has no fresh water.

They sailed the next day. A strong land breeze carried the ships to a nearby port protected by a coral reef, which Columbus had named Puerto Santa Gloria in 1494. Don Ferdinand describes their entrance:

> Coming inside and being unable to keep the ships afloat any longer, we ran them as far up the beach as we could. Putting the ships alongside each other, we lashed them together so they could not move. They filled with water almost to the deck. The quarterdeck and forecastle were turned into defensive positions against the Indians. At that time there were no Christians on Jamaica.

At Santa Gloria (today St. Ann's Bay) ended the epic of the great discovery, though not the life of its protagonist, which even more at Santa Gloria was filled with ordeals and dramatic episodes. On that beach Columbus spent a whole year, from 25 June 1503 to 28 June 1504. It was a year of problems, misery, hopes, and fears, of illusions and disappointments, of splendid demonstrations of courage as well as abject cowardice. Relations with the Indians, primarily peaceful, contrasted with relations among the Spaniards, which degenerated from criticism and murmuring into rebellion and open warfare. A year on the beach of Santa Gloria! A seemingly unending series of dawns, days, sunsets, and nights of hope, suffering, and desperation.

When Columbus and his men beached the two remaining caravels at Santa Gloria on 25 and 26 June, they did not imagine they would stay a whole year. They could not have had illusions, however; several months' residence would have been inevitable. Cut off from the world, they needed to reestablish ties with Hispaniola, the only place in the New Lands where Christians could be found.

The first problem was securing food. Of the 140 men and boys who sailed on the fourth voyage, 6 had died or deserted before reaching Veragua, 12 were killed there, and 6 had died later, either from wounds or disease. That left 116 mouths to feed. It would have been dangerous to let the sailors loose in the countryside to secure provisions, because that would have produced raids and new wars with the Indians. Hence the Admiral's decision, unpopular but justified, to prohibit the men from straying off the beach. The task of scouting the area to organize a constant flow of food was entrusted to Diego Méndez, who managed to establish contracts with the neighboring caciques. Every day canoes came laden with fish, *hutías,* game, and cassava bread and went back with pins, knives, combs, scissors, mirrors, hawks' bells, glass beads, and other trinkets that meant nothing to the givers but delighted the recipients. Méndez obtained something else of great importance. At the eastern end of the island, he made friends with the cacique and traded a brass basin for a canoe with six oarsmen and supplies.

The canoe was necessary for solving the other fundamental problem, establishing contact with Hispaniola. There was no hope that a caravel would be sent to search for the lost men. Ovando, governor of Santo Domingo, was hoping that the embarrassing Genoese would disappear for good. Nor was there any hope that some exploring ship would come to Jamaica. The reason for the lack of interest is clear: these islands, as Columbus realized, have no gold.

The only hope of rescue, then, was to send a messenger to

Hispaniola to hire a caravel. But the single launch saved at Belén had been lost in the storm. Therefore Méndez's canoe was providential. The Admiral decided that Méndez, courageous and capable, should make the attempt. That was at the beginning of July 1503. On 7 July Columbus closed himself in his cabin built on the bridge and wrote a long letter to the monarchs, known as the *Lettera Rarissima* because it was discovered much later, at the end of the eighteenth century. This letter, which I have already mentioned briefly, has received differing appraisals. It is filled with geographical, historical, cosmographical, philosophical, and theological considerations and references. In places it is disconnected, but it cannot be dismissed, as some have done, as the ramblings of a madman. On the contrary, it contains some original perceptions, accurate and brilliant, that merit close attention. To single out the most important, in this letter Columbus calls the "measureless mainland" discovered at Venezuela in 1498 "another world." It was that phrase that opened the door of recognition in the encounter between the Old World and the New, as I will discuss in the last chapter. Columbus entrusted the letter to Méndez along with a brief message to his friend Friar Gaspar Gorricio at the convent of Las Cuevas in Seville.

Diego Méndez put a false keel on the great canoe, smeared pitch and grease on the bottom, raised the breakwaters in the prow and stern to keep the waves from swamping it, and made a mast and sail. He set out with a sailor and six Indians. When he reached the eastern cape, he stopped to wait for good weather, and Indians attacked. Fortunately, they decided to play a ball game to determine who should kill him and who should take the booty, and he managed to escape. Returning to the beach, he found the canoe, raised the sail, and with the trade wind, which luckily was blowing, returned to the beached ships.

He tried again but this time arranged for protection until he set out to sea. Captain Bartolomeo Fieschi, a Genoese, volunteered to accompany Diego to Hispaniola in another large canoe and return to reassure the men stranded at Santa Gloria. In addition, Bartholomew Columbus offered to protect them by following on land with seventy men as far as Cape Jamaica. The two canoes each had six Spaniards with swords and shields, food, and ten Indian oarsmen. The Spaniards advanced to the eastern end of the island, Fieschi and Méndez by sea and Bartolomew by land. There they waited four days for the rough seas to quiet down, and then Méndez and Fieschi began the crossing to Hispaniola.

The sea was unusually calm, and this time they succeeded. In August 1503 Méndez reached Governor Ovando in the interior of Hispaniola, where he was fighting the Indians, but not until the end of May 1504 was the faithful Méndez allowed to buy a ship and supplies and send it to the Admiral—nine months of waiting! What can explain the delay? It is certain that Ovando was not saddened to learn that the foreign Admiral was shipwrecked on Jamaica. His arrival with news of fresh discoveries might induce the monarchs to reinstate him in his viceregal powers, stripping Ovando of the office of governor. Ovando detained Méndez with the excuse that he was busy putting down the Indian revolt, which he did by hanging and burning alive eighty caciques and other leaders.

In the nine months of waiting at Santa Gloria, Columbus and his men looked anxiously out to sea every morning for a sail, but in vain. The sailors began to fear that Méndez and Fieschi were dead or that they had reached their goal but the governor had refused aid. The hot, humid climate, a shortage of meat, and the lack of wine wore down many sailors, who lay sick. Columbus himself could not stand up. Naval exercise was impossible because the ships were beached, going ashore and wandering around the island was absolutely prohibited, there was not enough space for target practice, and gambling was strictly forbidden. The only duty was a turn as one of two sentinels.

Francisco de Porras and his brother, Diego, stirred up the men against the Admiral. They nursed a grudge against him, knowing he thought little of them. Repeating old gossip, they said he had been exiled from Spain for his mistakes and that Méndez and Fieschi had been sent not to Ovando to ask for ships and aid but to the monarchs to try to rehabilitate him, citing as proof the fact that Fieschi had not returned. The Porrases suggested attempting the same course Méndez had followed, claiming that the Admiral could not oppose the plan; if gout prevented him from going he could stay and take his chances. Seduced by these arguments, some of the men decided to seize ten canoes the Admiral had bought to hinder the Indians in attacking the ships in case of war.

On 2 January 1504 the rebels took up arms. Francisco de Porras entered the cabin and said to Columbus, "Sir, why don't you want to go to Castile? Why are you content to let us all perish here?" The Admiral replied that he did not see how they could leave until those who had gone to Hispaniola sent a ship and that he wanted to return to Spain more than anyone did, for his own good and for everyone else's. He asked Porras if he knew some other means of getting out of there alive. The rebel leader made an insolent reply and, turning his back, cried out, "I'm going back to Castile! Whoever wants to save himself can follow me!" From all sides the armed conspirators came, occupied the castles and tops, and plundered the magazines and armory.

Columbus tried to get out of bed and go to the site of the tumult but fell face down. He tried to get up and fell again. Four officers and his son Ferdinand lifted him back into bed. Meanwhile, Bartholomew ran up with a halberd. He wanted to attack the traitors, but the other loyal officers forced the weapon from his hand and dragged him to his brother's cabin, begging Captain Porras to be quiet and leave since he had what he wanted. The forty-eight rebels seized the canoes and left.

The many sick men, hearing the others leave, felt abandoned. Columbus, held up by the arms, went to the sick bay and comforted them with his presence. From then on he visited the sick every day, reawakening in them a strong faith in God, pointing out, as best he knew, remedies to everyone's ailments, and sometimes nursing them with his own arthritic hands. They needed such comfort, because the damp straw on which they lay and the swarms of gnats and mosquitoes made their sufferings intolerable.

The mutineers followed Méndez's course along the coast, attacking the Indians and stealing everything they could. When the Indians protested, the Spaniards told them to go to the Admiral and make him pay for the things taken, killing him if he refused, for they were acting on his orders. They added that the Spaniards hated Columbus for his tyranny and that, being an implacable enemy of the Indians, he would take away their freedom, causing a thousand misfortunes on the island; removing him from this world would help everyone.

The forty-eight reached the end of the island and, with Indian oarsmen, left for Hispaniola. They were scarcely four leagues out when the sea grew rough, and they turned back out of fear. Water came into the canoes and threatened to swamp them, so they threw their goods and clothes overboard. The weather continued to grow worse, and not wanting to lose their weapons and provisions, they decided to lighten the canoes by killing the Indians and throwing them overboard. Before the slaughter could begin, the Indians dove overboard and tried to keep up with the canoes at a distance. But it was a long way back to land, and the Indians, crying and begging, tried to hang on to the boats while they caught their breath. Apparently some Spaniards cut off the Indians' hands with swords. It is given for certain that eighteen Indians were killed.

Back on Jamaica, Porras and his rebels waited a month for good weather, but favorable spells were brief, and new storms forced them back twice. In desperation they abandoned the canoes and returned to Santa Gloria, again sacking the villages on the way. The Indians associated the rebels with Columbus and refused to bring provisions to the ships. On the beach of Santa Gloria the light trades continued to blow without respite, no longer a wind of relief and hope but of desperation.

39 | *The Last Crossing and Death*

*I*n February 1504 it was impossible to see a solution to the hellish pains afflicting Columbus and those faithful to him. Everyone was desperate. Leaving the redoubt to procure supplies meant exposing oneself to continual danger, ambushes, and battles either with Porras's rebels or the Indians, now decidedly hostile. Remaining holed up on the ships meant dying not from thirst—because periodic rains supplied water—but from hunger.

Once again the leader's instinct surfaced. Among the few books aboard ship was a copy of Regiomontanus's *Ephemerides*. Printed at Nuremberg before the turn of the century, it predicted eclipses for the next thirty years, among them a total lunar eclipse on the night of 29 February 1504. Three days before that date, Columbus called together some caciques and many notables and, as Don Ferdinand tells it,

> let them understand through an interpreter that God lived in heaven and they were his subjects. He protected the good and punished the wicked. Seeing the rebellious Christians, he had not allowed them to reach Hispaniola, while Méndez and Fieschi had. As for the Indians, seeing the little care they had taken to bring food to the Spaniards, God was angry and had

decided to send famine and pestilence among them. He would give a clear sign from heaven so they should know without doubt that punishment would come from His hand. Three nights hence they should pay careful attention to the rising moon, and they would see it angry and inflamed, signifying the misfortune God would send them.

The eclipse occurred as predicted.

> The Indians were terribly afraid. With great cries and wailing they came running from every side to the ships, loaded with food and begging the Admiral to intercede with God in any way he could. The Admiral said that he wanted to speak for a little while with his God and retired to his cabin while the eclipse grew. When he saw that it was beginning to wane he came out, saying that he had beseeched his God, giving his word that from thenceforth the Indians would be good and treat the Christians well, bringing food and other necessities.

The Admiral measured with the hourglass the duration of the eclipse so he could compute the longitude of Jamaica. His calculations he reported in the Book of Prophecies:

> On Thursday, 29 February 1504, when I was in the Indies on the island of Jamaica in the port of Santa Gloria, there was a lunar eclipse. Since it began before sunset I could observe only its end, when the moon had just regained its full light, and that occurred two and a half hours after nightfall, five half-hour glasses of a surety.

Taking the exact time of the eclipse in Cádiz from the almanac, Columbus calculated that "the difference between the center of the island of Jamaica in the Indies and Cádiz in Spain is seven hours and fifteen minutes; that is, at Cádiz the sun sets seven hours and fifteen minutes before it does in Jamaica."

It was the usual trick. He had to show that the New Lands lay well beyond the line agreed to under the Treaty of Tordesillas and were therefore Asian—and thus, Spain's—so he wrote down seven hours and one-quarter instead of four and three-quarters as it actually is. That it was a trick is evident from examination of his calculation of the latitude. In contrast to the situation on the first voyage, he was not preoccupied by latitude disputes with the

Portuguese because the boundary line between the possessions of the two Iberian nations now ran north-south instead of east-west. His calculation of the latitude is nearly perfect: "In the port of Santa Gloria, Jamaica, the altitude of the polestar was 18° when the Guards were in the position of the arm." The exact latitude of the bay of Santa Gloria is 18°26'45'', so Columbus was off by less than a half-degree. It is true that he had the benefit of a stable platform and an entire year to repeat the observations and obtain an average. Nevertheless, this is one of the most precise calculations of latitude we know of from the early sixteenth century.

The episode of the eclipse merits some consideration. In the unhappy conditions in which he found himself, Columbus was not only once again a leader but a good geographer, an acute investigator of natural phenomena, and an ingenious cosmographer. Proof of that is his calculation of a nearly exact latitude, which also proves that when he gave the latitude of Cuba as 42° he did not make an error but, as I have said, deliberately lied in order not to offer an opportunity to the Portuguese or help in any way rival discoverers who might follow. Here on the beach of Santa Gloria he no longer had a need to lie about the latitude, and his figures were exact.

Though the Genoese had mastered it, the situation was still bleak. The suffering, fears, and murmuring intensified with the passing of time, and exasperation set in. One Master Bernal, an apothecary and physician for the fleet who was already suspected of poisoning some sick men for revenge, resolved to assassinate the Admiral lest he bring charges against him at court in Spain. He attracted four sailors with his scheme and hatched a plot to seize the new canoes that had been bought from the Indians and attempt the crossing to Hispaniola. The night he had chosen to carry out his plan a sail appeared. The joy of the crews filled the conspirators as well, who ran to see the small brigantine that anchored a short distance from the beach. A boat came to the *Bermuda,* and the oarsmen asked for a line. They sent up a barrel of wine, half a side of salt pork, and a dispatch. Then the officer asked in a loud voice to talk to Columbus.

The officer was Escobar, an accomplice of Roldán's, condemned to death for his part in the rebellion but later rewarded for having betrayed Roldán's trust. Columbus, although offended by the choice of messenger, came out of his cabin. As soon as he saw Columbus, Escobar called out that for the moment his governor did not have enough ships to fetch him and his men, but he would get them as soon as possible. If he wanted to write to Ovando he should do so right away, because the brigantine had to return without delay. Receiving the letter addressed to Ovando, in which Columbus recounted Porras's rebellion and warmly recommended Méndez and Fieschi, Escobar returned to his ship. Raising anchor and hoisting sail, the brigantine disappeared into the night.

This first expedition sent by Governor Ovando seemed peculiar. For a large number of hungry and sick people, he sent a barrel of wine and half a side of salt pork, and he had appointed as commander of the ship Diego de Escobar, a former lieutenant of the rebels under Roldán and therefore picked intentionally, for the governor knew very well that he was an enemy of the Admiral "for past deeds." As Las Casas observes, Escobar was under orders not to board the beached ships, not to go ashore, and not to speak with any of Columbus's men.

The disappointment among the shipwrecked men was great, but once again the Admiral proved master of himself. He said that because the brigantine was too small to take everyone, he had chosen to stay until Méndez could send a ship large enough. Then he attempted reconciliation with Porras's mutineers. Two men were sent to the rebel camp with a large part of the pork sent by Ovando as proof that the ship had come and with an offer of a general pardon. Porras made so many conditions and requests—so much food and so many clothes and so much space on the ship— that the messengers were outraged and broke off negotiations. The mutineers then marched on Santa Gloria, convinced they could easily seize the beached ships. Columbus entrusted the defense to Bartholomew. Gathering fifty men, the *adelantado* dressed them in armor and led them over the hill behind the beach to engage the rebels immediately.

Porras, counting among his followers the healthiest and strongest men, laughed when he saw the soldiers come out of the sick bay to fight him, and he was confident of victory. But he so feared Bartholomew that he ordered six of his best men to attack him together and kill him. Many armed Indians stayed at a distance, watching the battle between the palefaces. It was Sunday, 19 May

1504. When the two lines came together, Francisco de Porras led the assault, crying "Kill! Kill!" The strongest advanced on Bartholomew and surrounded him, but with one stroke he killed the pilot Juan Sánchez and with incredible swiftness laid at his feet the five others who had sworn to kill him. Porras then came up and dealt Bartholomew a heavy blow with his sword, breaking Bartholomew's shield and wounding him in the hand. Porras's blade penetrated the shield up to the hilt and he could not withdraw it. Bartholomew could have killed him but spared his life. Porras made a break for freedom and Bartholomew knocked him down, disarmed him, and gave him to his men as a prisoner. Bartholomew then led a strong counterattack and killed Juan Barba, the first to draw sword against the Admiral. The rest of the rebels fled. On Columbus's side only one man died, a steward of the Admiral's who received a slight wound in the side and whom everyone thought would live. By contrast, Pedro de Ledesma, one of the rebels, survived extraordinary wounds; his story merits telling. He had a head wound so severe one could see his brains; an arm hung down uselessly from his shoulder, like a falling partridge; one side of his thigh hung down his leg like an untied shoe; and his sole was cut like the bottom of a broken slipper. The similes are from Don Ferdinand and Las Casas. The latter continues:

> As he lay on the ground the Indians came up to see and touch the great wounds Spanish swords could make. But when they disturbed him, Pedro cried out, "Beware! I can get up!" and the Indians fled because his mutilated body was still so strong and his voice so powerful. He lay on the ground the day of the battle and all of the next day, when his companions found him. A doctor treated his wounds with oil instead of turpentine for eight days, and every day he found new wounds. In the end Pedro recovered. I saw him, as healthy as if nothing had happened, but a few days later I learned that he had been killed in a brawl.

The vanquished sought a pardon, and the Admiral granted it on two conditions: that Francisco de Porras remain in irons and the others not stay on the ships, where there was not enough food, but live elsewhere until the ever-expected ship should arrive.

246

Don Ferdinand and Las Casas agree that the rebels surrendered on 20 May 1504. It was also in May that Méndez finally managed to outfit a rescue expedition. Ovando had not allowed him use of a caravel at Santo Domingo, and so he had had to await the arrival of ships from Spain. After a long wait, three ships finally arrived. One of them, a *caravelón* ("little caravel"), Méndez hired, furnished with food, and sent to Jamaica commanded by Diego de Salcedo. Following Columbus's orders, Méndez returned to Spain on one of the other ships with the letters for the monarchs and Father Gorricio. The *caravelón* arrived at Santa Gloria toward the end of June 1504. In that ship, writes Don Ferdinand, "we embarked, friends and enemies." They sailed on 28 June, having been at Santa Gloria a year and four days. With a bad mainmast and poor caulking, the *caravelón* barely stayed afloat. It took a month and a half to reach Santo Domingo.

On 13 August 1504 Ovando received Columbus civilly enough, but he was simply following protocol. One of his first acts was to free the Porras brothers, clearly demonstrating that Columbus, having no authority in the Indies, could not mete out punishment. Although claiming his rights and powers to the end, Columbus resigned himself. Thus, with an attitude of sad resignation, ended the adventure of the grand discovery.

The brief notes that follow ignore additional discoveries being made at the time by other bold Spanish navigators in the wake of the four great Columbian voyages. These notes concern only the last two years of Columbus's life, years troubled by illness and stubborn, painful, fruitless attempts to be reinstated in the rights and privileges he still believed were his.

12 September 1504: Columbus embarks at Santo Domingo for Spain. With him are his son Don Ferdinand, his brother Bartholomew, and twenty-two other men. Some of the survivors from Santa Gloria embark on the *caravelón* that rescued them from Jamaica, while most remain at Santo Domingo. Some would be among the first colonists of Puerto Rico.

7 November 1504: Columbus reaches Sanlúcar de Barrameda, at the mouth of the Guadalquivir. Sick again with the gout, he is taken to Seville.

26 November 1504: At Medina del Campo Queen Isabella dies. She had listened to the unknown sailor, sensed his genius, defended his undertakings, and honored his incredible success.

May 1505: Christopher and Bartholomew Columbus go to the court, in Segovia, and receive a dignified but cold audience from King Ferdinand. At the Admiral's insistence, the king allows him to designate a mediator for his interests. Columbus chooses Father Deza, archbishop of Seville, the Dominican who supported him from the time they met at Salamanca through the conclusion of the laborious negotiations with the king for the first voyage of discovery.

For a year Columbus lives with hopes and illusions, disappointments and heartbreaks. He follows the court to Valladolid, where he attempts to gain an audience with the new sovereigns of Castile, the Infanta Juana and Philip of Austria, her husband. He is not poor, as legend would have it; he has money and is surrounded and assisted by family, friends, and servants. But he is abandoned by the court and forgotten by the public.

20 May 1506: The greatest sailor of all time, the brilliant protagonist of the greatest adventure in history, dies at Valladolid on the vigil of the Ascension. His last words, when given extreme unction, were *"in manus tuas, Domine, commendo spiritum meum"* ("into your hands, O Lord, I commend my spirit").

A local, handwritten chronicle has this entry: *"El Almirante Cólon, que descubrió las Indias, otras muchas tierras, morió en esta villa miercoles víspera de la Ascensión, 20 de Mayo de 1506."* ("The Admiral Columbus, who discovered the Indies and many other lands, died in this city on Wednesday, the vigil of the Ascension, 20 May 1506".) Spain, Europe, and the rest of the world did not receive news of his death.

The place where Columbus spent his last weeks was certainly in the center of Valladolid. A stone on one of the remaining walls of an old house reads *"Aquí murió Colón"* ("Here died Columbus"). The funeral rites were celebrated in the church of Santa María de la Antigua. The body was temporarily buried in the cloister of San Francisco (the chapel of Luis de la Cerda). There it remained until 11 April 1509, when it was transferred to the monastery of Las Cuevas, Seville, one of the greatest monasteries in the city. Father Gorricio, Columbus's friend and confidant, was there. The body stayed there for a few decades until the decision was made that its final resting place should be in the lands he had discovered, more specifically in what was the pillar of the Hispanicization of the

Americas in the sixteenth century, Hispaniola. The year of its removal is uncertain; it could have been any time between 1537 and 1559. For a time, then, in the city of Santo Domingo—the only one of those founded by the Admiral or his brothers whose name recalls the Discoverer's ascendancy—lay Columbus's remains and those of his son Diego; his brother Bartholomew, the *adelantado;* the third admiral, Don Luis; and the third admiral's son, Don Cristóbal. In 1795, with the Treaty of Basel, Spain ceded to France its portion of Hispaniola, and the duke of Veragua decided to have the body of the first Admiral of the Ocean Sea taken to Havana. The remains were solemnly put on the brig *Descubridor* and transferred to Cuba. In Havana they were deposited near the altar of the gospel in the cathedral, under a stone with the following inscription:

> *O Restoe é Imagen del grande Colón*
> *Mil siglos durad guardados en la Urna*
> *Y en la remembranza de Nuestra Nación.*

> The remains and effigy of the great Columbus,
> For a thousand centuries will you endure in the urn
> And in the memory of our nation.

But even at Havana Columbus's remains, or supposed remains, did not find peace. The United States occupied Cuba in 1898, and the Spanish government had Columbus's remains brought back to Europe, where, after a solemn crossing of the Atlantic, they were finally deposited on 19 January 1899 in the monumental tomb built in Seville Cathedral by the sculptor Arturo Mélida on the fourth centenary of the discovery of America.

I say "remains or supposed remains" because in 1877 the entire question of the identity of the remains of the great Discoverer was turned upside down by a sensational but detailed explanation by Monsignor F. Rocco Cocchia, bishop of Oropa and apostolic delegate to Santo Domingo,[1] who asserted (with the support of other Genoese living in Santo Domingo) that in the presbytery of

---

[1] His full title was Monsignor D. Fr. Roque Cocchia of the Order of Friars Minor Capuchin, bishop of Oropa, delegate of the Holy See to the Republic of Santo Domingo, Haiti, and Venezuela, and apostolic vicar of the Archdiocese of Santo Domingo.

the cathedral he had found the tomb of Don Luis Colón and, nearby, that of the great navigator. Remembered for the famous "Lettera a Cesare Cantù sulla scoperta delle ossa di Cristoforo Colombo," published in 1877 in the *Giornale ligustico di archeologia, storia e belle arti,* Cocchia maintains—and several experts agree today—that the Admiral's remains never left Santo Domingo Cathedral. Those transferred to Havana were Don Diego's, either by mistake or through a ruse by the Dominicans, who ran the cathedral in 1795 and wanted to keep these most precious remains. In Santo Domingo, then, some still maintain, rest the Admiral's ashes, of which Genoa took a small part (as did Venezuela and the University of Pavia) in 1878, thanks to the initiative of the consul of the Kingdom of Italy, Luigi Cambiaso, a Genoese.[2]

In Spain, however, many people are convinced that the Admiral's remains were indeed transported to Havana in 1795 and that Cocchia's "revelations" do not merit consideration. Some believe Columbus is still buried on the grounds of the monastery of Las Cuevas, while others fantasize that his remains are at Valladolid, Puerto Rico, or elsewhere. As with his birth, so in death Columbus is the subject of myth; dilettantes have multiplied the fantastic theories and created outright fables. I maintain that what remains of the great navigator is in the sepulcher at Santo Domingo, though we cannot be as sure of this as we are of his Genoese origin, now proven both by documents and cultural evidence.

---

[2]Venezuela took some because on its coasts Columbus discovered the South American mainland in 1498, the University of Pavia because in 1878 people still believed a fantastic invention of Don Ferdinand's: in the *Historie,* to honor his father's memory and deny his humble origin, he says that his father studied at that university. People today are not ashamed of humble origins as they were then.

40 | Columbus the Man, Protagonist in the Great Undertaking

*T*here are no true portraits of Christopher Columbus. There are, however, over eighty statues or paintings, each quite different from the others because the artists were inspired by their own imagination, sometimes taking into account the few but essential descriptions about the physical appearance of the Genoese left to us by those who knew him. These descriptions are four.

The first is given to us by his son Don Ferdinand, born when Christopher was thirty-seven or thirty-eight years old. In the *Historie della vita e dei fatti di Cristoforo Colombo,* he writes as follows:

> The Admiral was well formed, taller than average with a long face and rather high cheeks, neither fat nor skinny. He had an aquiline nose, light eyes, fair skin, and a healthy color. In his youth he had blond hair, but when he reached thirty it all turned white.

The second description is by Las Casas, who saw Columbus in person at Santo Domingo in 1500, when the latter was about fifty. Las Casas writes as follows in the *Historia de las Indias,* chapter 2:

> Concerning his person and outer appearance, he was tall, above average, his face long and authoritative, his nose aqui-

line, eyes blue, and complexion clear, tending to ruddy. His beard and hair were blond when he was young, but they turned white almost overnight from his travails.

The third description is by Oviedo, who met him when Columbus was about forty. The following passage is from the *Historia general y natural de las Indias:*

> A man of good stature and a fine appearance, taller than average and strong. His eyes were bright and his other features were well proportioned. His hair was very red, his visage reddish and freckled.

The last description is that of the Venetian Angelo Trevisan, chancellor and personal secretary to the Venetian ambassador to Spain. Trevisan probably saw the Genoese navigator when the latter was fifty: "Christopher Columbus, a Genoese, a tall man of distinguished bearing, reddish, with great intelligence and a long face." The word here translated "distinguished" *(procera)* in fifteenth-century Italian meant "tall," but it could also be used in its Latin sense of "aristocratic."

Face long, cheeks rather high without being fat (Don Ferdinand); long face (Las Casas); long face (Trevisan). His high, wide forehead gave him an appearance considered aristocratic by Trevisan and authoritative by Las Casas. His nose was aquiline, as Don Ferdinand and Las Casas attest. His eyes were light (Don Ferdinand), blue (Las Casas), or lively (Oviedo), indicative of great intelligence (Oviedo and Trevisan), and of eloquence and pride (Las Casas and De Barros).

There remains the problem of his coloring. We can be certain of some elements. His hair was white after he was thirty. Don Ferdinand, Las Casas, Oviedo, and Trevisan—the four who saw him in person—knew him when his hair had already turned white. This explains why they differ on the color of his hair in his youth. According to Don Ferdinand and Las Casas it was *rubios,* which in Castilian means "blond"; one is at a loss to explain why some English speakers have translated it "red." Perhaps they were influenced by Oviedo, who speaks of his "very red hair," and by the color of his face, which all say tended toward ruddy. Dario Guglielmo Martini was justified in saying he had red cheekbones. In fact, Don Ferdinand, in the *Historie,* says "white, burning with a vivid color"; Las Casas, "complexion clear, tending to ruddy"; Oviedo, "reddish and freckled face"; Trevisan, "red." I tend toward the theory that the young Columbus's hair was more red than blond, as Don Ferdinand and Las Casas say, perhaps being more attracted to blond.

More important than his appearance were the great Discoverer's sensory abilities. He had an exceptional sense of smell; that is the most undeniable fact about his physical characteristics. All his writings indicate that. Many who knew him extolled his extraordinary olfactory ability and left accounts of his acute sensitivity to odors. Some have considered it affectation, but it was simply a highly developed sense that was a fundamental and determining component of his sixth sense, his sense of the sea.

Just as extraordinary were his sight and hearing. He ruined his sight during the crossing of the third voyage (1498), when he spent twenty-seven afternoons in July on deck, staring into the sun to make out the course from east to west. He developed ophthalmia, but he did not lose the outstanding, incredible maritime abilities he had acquired in his youth in the waters of Liguria and the Mediterranean and perfected in the Atlantic.

So much for his physical appearance and abilities. The discussion must be much longer and more complex when considering his character, psychology, and moral qualities. On these subjects hundreds, perhaps thousands, of essays and articles have been written over the last five centuries. There have been many novels, plays, and even lyric operas. Among the literary works, bound not by historical facts but only poetic inspiration, two stand out: Paul Claudel's *Le livre de Christophe Colomb* and Alejo Carpentier's *El harpa y la sombra*. These two authors interpret reality in a completely distorted fashion, at times altering history and at others scrupulously respecting it. Both books are unparalleled works of art, sufficient to ensure their place in world literature. They make a perfect antithesis: Claudel's Columbus hears voices like St. Joan of Arc, whereas Carpentier's is a fraud, a liar, a thief, and a womanizer. Two artistic interpretations, they are to be read without concern for the real Columbus, without regard for any myths of glorification or attempts at defamation.

On the level of scrupulous, rigorous historicity, Columbus was neither a saint nor a shrewd politician. His misfortunes cannot be explained as simply bad luck, caused by the maliciousness of his enemies and the envy of those who could not abide a foreigner of modest origins being granted such privileges and high honors. He was neither inept nor inefficient, but he lacked the two essential gifts of a politician: the capacity to make firm decisions for the long run and a keen knowledge of human nature, indispensable for putting the right people in the right position.

Some have called Columbus a man of the Middle Ages, while others have claimed him for the Renaissance, saying that his soul was superior to the century in which he lived. In reality he bestrode the two ages: his theoretical approach to philosophy, theology, and even science was medieval, whereas his zeal for scientific investigation, keen interest in nature, and capacity for accepting phenomena previously unobserved or unexplained were peculiar to the Renaissance. Renaissance too—as I have already amply explained—was his economics, typically mercantilistic and capitalistic, at least until the confused developments of the third voyage at Santo Domingo.

Psychologically he was a modern man. Concrete and pragmatic to the point of being overmeticulous, he elaborated his projects only after he had acquired direct experience, and from it sprang the conception for his grand design. In short, he had a modern psychology but roots in the Middle Ages.

The same can be said about his spirituality. He was a Christian and Catholic in the modern sense yet influenced by medieval teachings. His faith was strong, sincere, and inexhaustible, pure at all times and untainted by superstition and hypocrisy in the most demanding of circumstances. He was at times a fanatic or, as we would say today, a true believer. But his fanaticism never violated the eternal principles of the Christian and Catholic worldview. He was never particularly fond of the clergy. In defense of true Christianity, he quarrelled with priests, friars, and bishops, but by the same token a few friars and bishops gave him their friendship throughout his life, among them the Franciscan Father Antonio de Marchena. Marchena was also a leading figure in the greatest adventure in the history of discovery.

Confronted with the incredible mystery of a fourth continent, Columbus did not locate the Transcendent (purgatory) in the Immanent (the southern hemisphere), as Dante had done. Instead, he resorted to the idea of the earthly paradise, of which even a skeptic like Amerigo Vespucci had to admit, "if ever it existed it could have been only in these places."

When beset by mortal danger in storms he turned to the Madonna and saints as practicing Catholics have done throughout time—in the Middle Ages, the Renaissance, and the modern era. When he was wounded by jealousy, meanness, greed, and human wickedness, and especially when he was misunderstood or suffered what he considered injustice from the Spanish monarchs, the Admiral always reacted with Christian humility and with the resignation of the believer who looks beyond the limits of earthly life.

He was especially devoted to the Madonna and St. Francis. He knew to perfection the New Testament and many passages of the Old. Faced with the most terrible danger he had ever seen in his daily experience of love and war with the sea, and realizing that there was no hope left in the natural order, Columbus called directly on the Creator, the Word, reciting the first verses of the Gospel of St. John. This incident is important, because it shows that the cults of the Madonna and St. Francis were not the fruit of superstition but part of a systematic and rigorous religious nature.

Finally, it must be repeated that his continuous, obsessive search for gold and riches was always directed toward a very definite goal: a crusade to reconquer the Holy Sepulcher. This crusading spirit was not medieval. It was new, revived by the psychological trauma of the fall of Constantinople, the capital—along with Rome—of Christianity. The spirit of the new crusade aspired not only to reconquering the Holy Land but to much more, to rejoining that which had been divided, to bringing the world back to the unity it had had under the Roman eagle and which continued with the conversion to Christianity. All the barbarians—Germans, Slavs, even Vikings and Tartars—had found a place in Christianity, but Islam had disrupted the world, splitting Christianity. The subsuming of his plans into the religious ideal of a new crusade also had its roots in Genoa, where the desire for a crusade was felt at the beginning of the second half of the fifteenth century; it was strengthened when he came to the Iberian Peninsula, where he met Christians who had escaped the oppression of Islam.

The Christian and Catholic conception of the world constituted the essential and primary pillar of Columbus's personality. There is no contradiction between this assertion and the equally categorical one that he was no saint. For that status his faith, though unshakable, was not enough, nor were his humility, resignation, and occasional generosity, for he also demonstrated pride, avarice, suspiciousness, almost meanness, partiality for friends and relatives, and indifference to and direct participation in the horrendous institution of slavery. He was above all proud; his mystical conception of himself and his mission carried him in the last years of his life to the belief that he was the man who would open the door to the third age, that of the Holy Spirit, prophesied by Joachim of Floris. His faith was as strong as his charity was weak and intermittent; he was not a major or even a minor saint; he was—and it is not a small achievement—a convinced, profound, and constant defender of the faith.

The image of Columbus as a mere "adventurer" is false. There was adventure in his life, certainly. He never refused it but sought it repeatedly, living with a contempt for danger, with the daring and courage of one confident of his own powers and sure of divine aid. The first transatlantic voyage was without doubt a fabulous adventure, but in a certain sense his early voyages to Chios, Iceland, and Guinea were too. The third voyage was also an adventure, voluntarily pursued in the torment of the doldrums and the incessant, torrid heat of the tropics. But his greatest feat—or rather series of feats—was the fourth voyage, undertaken, when his star was setting, with the intention of circumnavigating the globe. It concluded with two worm-eaten vessels beached for a whole year at Santa Gloria, Jamaica, on a beach as open as one could find anywhere in the world.

Nor were all his adventures at sea. Was not his leaving Portugal for Spain and persisting for seven years—never admitting defeat—in his effort to gain support of his grand design an adventure? His expedition in the Vega Real and the founding of San Tomaso in the center of a land as unknown as the ocean was another daring feat. His whole life was a marvelous adventure, albeit a mixture of joy, unhappiness, and anguish. But those who call him an "adventurer" do so to diminish his merits, trying to credit sheer luck and chance with his success. In this sense Columbus was anything but an adventurer. His merits are indeed tied to his successes, but they were the cause, not the effect.

256   History would be distorted if we ignored one particular aspect of Columbus's character: his exceptional gift as a sailor. I have

many times had occasion to linger on facts, episodes, and judgments that amply prove my assertion. Columbus not only discovered America, he discovered the routes between Europe and the Gulf of Mexico. During the days of sail, ships leaving from Spain, Portugal, France, or Italy for Mexico, the mouth of the Mississippi, any island of the Caribbean, or Colombia or Venezuela followed the route Columbus took on the first voyage. To return they went north of the Sargasso Sea on the parallel of the Azores. Even today, anyone who wants to cross the Atlantic by sail chooses the route of Columbus's second voyage, from the Canaries to Guadeloupe.

The discovery of the routes is tied to the discovery of the trade winds, of which I have already spoken at length, just as I have pointed out that Columbus was the first to face the Sargasso Sea without fear, to have an inkling of the Gulf Stream, and to discover the western magnetic declination. But above all he was the one to begin, in the modern era, navigation in the open sea: first and determined, he dared to go out of sight of land for long periods of time.

I have already said that he possessed to an exceptional degree the physical gifts of the mariner. Michele da Cuneo writes as follows: "Just by seeing a cloud or a star at night he could tell what was coming up and if there would be bad weather. He commanded and stood at the helm, and when the storm was over he raised the sails himself while the others slept."

There is a spectacular proof of these extraordinary, almost magical, maritime abilities. During the fourth voyage Columbus found himself off Santo Domingo. He learned that thirty Spanish ships were about to sail for Europe with a large shipment of gold. He immediately sent word that they should wait because a tremendous storm was about to break. There seemed, however, to be no obvious sign to support his prediction. Sea and sky did not appear menacing, and the wind blew favorably for sailing east. The Spanish laughed at his worries, and the powerful armada set sail. But before it reached the eastern end of Hispaniola, the sky grew dim, the sea flat and dark, and the air suffocating. Thus did the storm announce itself, but the flat calm allowed no turning back. The heavily whirling hurricane shook masts and keels and smashed everything on board. The greater part of the fleet was lost with all hands and an enormous amount of gold. Only four ships managed to limp back to Santo Domingo. Others, badly battered, took refuge in the bays and roadsteads of the southeastern coast.

A single ship, the smallest and worst of them all, the *Guecha*, was unscathed. It continued to Spain, oblivious of the fate of the other ships. Aboard it was Columbus's agent, Alonso Sánchez de Carvajal, who was carrying about four thousand gold pesos surrendered by Bobadilla on orders from the monarchs for Columbus. That was the only gold of the great quantity shipped on that occasion from Santo Domingo that arrived in Spain, where it was consigned to Columbus's son Don Diego. Besides the surprising fact that only Columbus's gold was saved from the hurricane there was another, equally surprising. All four of the Discoverer's ships, even the *Santiago de Palos,* which he had wished to trade, managed to save themselves.

The haughty foreigner was now also a seer, a witch able to conjure up a hurricane and make it sink his enemies' ships while leaving his untouched. Obviously, Columbus was not a witch, and it is just as apparent that through mere chance the only ship that managed to save itself and reach Spain was the one carrying his gold. But it is not obvious that Columbus sensed the approach of a hurricane, a phenomenon completely unknown in the Old World. He had experienced only one before, seven years earlier. Thus, he demonstrated yet again his matchless reading of the sea.

Among the greatest Columbus scholars, Thacher, Harrisse, Caddeo, De Lollis, Revelli, Morison, Ballesteros Beretta, Madariaga, and Nunn fully confirm Las Casas's judgment: "Christopher Columbus surpassed all his contemporaries in the art of navigation." Just a handful disagree with that assessment. The most drastic critic of Columbus's sailing skills was Vignaud, whose nautical experience seems to have been limited to outings on passenger steamers on the Seine River. The great French explorer Charcot calls Columbus "a mariner who had '*le sens marin,*' that mysterious and innate ability that allows one to pick the right course in the middle of the ocean. . . . The dogs have barked and will continue to do so, but the caravels have sailed into history. The achievement of Christopher Columbus is so great it moves one to the point of rapture." Such is one great sailor's judgment of another, of the man who, except for Cook, has no peer among the sailors of all time.

Columbus was also a geographer, mostly self-taught. It is not surprising or unimportant—as some say quite thoughtlessly—that he was born in Genoa. In his childhood there he learned the first elements of navigation, and in Genoa and Savona he acquired that familiarity with the problems of the sea and navigation that was second nature in the traditions of the republic. Genoa was a leader in navigation not only in the Mediterranean but in all of Christendom. Then, with his first voyages and especially the prolonged Atlantic experiences, Columbus developed an acute sense for geography and unveiled many of its problems. He demonstrates in his writings how inclined he was toward geography and how cleverly he often solved problems related to it.

Alessandro Humboldt points out Columbus's quick grasp of natural phenomena. Once in a new world and under a new sky he studied closely the land and vegetation, the habits of the animals, the variations in temperature and in the earth's magnetism. The entries in his *Journal* touch on nearly all the subjects of interest to science in the late fifteenth century and early sixteenth. Although he lacked a solid preparation in natural history, Columbus's instinct for observation developed in many ways from his contact with exceptional physical phenomena. A self-taught man without formal education, he nevertheless became a great geographer.

Columbus was a genius in the full sense of the word. He had not only a sense of the sea and an acute sensibility for geography but an unshakable faith and a limitless desire for glory, a character strong willed and tenacious almost to the point of foolhardiness. He was courageous, patient, imaginative, and possessed an excellent memory. In crises he usually managed to use his intuitions and many abilities for effective action as only geniuses can.

All of this explains how he could conceive of the grand design to reach the Orient by sailing west. This explains how he could give up family, gain, and the main component of his dreams, the sea, for the best years of his life, the ages thirty-four to forty-two. This explains how he was able to carry out the four great Atlantic voyages: directing, commanding, resisting, showing clear perception, and making prompt decisions when faced with the fury of the elements and the rebellions of men.

Firm and unshakable in his convictions and judgments, Columbus dealt with the king of Portugal, the Spanish monarchs, and the Genoese, Florentine, and Jewish bankers almost as an equal. He was not conceited but perfectly aware of his own merits and of the strength of his ideas. Had he been conceited he would not have gained the friendship of Father Antonio de Marchena and Father Juan Pérez. Had he been conceited he would not have won so many friends, protectors, and admirers at the Spanish court; he would not have obtained the sympathy and trust of Queen Isabella, a woman of exceptional intelligence and rare virtue. Had he been conceited he would not have convinced Martín Alonso Pinzón, that shrewd and expert Paleñan captain who shares credit and glory for the success of the first voyage; through him Columbus recruited most of his men for the first voyage. Had he been conceited he would never have had, even in the most vexing situations, the respect of the sailors, most of whom obeyed him even under the trying conditions of the tragedy at Santa Gloria.

Columbus's success was not a product of chance. He was not, as is so often repeated, the navigator who left in search of new lands without knowing precisely where they were. True, he found America on his way, but it is also true that he was a discoverer and the inventor of a new idea, or a new perspective, until then unknown to the Old World and its civilizations—Greco-Roman-Christian, Arabic-Islamic, Indian, Chinese, and Japanese.

The Columbian discovery was of greater magnitude than any other discovery or invention in human history. Europeans realized that in the sixteenth century. In the centuries since then, the importance of Columbus's discovery has continued to swell, both because of the prodigious development of the New World and because of the numerous other discoveries that have stemmed from it. It was after Columbus's voyages that the task of integrating the American continents into Greco-Roman-Christian—European—culture was carried out. Notwithstanding errors, egoism, and unheard-of violence, the discovery was an essential, in many ways the determining, factor in ushering in the modern age. It was brought about first and above all by the Spanish and then by the Portuguese, French, English, Italians, Irish—to some extent by all the peoples of Europe. But this recognition cannot diminish the value of the inception of that task, which was Columbus's discovery.

Nevertheless, nearly every year the argument against the value of Columbus's undertaking and his claim to priority breaks out anew in the European and American press. Who reached America first? Couldn't someone have found the Atlantic route before Columbus? Didn't the Norsemen reach Greenland and Canada? It is an argument completely without justification from a scientific point of view. The problem is not a sporting match but a historical consideration. It is not a question of who the first European was to set foot on some beach on the American mainland, but who was the person who brought the new continent to the awareness of the old continents, who thrust it suddenly and overwhelmingly into the development of civilization, effecting a decisive turning point in human history.

The first humans probably reached American soil via the Bering land bridge in the Upper Paleolithic era, about twenty to twenty-five thousand years ago. When Christopher Columbus landed on the island of San Salvador in the Bahamas, the American continents were populated by several million people, from the extreme north to the extreme south. That population was well established, for great civilizations had prospered for centuries over vast territories, while other civilizations of equal stature had already fallen or were decaying.

Thus, the discussions of who was the first to arrive in America are superficial and scarcely scientific. Not one but millions and millions of people had arrived, or rather were descended from the many couples that had come during the millennia before 1492. The only serious question is whether some navigator from the Greco-Roman-Christian civilization or from cultures of the Middle East reached here before Columbus. But casual contacts by single Europeans or Africans or Asians with the New World could not affect, much less diminish, the value of Columbus's discovery. Nor do the undoubtedly sensational undertakings that constitute the lost discovery of the Norsemen affect it. Here we are faced with unimpeachable historical facts. But even these historical facts assure us that none of the Norsemen who touched the frozen lands of Labrador or reached Nova Scotia and Massachusetts recognized that he had found a new world or made Europe—and with it the rest of the Old World—aware of it. Similarly, no one in that part of the Old World that looks out at the Pacific Ocean or the Indian Ocean, no one in the Oriental civilizations of China and India, knew anything about the existence of the New World.

The most memorable undertakings of the Norse in the northwest Atlantic had no lasting effect on the history of humankind.

The American mainland remained wrapped in mystery. That veil of mystery was torn asunder only by the genius, tenacity, and faith of Christopher Columbus. And so Columbus, and Columbus alone, was truly the *"élargisseur du monde,"* as Claudel said, "he who widened the world." He invented the idea and brought it to fruition.

Columbus gave the Old World two great revelations. One was foreseen by some scholars and expected by some sailors, but no one had the courage to verify it: beyond the Ocean was not the abyss but more land. Columbus landed there on 12 October 1492, beginning a new era. The other revelation, fabulous and fantastic until then, Columbus received at the mouth of an immense river, the Orinoco. That evening, 15 August 1498, he wrote in his *Journal:* "I think that this is a vast mainland, unknown till today." A few years later he would write, "Your Highnesses are masters of these vast lands, which are another World." "Another world, a new world": only with Columbus's undertaking did Europe, Islam, India, China, and Japan learn of the existence of a New World. And that changed the course of human history profoundly.

What would human history have been without the great discovery of that year? The question is fruitless, for no valid history is based on *ifs*. It is also silly, because there is no doubt that if the Genoese had not realized his fantastic plan in 1492, some other navigator from Christendom, caught up in the fever for voyages and exploration of those decades at the end of the fifteenth century and the beginning of the sixteenth, would have revealed to the Old World the existence of the New.

There remain, then, three solid facts:

1. It was the genius of Christopher Columbus that conceived the plan of crossing the Dark Sea, opening the way for the enlargement of the world.
2. It was coincidence that Genoa—home of the Vivaldis, of Lanzarotto Maroncello, Antoniotto da Noli, and Nicoloso da Recco, of the best cartographers of the Mediterranean, of victorious fleets in the Tyrrhenian, Adriatic, Aegean, and Black seas and in the Crusades—gave birth to the man that the world would recognize as the mariner par excellence, one of the two greatest sailors of all time (the other being Cook).

3. Columbus was not the only genius in fifteenth-century Italy. True, Italy was not yet a state; it had not yet achieved political unity. Nor had it attained unity in a spoken language. We have seen that when Columbus left Liguria he knew Genoese and some rudiments of the Latin of the time. He learned Italian, that is, Tuscan, in Spain while discussing his plans with Monsignor Geraldini, from Umbria, and organizing his voyages with Berardi, Vespucci, and other Florentines. Italy did not yet have a unified spoken language, but it did have a unified literary language, from the Veneto to Sicily, from Puglia to Liguria, from Calabria to Ticino, today a Swiss canton.

There was already an Italian culture. And Columbus was not an isolated product of fifteenth-century Italian culture, of which Genoa was an essential part. Christopher Columbus of Genoa was the greatest and most spectacular actor at the beginning of the modern age. Beside him, enlarging the boundaries of geography, philosophy, politics, science, art, and music, stand a host of Italian geniuses, his contemporaries. Columbus was born about 1451: six years earlier Botticelli; two years earlier Lorenzo de' Medici and Ghirlandaio; a year later Leonardo da Vinci and Savonarola; two years later Giuliano de' Medici; three years later Amerigo Vespucci, Pinturicchio, and Politian. While Columbus was having his first nautical experiences in the Ligurian and Tyrrhenian seas, Pico della Mirandola (1463) and Machiavelli were born (1469). While he was conceiving the idea of reaching the Orient through the west, Ariosto (1474), Michelangelo (1475), and Titian (1477) were born. While he was reaching San Salvador (1492), Piero della Francesca was dying. While he was searching for the strait to circumnavigate the globe, Benvenuto Cellini was born (1500). The year before he died, Raphael was born. The year he died Mantegna died. A few years later Pier Luigi da Palestrina was born, who opened the boundaries onto new musical spaces.

If these names were omitted from history the Italian Renaissance would disappear. Without the Italian Renaissance there would have been no modern age. Christopher Columbus symbolizes the creative genius of Italy shaping the beginning of the modern age.

For Further Reading

Readers who wish to deepen their knowledge of the Columbian experience can find the documentation in two works supported by numerous illustrations both of documents and places: Paolo Emilio Taviani, *Cristoforo Colombo, La genesi della grande scoperta,* two volumes (Novara: Istituto Geografico De Agostini, 3rd edition 1988), and *I viaggi di Cristoforo Colombo,* two volumes (Novara: Istituto Geografico De Agostini, 1985). Both works are also available in economical editions (complete text but without illustrations) published by the Istituto Geografico De Agostini. Spanish, French, and English versions of the first work have already appeared (the English version is *Christopher Columbus: The Grand Design* [London: Orbis, 1985]). The English version of the latter work is forthcoming.

The best biography of Columbus in Spanish is that by Antonio Ballesteros Beretta, *Cristóbal Colón y el descubrimiento de América,* 2 volumes (Barcelona-Buenos Aires: 1945).

The best biography in English is by Samuel Eliot Morison, *Admiral of the Ocean Sea: A Life of Christopher Columbus* (Boston: 1942).

The French biography by Jacques Heers, *Christophe Colomb* (Paris: 1981) has gaps; however, it can be recommended for its serious and thorough study of the Genoese, Spanish, and Portuguese economic environment.

For those who wish to read the *Journal* of the first voyage I suggest the edition edited by Gaetano Ferro, *Cristoforo Colombo, Diario di bordo. Libro della prima navigazione e scoperta delle Indie* (Milan: 1985).

For readers who wish to specialize in the study of the Columbian and contemporary discoveries, I recommend the *Nuova Raccolta Colombiana*, edited by the Ministry of Cultural Affairs and the National Committee for the Celebrations of the Fifth Centenary and published by the Poligrafico dello Stato, Rome. Publication of this series, which will run to over twenty volumes, began in 1988.

Index

Africa, 58, 115
Albertus Magnus, 18
Alexander VI, 214
Alfonsine Tables, 66
Aloe, 113–14, 146
Anguilla [island], 148
Another world. *See* Venezuela
Antigua, 148
Antilia [island], 59–60
Antilles, 145, 148–49, 169–70, 207, 215. *See also name of specific island*
Arabs, 18
Arana, Beatriz de, 65, 68–71, 132, 184
Arana, Diego de, 83, 132, 151, 174
Arana, Rodrigo de, 68–69
Arctic Circle, 18
Aristotle, 18, 42–43
Asia: and the Capitulations, 211; Columbus's need to find, 163; Columbus's persistent belief that he had discovered, 221, 222–25; and cosmography, 190–91; Cuba as, 105–10, 164–66, 190–91; evidence of having reached, 105–11, 165–66, 190–91; and gold discoveries, 163; Polo's voyage to, 17; swearing ceremony about, 164–65
Aspa, Father, 81
Astronomy: Columbus's studies/understanding of, 13, 39, 41; and the first voyage, 134
Averroës, 42
Azores, 39–40, 43, 44, 47–48, 49, 58, 60, 91

Bahamas: Columbus's enthusiasm for the, 112; and evidence of having reached the East, 105; and the first voyage, 95, 105, 112; and gold, 126, 162; indians of the, 121–25, 170–71; palms in the, 115; reports about the, 139
Balboa, Vasco Núñez de, 193, 234
Ballester, Miguel de, 204–5
Banco San Giorgio, 31, 77

Bankers, 78, 207, 259–60
Barba, Juan, 246
Bariay Bay, 110
Baza, siege of, 73–74
Beans, 118
Behaim, Martín de, 51–52
Belén, 227–28, 231–34, 235
Berardi, Gianotto, 80, 81, 192, 263
Beretta, Antonio Ballesteros, 98n, 258
Bermejo, Juan Rodríguez, 98–99
Bernáldez, Andres, 66, 67, 165, 178, 186, 208
Birds, 94–95, 97, 146
Bobadilla, Beatriz de, 87–89, 144
Bobadilla, Francisco de, 206, 207, 208, 210, 212, 258
Boil, Father, 153, 158, 173, 174, 176, 177, 178, 185, 186, 187
Borgognone, Giovanni, 178
Borromeo, Federico, 183
Bradford, Ernle, 7, 227
Braudel, Fernand, 9
Brazil, 140, 193
Bristol, England, 20–21

Cabo de las Palmas, 115
Cabot, John, 213
Cabral, Pedro Alverez, 58, 140
Cabrero, Juan, 78, 79–80
Calabrés, Anton, 132
Cambiaso, Luigi, 250
Canary Islands, 40, 44, 46, 58, 105, 106, 191–92. *See also* Gomera
Canoes, 124–25, 217–18, 237
Caonabó, 152, 175, 178, 179–80
Cape Verde Islands: early voyages to the, 19, 37, 39, 46–47; and evidence of western lands, 46–47; and the third voyage, 188, 191–92, 196; winds in the, 46–47
Capitulations of Santa Fe, 81, 82, 84, 207, 208, 210–12

Capo Gracias a Dios, 220
Caraci, Giuseppe, 26
Caravels, introduction of, 16
Carib [Isle of Women], 134
Caribs [Cannibals], 122, 146–47, 149, 152–
  53, 154, 176, 183–84. *See also* Caonabó
Carpentier, Alejo, 253
Cartography, 16–17, 262. *See also name of
  specific person*
Castagno, Francesco, 81
Cathay. *See* Asia
Cayman Brac, 236
Celts, 22
Central America, 219, 234. *See also name of
  specific country or island*
Chanca, Dr., 146, 148, 150, 152, 156
Chios, 12–13, 114, 256
Chiriquí, 222–25
Christianity, 112, 178
Cibao, gold in the, 160–63, 226
Cinnamon, 146
Cipango. *See* Asia
Circumnavigating the world: as the objective of
  the fourth voyage, 213–15, 224–25, 256
Claudel, Paul, 56, 253, 262
Coca, 118–19, 218, 230–31, 234
Cocchia, F. Rocco, 249–50
Cólon, Diego [indian translator], 122
Cólon, Luis [grandson], 226
Colonizers, 168–70. *See also* Belén; La Isabela;
  La Navidad
Cólon y Toledo, María de, 226
Columbus, Bartholomew [brother]: as *adelanta-
  do,* 174–75, 187; arrest of, 207–8, 209–
  10; and Belén, 231, 232; and cartography,
  16–17; expedition of, 174; and Ferdinand's
  audience after the fourth voyage, 248; and
  the fourth voyage, 215, 217, 219, 228–34,
  238–39, 240, 245–46, 247; and La Isabela,
  158–59, 174–75, 181, 183; and proposals
  for the first voyage, 64, 76, 77; remains of,
  249; returned to Spain, 207–8, 209; and
  Santo Domingo, 185, 204, 206, 207–8; as
  support for Columbus, 68, 71; youth of, 3
Columbus, Christobal [great-grandson], 249
Columbus, Christopher: as an admiral, 100; as
  an adventurer, 256; arrest of, 207, 209–10;
  attempted assassination of, 244–45; birth of,
  2; burials of, 248–49; canonization for, 184;
  character of, 21, 98, 164–66, 253–60; and
  credit for discoveries, 136–37; cultural roots
  of, 7–10, 263; death of, 248; debts owed,
  211; as "divinely chosen," 128, 137, 256;
  education of, 4, 10; family background of,
  1–2; as the "first," 260–62; as a genius,
  259–60, 262, 263; health of, 196, 210, 217,
  219, 227, 239, 247, 252; honors/rewards of,
  210, 212, 247, 248, 258; humility of, 260–
  62; as a ladies man, 70, 88; marriage of,
  31–32; as an obstacle to Spanish expansion,
  206–7; obstinacy of, 108–10, 187, 234,
  247; personality of, 65, 88, 184, 196, 207,
  255–56; physical appearance of, 109–10,
  255, 256; importance of, 251–53; relieved
  of command in Santo Domingo, 206; as a
  sailor, 13, 41, 49, 256–58, 262; as a seer,
  257–58; sensory abilities of, 252; spirituality
  of, 62, 254–56; youth of, 4–6, 9, 10, 12
Columbus, Diego [brother]: arrest of, 207–8,
  209, 210; and the church, 215; and La
  Isabela, 158–59, 171–72, 174; and Santo
  Domingo, 206; and the second voyage, 158–
  59, 171–72, 174, 178; youth of, 3

Columbus, Diego [son], 33, 60, 62, 63, 69, 70,
  192, 249, 250, 258
Columbus, Domenico [father], 1–2, 5, 10, 11–
  12, 185
Columbus, Felipa Moniz Perestrello [wife], 31–
  32, 60
Columbus, Ferdinand [son]: birth of, 69; and
  the fourth voyage, 215, 247; legitimacy of,
  69, 184; named after the king of Spain, 71
Columbus, Ferdinand [son]—*Historie della vita
  e dei fatti di Cristoforo Colombo:* and Bartolomeo Perestrello, 32; and Columbus's early
  voyages, 14–15; and Columbus's marriage,
  31–32; and Columbus's physical appearance,
  251–53; and Columbus's studies, 43–44; and
  Columbus's studies, 43–44; and evidence of
  western lands, 48, 49; and family life, 33;
  and Fernao Dulmo's voyages, 59–60; and
  the first voyage, 116, 118, 122, 124–25;
  and the fourth voyage, 216, 217, 219, 222–
  23, 229, 230, 231, 236, 240, 242–44, 246–
  47; and La Isabela, 167, 181–82; and La
  Navidad, 151–52; and roundness of the
  earth concept, 42; and Santo Domingo, 206;
  and the second voyage, 146, 148, 162; and
  the third voyage, 206; and Toscanelli, 53
Columbus, Luis [grandson], 249–50
Columbus, Susanna Fontararossa [mother], 2,
  3, 5
Commission system, 205–6
Constantinople, fall of, 52, 255
Cook, James, 258, 262
Coral reefs, 99–100, 131, 227, 234, 236
Corn, 115, 116
Correa, Pedro [brother-in-law], 32, 43
Cortés, Hernando, 205
Cosa, Juan de la, 82, 130, 131, 164, 193, 207,
  211
Cosmography, 65–66, 190–91, 195, 199–
  200, 244
Costa Rica, 220
Cotton, 115, 119–20, 146, 177
Coup d'état, at Santo Domingo, 204–12
Criminals, as sailors, 82
Crusades, 80, 255
Cuba: as Asia, 105–10, 164–66, 190–91;
  and Christianity, 112; colonizers in, 169–70;
  Columbus lands in, 111–12; Columbus's dis-
  interest in, 216; and Columbus's remains,
  249, 250; description of, 112; discoveries in,
  114–15, 116–17, 118, 119–20, 122, 168;
  as a fascination, 110; and the first voyage,
  104–10, 111–12, 114–15, 116–17, 118,
  119–20; and the fourth voyage, 236; and
  gold, 126; indians in, 118, 121–25, 170–
  71; as a pillar of the Spanish Empire, 148;
  reports about the, 139; and the second
  voyage, 164, 168
Cuneo, Michele da: and Beatriz de Bobadilla,
  87–88; and Columbus's character, 257; Columbus's friendship with, 185; and La Isabela,
  167–68; and the second voyage, 144, 146,
  148, 160, 162, 171, 178; and slaves, 178
Cusanus, Nicolaus, 51, 52, 56

Dead reckoning, 39
De locis habitabilibus [Julius Capitolinus], 66
Deseada [island], 144, 145
Deza, Diego, 74, 78, 79–80, 248
Díaz, Bartolomeu, 58, 77, 164–65, 193
Díaz, Dinis, 19
Díaz de Isla, Ruy, 170

Index

Diego de Valera, Mosen, 83
Di Negro family, 10, 14–15, 30, 81
Disease, 168, 169–70, 176, 179, 182–83
Dog Island, 148
Doldrums, 40–41, 47, 201, 256
Dominica [island], 144, 145
Dominican Republic, 155, 156, 162, 169–70.
  See also Hispaniola
Doria family, 10, 81
Duela, Juan de la, 158
Dulmo of Terceira, Fernao, 59–60
Durlacher-Wolper, Ruth, 98

Earth: not a perfect sphere, 201–3; as round,
  17, 42–50, 51, 53–56, 62, 64–65, 84
Eckels, A., 202
Eclipses, 242–44
Egypt, 18
Elmina, 36–38, 48–49
Encomienda [commission system], 205–6
England, 14, 20, 64, 76, 77, 211
Enríquez, Alfonso, 75
Eric the Red, 23
Esbarroya, Luciano and Leonardo, 69
Escobar, Diego de, 244–45
Escobedo, Rodrigo de, 100–101, 132
Estreito of Funchal, Joao, 59–60
Ethiopia, 17
Eugene IV [pope], 55–56

Ferdinand [King of Spain]: and Columbus's arrest, 209, 210; and Columbus's naming his
  brother adelantado, 174–75; Columbus's
  relationship with, 186, 204, 206–7, 209,
  210–11, 248, 255, 259–60; Columbus's reports to, 175–77, 199–200, 201, 238, 247;
  and Ferrer, 190; and the fourth voyage,
  214–15, 238, 247, 248; and the Santo
  Domingo coup d'état, 206–7, 209, 210–11;
  and the second voyage, 175–77, 186–87;
  and sponsorship of the first voyage, 64–65,
  68, 73–74, 80; and the third voyage, 199–
  200, 201; and the welcome home, 140–41
Fernandina [Long Island], 104, 105, 118, 123
Ferrer, Jaime, 189–92, 194
Fieschi, Bortolomeo, 238–39, 242
First voyage: and the Azores, 137; and the
  Canary Islands, 191–92; capitulations [the
  agreement] for the, 81, 82, 84; colonizers on
  the, 131–33; and Columbus's character,
  256, 260; Columbus's demands for the, 59,
  79, 81, 82; discoveries on the, 113–20,
  122–25; and evidence of reaching Asia,
  104–11; financing of the, 73, 78–79, 80–
  82; and gold, 102, 104, 105, 106, 111, 120,
  126–29; Gómara as the departure point of
  the, 86, 89; and the indians, 101–3, 106,
  121–25, 183; and land sightings, 95, 97–
  99; and the Milione, 99, 106–7, 108; motives for the, 128–29; mutiny rumors about
  the, 90, 91, 93–96; objectives of the, 84,
  107; proposals for sponsorship of the, 64–
  65, 68, 73–74, 75, 76–78; and the return
  voyage, 133, 134–38; route of the, 90–96,
  257; sailors on the, 82–84, 86, 90, 91, 93–
  96, 113, 126, 168–69; ships for the, 73,
  82–83; and the welcome home, 139–42.
  See also Bahamas; Cuba; San Salvador
Fischer, J., 26
Fonseca, Juan de, 178
Fourth voyage: and Chiriquí, 222–25; and
  coca, 218, 230–31, 234; and Columbus's

character, 256, 257–58; and Columbus's
  health, 196, 217, 219, 227, 239; and the
  crossing, 215–16; discoveries of the, 216–
  21, 222–25, 234; and dissension among the
  Spanish, 237–41, 244–47; and gold, 222,
  225, 226–30, 231, 234, 237, 257–58; and
  Hispaniola, 215–16; and indians, 217–19,
  220–21, 228–29, 230, 231–34, 237–41;
  objective of the, 213–15, 224–25, 256;
  preparations for the, 213–15; and the return
  trip, 247; and sailors, 215, 233, 237, 239–
  41; and Santa Gloria, 236–41, 242–47;
  Spanish monarchs approve the, 214–15
Fund for the Crusades, 80

Galway, Ireland, 21, 28, 44–45
Gambia River, 18
Genoa: as a banking center, 31, 77, 80; as a
  capitalistic city, 10; as a cartography/
  cosmography capital, 16, 259; as Columbus's
  cultural homeland, 7–10; and Columbus's
  importance, 262; Columbus's last visit to,
  31; and Columbus's proposal for an expedition, 31, 76–77; and Columbus's remains,
  250; description of, 3–4, 7–8; and gold,
  129, 162; government of, 11; and Italian culture, 263
Geography: Columbus's interest in, 21, 65–66,
  191, 258–59; and evidence of having
  reached Asia, 107–8, 165–66; main principles of, 17; and the second voyage, 149; and
  the third voyage, 195, 196; of Venezuela,
  197
Geraldini, Monsignor, 75, 197, 263
Ghana. See Elmina
Ginger, 146
Gnupson, Eric, 24
Godfrey, W. S., 25
Gold: Columbus's obsession about, 128, 255;
  Columbus's personal, 258; and Columbus's
  spirituality, 255; and the crusades, 255; as
  evidence of having reached Asia, 105, 106;
  and Ferrer's views, 191; and the first voyage,
  102, 104, 105, 106, 111, 120, 122, 126–29;
  and the fourth voyage, 222, 225, 226–30,
  231, 234, 237, 257–58; and La Navidad,
  150, 151, 153–54; as proof of discoveries,
  140–41; and the second voyage, 128, 129,
  153–55, 160–63, 175, 177, 182–83, 186–
  87; trade in, 36–37; and the tribute system,
  182–83
Gómara [Canary Islands], 67, 86, 89, 143–44
Gonzales de Mendoza, Pedro, 141–42
Gorricio, Gaspar, 238, 247, 248
Gorvalán, Ginés de, 160
Granada, 73–75, 116
Grand Design: and Columbus's character, 109,
  254, 256, 259; and Columbus's importance,
  262; and evidence of western lands, 33–35,
  36–41, 42–49; and the genesis of the plan
  for discovery, 66; India as the objective of
  the, 163; and inhabitants of the southern
  hemisphere, 36–38, 49–50; as an obsession
  with Columbus, 60; and scholarly studies,
  42, 65–67; and the shipwreck at Lagos, 15–
  16; and superstition, 49–50; and Toscanelli's views, 42, 49, 56
Great Inagua [island], 111
Greeks, 18
Greenland, 18, 23, 24, 26, 27–28, 29, 44
Guacanagarí [Taino chief], 127–28, 131, 151,
  152–53, 178, 179, 181

Index

Guadalupe, Spain, 65
Guadeloupe, 145–46
Guanaja Island, 217–19
Guinea, 39, 43, 48–49, 105, 115, 116, 117, 122, 162, 256
Gulf Stream, 23, 257
Gutiérrez, Pedro, 97, 132
Guyana, 193
Guzmán, Enrique de, 72

Haiti, 111, 116, 117, 126–27, 128, 130–31, 148, 153–55, 169–70. *See also* Hispaniola; La Navidad
Hammocks, 123
Havana, Cuba, 249, 250
Henry the Navigator [Prince Henry of Portugal], 16, 17, 32
Hispaniola: as Asia, 191; Columbus lands on, 113; Columbus prohibited from landing in, 215–16; description of, 113; discoveries on, 113–15, 122, 167–68; and the first voyage, 113–15; and the fourth voyage, 215–16, 236, 237–38, 240; and gold, 127–28, 162, 186–87; as important for future expeditions, 207; indians on, 121–25, 170–71, 173–84; mastic on, 114; reports about, 139; and the second voyage, 162, 164, 167–68, 170–71; and the third voyage, 201; and the Treaty of Basel, 249. *See also* La Isabela; Santo Domingo
Hojeda, Alonso de, 160, 179–80, 181, 193, 207, 211, 212
Holm, Olaf, 231
Honduras, 119, 219
La Huerta [island], 220
Humboldt, Alessandro, 259

Iceland, 22–29, 30, 44, 49, 256
Incense, 146
Incest, 171
India: and the Capitulations, 211; Greeks voyage to, 17; as the objective of the first voyage, 84; as the objective of the fourth voyage, 213–15, 224–25, 256; as the objective of the Grand Design, 163; and the riches of the Orient, 191; Vasco da Gama's voyage to, 58, 214
Indians: characteristics of, 121–25; and Christianity, 178; Columbus's reports about, 175–76; and the commission system, 205–6; in Europe, 139, 178, 186; as evidence of having reached Asia, 105, 106–7; and the first voyage, 101, 102–3, 104, 105, 106–7, 121–25, 183; and the fourth voyage, 217–19, 220–21, 228–29, 230, 231–32, 237–41, 242–44, 245; genocide of, 182–83; as inferiors, 183–84; nakedness of, 101, 106–7, 122–23, 126, 181; as proof of discoveries, 140–41; racial characteristics of the, 104, 106–7; and the second voyage, 149, 173–84, 186; as serfs, 205–6; and sexual issues, 170–71; as slaves, 102–3, 121, 176, 177–78, 183–84, 206; and the third voyage, 197, 204, 205–6, 208; and tobacco, 118; *See also* Caribs; Indian-Spanish relations; Tainos; Women; *name of specific island or country*
Indian-Spanish relations: and La Isabela, 173–76, 178–82; and war, 175–76, 178–82, 184, 231–34, 239; and women, 150–53, 171–72, 174
Ingstad, Helge, 26
Inter caetera [papal bull, 1493], 188

Ireland, 21, 23, 44–45
Iron, 101, 106–7
Isabela [Crooked Island], 104, 105
Isabella [Queen of Spain]: and Columbus's arrest, 209, 210; and Columbus's naming his brother *adelantado*, 174–75; Columbus's relationship with, 70, 88, 186, 187, 204, 209, 210–11, 247, 255, 259–60; Columbus's reports to, 175–77, 199–200, 201, 238, 247; death of, 247; and Ferrer, 190, 191; and the fourth voyage, 214–15, 238, 247; and the Santo Domingo coup d'état, 206–7; and the second voyage, 186–87; and sponsorship of the first voyage, 64–65, 68, 73–74, 75, 82; and the third voyage, 199–200, 201; and the Treaty of Tordesillas, 188; and the welcome home, 140–41
La Isabela [colony], 155–60, 166–70, 171–76, 178–82, 184, 185
Isla de Colón, 222
Isla de Gracia, 197
Islands: as an indication of land mass, 149, 166
Isla Sancta, 197
Italian Renaissance, 263
Ivory Coast, 37

Jamaica, 121, 148, 164, 168, 169–70, 191, 216, 237. *See also* Santa Gloria
Japan. *See* Cipango
Jardines de la Reina, 236
Joachim of Floris, 128, 256
John II [King of Portugal], 43, 57–60, 139–40, 259–60

Kensington Stone, 24–25

Labrador, 24, 27
Lagos, Portugal: Columbus as shipwrecked at, 15–16
Landino, Christoforo, 66
Lanzarote [island], 31
Las Casas—*Historia de las Indias:* and Columbus as a sailor, 258; and Columbus's arrest, 208; and Columbus's belief he had reached Asia, 108; and Columbus's demands, 59; and Columbus's marriage, 31–32; and Columbus's obstinacy, 109; and Columbus's physical appearance, 251–53; and the first voyage, 118, 119–20, 142; and the fourth voyage, 216, 222, 231, 245, 246–47; and Guzman, 72; and indians, 123; and La Isabela, 170, 173, 181; and La Navidad, 151–52, 153; and Medinaceli [Luis de la Cerda], 72–73; and Perestrello [Bartolomeo], 32; and the second voyage, 144, 146, 148, 161–62; and the Spanish council for the first voyage, 75; and the third voyage, 192, 198, 199, 201; and Toscanelli, 53, 54
Ledesma, Pedro de, 234, 246
Leme, Antonio, 43
Lettera Rarissima, 238
Liberia, 36, 37
Liguria, 7–8, 114. *See also* Genoa
Little Cayman [island], 236
Lives [Plutarch], 66
Long Island, 118
Luperón [city], 155

Madariaga, Salvador de, 142, 166, 258
Madeira, 32–35, 38–39, 44, 46, 49, 58, 105, 188
Madonna, cult of the, 255

Index

Magnetic declination, 90, 91, 92–93, 201–3, 257
Malay Peninsula, 165
Manioc, 116, 117, 122, 182–83
Manzano, Juan, 79
Manzoni, Alessandro, 183
Marchena, Antonio de, 58, 61–67, 70, 71, 74, 78, 83, 84, 254, 260
Marchena, Juan Pérez de, 61, 62, 74, 78, 82, 260
Margarit, Mosén Pedro, 163, 174, 177, 178, 185, 186, 187
María Galante [ship], 143, 144, 145
Marinus, 42–43
Maritime routes: Columbus discovers, 41, 257; of the first voyage, 90–96, 257; of the fourth voyage, 215–16; and return voyages, 133, 134–38, 185–87, 207–8, 209; of the second voyage, 143–44, 185–87, 257; of the third voyage, 194, 196
Marocello, Lanzarotto, 31
Martín, Andrea, 209
Martini, Dario Guglielmo, 252
Martinique, 215
Martyr, Peter, 76, 113, 115, 116, 146, 148, 160, 165, 172, 206
Mastic, 114, 119, 146
Mayan indians, 217–18, 219
Medina, Juan de, 132
Medinaceli, Luis de la Cerda, 72–73, 74, 82
Mélida, Arturo, 249
Méndez, Diego, 228, 229, 232, 233, 235, 237, 238–39, 242, 245, 247
Mendoza, Cardinal, 75, 190
Mercader, Honorato, 63
Mercantilism, 205, 254
Milione of Marco Polo [Francesco Pipino], 51, 55, 66, 99, 106–7, 108
Missionaries, 18, 23, 45, 62–63
Moltke, Erich, 25
Montserrat, 147–48
Morales, Alonso, 132
Morison, Samuel Eliot, 7, 25, 60, 227, 258
Morocco, 18
Moya, marquess of, 78
Muliart, Miguel [brother-in-law], 61, 63
Muñoz, Weckmann, 206

La Navidad, 131–33, 148, 150–56, 168, 171
Nearchus, 42
Nevis [island], 148
Newfoundland, 24, 27
Newport, RI, 25
Nicaragua, 220
Nile River, 18
Niña [ship], 82–83, 94, 111, 130, 131, 133, 134–38, 140, 155. *See also* Pinzón, Vicente Yáñez
Niño, Pero Alonso, 207, 211
Nobility: Columbus family and the lands of Veruga, 226, 234; Columbus's obsession with the, 32, 59, 70
Norse explorations, 18, 22–29, 261
North American mainland, 18, 24–26, 27, 28, 29, 219
Nova Scotia, 24, 27
Nubian Desert, 17–18

O'Keefe, J. A., 202
Ovando, Nicolás de, 205, 208, 212, 216, 237, 239, 245, 247
Oviedo—*Historia general y natural de las Indias*, 122, 170, 173, 183, 208, 252–53

Palm trees, 105, 110–11, 115
Palos, Spain, 80, 81–83, 86, 140
Panama, 225, 226–34
Pane, Roman, 158
Parrots, 104–5, 140–41, 146, 177
Peppers, 115
Perestrello, Bartolomeo [father-in-law], 32, 33
Perestrello, Violante Moniz [sister-in-law], 61, 62
Pérez, Diego, 132
Pérez, Juan, 219
Petti Belbi, Giovanna, 9
Philip II [King of Spain], 185
Piccolomini, Enea Silvio, 66
Pineapple, 146
Pinelli, Francesco, 10, 78–79, 80, 81
Pinta [ship], 82–83, 111, 137, 140, 155. *See also* Pinzón, Martín Alonso
Pinzón, Martín Alonso, 83–85, 95, 100, 111, 136, 137, 140–41, 155, 260
Pinzón, Vicente Yáñez, 84, 100, 111, 131, 207, 211, 212
Pirates, 217
Pliny, 42
Pohl, Frederick J., 26
Polo, Marco, 17, 42. See also *Milione*
Porras, Diego de, 239, 247
Porras, Francisco de, 239–40, 241, 245, 246, 247
Porto Santo [Madeira], 32–35, 38–39, 40, 43, 46, 49, 58, 188
Portugal: Azores as a colony of, 47; Columbus settles in, 30; Columbus shipwrecked in, 15–16; explorations by, 211; Spanish relations with, 177, 188–92, 215, 243–44; and the sponsorship of the first voyage, 76; and the Treaty of Tordesillas, 243–44. *See also* John II [King of Portugal]
Potatoes, 115, 116–18
Ptolemy, 18, 42–43, 63, 65, 202, 203
Puerto Baraoa, 112
Puerto Cayo Moa, 112
Puerto Gibara, 110, 111
Puerto Plata, 155, 156
Puerto Real [city], 153
Puerto Rico, 121, 148–49, 169–70, 247, 250
Punta Uvero, 110–11

Quibian [indian], 228–29, 230, 231–32
Quinto, Italy: Columbus's youth in, 5–6

La Rabida, 61–67, 70, 74, 140
Rafn, Carl, 24
Redonda [island], 148
Regiomontanus [Johann Müller], 51–52, 242
Reis, Piri, 76
Rico, Jácome el, 132
Rivarolo, Francesco, 81
Rock of Sintra, 138
Roldán, Francisco, 159, 204–5, 244–45
Routes. *See* Maritime routes; *name of specific voyage*
Rubber, 122
Russia, 18

Saba [island], 148
Sailors: as colonizers, 168–69; and Columbus's character, 256–58, 260; criminals as, 82; and evidence of western lands, 49; on the first voyage, 82–84, 86, 90, 91, 93–96, 113, 126, 168–69; on the fourth voyage, 215, 233, 237, 239–41; on the second voyage, 156; on the third voyage, 197; and

Sailors, *(cont.)*
tobacco, 118; and women, 126. *See also name of specific person*
Les Saintes [islands], 144–45
St. Ann's Bay. *See* Santa Gloria
St.-Barthelemy [island], 148
St. Croix, 148
St. Eustatius [island], 148
St. Francis, cult of, 255
St. Kitts, 148
St. Lucia [island], 215
St.-Martín [island], 148
Salcedo, Diego de, 247
Salvago, Christoforo, 14–15
Sánchez, Juan, 246
Sánchez de Carvajal, Alonso, 212, 258
Sánchez de Segovia, Pedro, 97, 100–101
Sandalwood, 146
San Michele [island], 137
San Nicolás [island], 113
San Salvador, 99, 100–103, 104, 105, 106, 118, 119
Santa Clara of Moguer, 136
Santa Fe: Capitulations of, 81, 82, 84, 207, 208, 210–12; special council of, 75
Santa Gloria [Jamaica], 236–41, 242–47, 256, 260
Santa Hermandad, 80
Santa María de Belén. *See* Belén
Santa María de la Concepción [Rum Cay], 104, 105, 106
Santa María of Guadalupe, 136
Santa María [island], 137
Santa María of Loreto, 136
Santa María [ship], 82, 130–31. *See also María Galante* [ship]
Santángel, Luis de, 78–79, 81
Santo Domingo: and Columbus's remains, 249–50; coup d'état at, 204–12; and the decline of La Isabela, 159; founding of, 185; and the fourth voyage, 215–16, 247; Spanish ships sunk at, 257–58
Saona: named in honor of da Cuneo, 185
Sargasso Sea, 90, 91–92, 257
Sargassum, 91–92
Savonne, Italy: Columbus family moves to, 11–12
Scholars: and Columbus's proposal of an expedition, 64–65, 66, 67, 68, 79; and roundness of the earth concept, 42; and superstition, 49–50. *See also name of specific person*
Scientific studies: of Columbus, 65–67, 254
Second voyage: and Asia, 149; and the Canary Islands, 191–92; Columbus's reports about the, 175–77; departure of the, 143–44; discoveries on the, 144–49, 177, 236; financing of the, 192; and geography, 149; and gold, 128, 129, 153–55, 160–63, 175, 177, 182–83, 186–87; and indians, 149, 173–84, 186; and La Navidad, 148, 150–56; and the return trip, 185–87; route of the, 143–44, 257; sailors on the, 156; size of the, 143; and slaves, 176, 177–78, 183–84. *See also* Isabela [colony]
Seneca, 42
Senegal River, 18, 19
Serra, Jaime, 63
Seville Cathedral, 249
Sexual issues: Columbus's writings about, 88; and indians, 170–71
Slaves, 102–3, 121, 176, 177–78, 183–84, 206, 256
Socotera [Socotra], 107

Solinus, 43
Southern hemisphere: as uninhabitable, 17–19, 37, 49–50
Spain: Genoese settlement in, 10; palms in, 115; and Portugese relations, 177, 188–92, 215, 243–44. *See also name of specific person or place*
Spices, 104, 105, 106, 114–15, 129, 177
Spinola family, 10, 14–15, 30, 81
Squarciafico, Teramo, 14–15
Squash, 146
Storms: and Columbus's character, 255, 257; Columbus's knowledge of, 39; and the first voyage, 111, 135–38; and the fourth voyage, 216, 220, 229, 236, 241, 257–58; and La Isabela, 172
Strabo, 42
Sumula confessionis [St. Antonino of Florence], 66
Sun, and evidence of western lands, 48
Superstition, 49–50, 159, 254
Swearing ceremony, 164–65, 166
Sweet potato, 116–17, 122
Syllacio, Nicolò, 148
Syphilis, 170

Tainos, 121–25, 149, 152–53, 154, 170–71, 177–78, 181, 182–83. *See also* Guacanagarí [Taino chief]
Talavera, Fernando de, 75, 78, 79–80
Terreros, Pedro de, 197, 216
Theology, 199–200, 254
Third voyage: and Columbus's arrest, 207; and Columbus's character, 256; and cosmography, 190–91, 195, 199–200; discoveries on the, 197–200, 201–3; and Ferrer, 188–92, 194; and geography, 195, 196; India as the goal of the, 187; and indians, 197, 204, 205–6, 208; and mercantilism, 254; preparations for the, 187, 193–94; and the return voyage, 207–8, 209; route of the, 194, 196; sailors on the, 197; and the Treaty of Tordesillas, 188–92, 194; and Venezuela, 195–200; and Vespucci, 192–94
Tides, 20–21, 45–46
Tisín, Juan de, 158, 178
Tobacco, 115, 116, 118
Tomatoes, 118
Torres, Antonio de, 170, 175–77, 178, 209
Torres, Juana de, 78, 209–10
Torres, Luis de, 132
Las Tortugas, 126–27, 236
Toscanelli, Paolo dal Pozzo, 42, 49, 51, 53–56, 108, 109, 190–91
Toscanelli, Piero dal Pozzo, 51
Tractatus de imagine mundi [Cardinal d'Ailly], 66
Trade winds, 39, 40–41, 46–47, 48, 94, 95, 130, 134, 155, 235–36, 257
Tragedies [Seneca], 66
Travels [John Mandeville], 66
Treaty of Basel, 249
Treaty of Tordesillas [1494], 188–92, 194, 243–44
Trevisan, Angelo, 252–53
Tribute system, 182–83
Tristan, Diego, 232, 233

Ulloa, Alfonso, 91
University of Pavia, 250

Valladolid, 248, 250
Vallejo, Alonso de, 209

Index

Variable winds, 40–41, 94
Vasco da Gama, 58, 214, 215
Vega Real, 181, 256
Venezuela ["Another world"], 110, 195–200, 238, 250, 254–55, 262
Veragua, 225, 226–34
Vespucci, Amerigo, 192–94, 254–55, 263
Vicente, Martín, 43
Virgin Islands, 148
Vivaldis, 31
Vizcaíno, Domingo, 132

Walter MacCrone Associates, 26

Western lands: evidence of, 34–35, 43, 44–45, 46–48, 49, 58
Winds, 40–41, 43, 46–48, 94, 95, 111, 130, 134, 155, 156, 220, 241. See also Trade winds
Women, 126, 150–53, 171–72, 174, 178, 219

Yale Map, 25–26
Yucatan Peninsula, 218

Zanzibar, 107
Zedo [goldsmith], 186–87

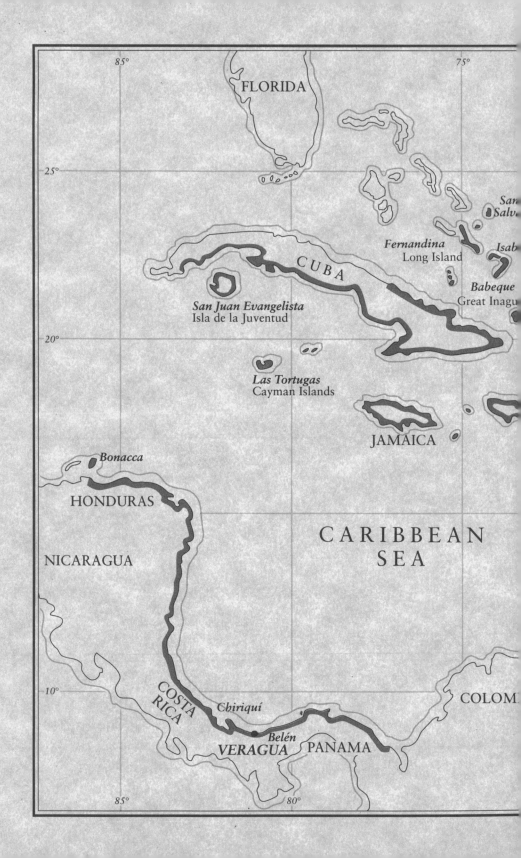